T0205972

Lecture Notes of the Institute for Computer Sciences, Social Informatics and Telecommunications Engineering

586

The LNICST series publishes ICST's conferences, symposia and workshops.
LNICST reports state-of-the-art results in areas related to the scope of the Institute.
The type of material published includes

- Proceedings (published in time for the respective event)
- Other edited monographs (such as project reports or invited volumes)

LNICST topics span the following areas:

- General Computer Science
- E-Economy
- E-Medicine
- Knowledge Management
- Multimedia
- Operations, Management and Policy
- Social Informatics
- Systems

Phan Cong Vinh · Hafiz Mahfooz Ul Haque
Editors

Nature of Computation and Communication

9th EAI International Conference, ICTCC 2023
Ho Chi Minh City, Vietnam, October 26–27, 2023
Proceedings

 Springer

Editors
Phan Cong Vinh
Nguyen Tat Thanh University
Ho Chi Minh City, Vietnam

Hafiz Mahfooz Ul Haque
University of Central Punjab in Pakistan
Johar Town, Pakistan

ISSN 1867-8211   ISSN 1867-822X (electronic)
Lecture Notes of the Institute for Computer Sciences, Social Informatics
and Telecommunications Engineering
ISBN 978-3-031-59461-8   ISBN 978-3-031-59462-5 (eBook)
https://doi.org/10.1007/978-3-031-59462-5

This Springer imprint is published by the registered company Springer Nature Switzerland AG
The registered company address is: Gewerbestrasse 11, 6330 Cham, Switzerland

Paper in this product is recyclable.

Preface

ICTCC 2023 (the 9th EAI International Conference on naTure of Computation and Communication), was held October 26–27, 2023 at Nguyen Tat Thanh University in Ho Chi Minh City, Vietnam, in fully online style, due to the travel restrictions caused by the worldwide COVID-19 pandemic. The aim of the conference is to provide an internationally respected forum for scientific research in the technologies and applications of natural computing and communication. ICTCC provides an excellent opportunity for researchers to discuss modern approaches and techniques for natural computing systems and their applications. These proceedings of ICTCC 2023 are published by Springer in the series of Lecture Notes of the Institute for Computer Sciences, Social Informatics and Telecommunications Engineering (LNICST; indexed by DBLP, EI, Google Scholar, Scopus, and Thomson ISI).

For this ninth edition of ICTCC, and repeating the success of the previous year, the Program Committee received submissions from authors in six countries and each paper was reviewed by at least three expert reviewers. We chose 12 papers after intensive discussions held among the Program Committee members. We really appreciate the excellent reviews and lively discussions of the Program Committee members and external reviewers in the review process. This year we had two prominent invited speakers, Issam Damaj from Cardiff Metropolitan University in the UK and Ngo Ha Quang Thinh from Ho Chi Minh City University of Technology, HCM-VNU in Vietnam. ICTCC 2023 was jointly organized by the European Alliance for Innovation (EAI) and Nguyen Tat Thanh University (NTTU). This conference could not have been organized without the strong support of the staff members of the two organizations. We would especially like to thank Imrich Chlamtac (University of Trento), Marica Scevlikova (EAI), and Stephen McGarry (EAI) for their great help in organizing the conference.

October 2023

Phan Cong Vinh
Hafiz Mahfooz Ul Haque

Organization

Steering Committee

Imrich Chlamtac   University of Trento, Italy
Phan Cong Vinh   Nguyen Tat Thanh University, Vietnam

Organizing Committee

General Chair

Phan Cong Vinh   Nguyen Tat Thanh University, Vietnam

Technical Program Committee Chair

Hafiz Mahfooz Ul Haque   University of Central Punjab, Pakistan

Web Chair

Nguyen Van Han   Nguyen Tat Thanh University, Vietnam

Publicity and Social Media Chair

Pham Van Dang   Nguyen Tat Thanh University, Vietnam

Workshops Chair

Vu Tuan Anh   Industrial University of Ho Chi Minh City, Vietnam

Sponsorship and Exhibits Chair

Abdur Rakib   Coventry University, UK

Publications Chair

Phan Cong Vinh   Nguyen Tat Thanh University, Vietnam

Local Chair

Bach Long Giang   Nguyen Tat Thanh University, Vietnam

Technical Program Committee

Technical Program Committee Chair

Hafiz Mahfooz Ul Haque   University of Central Punjab, Pakistan

Technical Program Committee Members

Anh Dinh	University of Saskatchewan, Canada
Ashish Khare	University of Allahabad, India
Bui Cong Giao	Saigon University, Vietnam
Cao Van Kien	Nguyen Tat Thanh University, Vietnam
Chernyi Sergei	Admiral Makarov State University of Maritime and Inland Shipping, Russia
Chien-Chih Yu	National ChengChi University, Taiwan
Dang Thanh Tin	Ho Chi Minh City University of Technology, Vietnam
David Sundaram	University of Auckland, New Zealand
Do Thi Thanh Dieu	Nguyen Tat Thanh University, Vietnam
Gabrielle Peko	University of Auckland, New Zealand
Giacomo Cabri	University of Modena and Reggio Emilia, Italy
Hafiz Mahfooz Ul Haque	University of Central Punjab, Pakistan
Harun Baraki	University of Kassel, Germany
Hiroshi Fujita	Gifu University, Japan
Huynh Xuan Hiep	Can Tho University, Vietnam
Hyungchul Yoon	Chungbuk National University, South Korea
Issam Damaj	Beirut Arab University, Lebanon
Kurt Geihs	University of Kassel, Germany
Le Hoang Thai	Ho Chi Minh City University of Science, Vietnam
Le Hong Anh	University of Mining and Geology, Vietnam
Le Xuan Truong	Ho Chi Minh City Open University, Vietnam
Manish Khare	Dhirubhai Ambani Institute of Information and Communication Technology, India

Muhammad Athar Javed Sethi	University of Engineering and Technology Peshawar, Pakistan
Ngo Ha Quang Thinh	Ho Chi Minh City University of Technology, Vietnam
Nguyen Thanh Hai	Can Tho University, Vietnam
Om Prakash	Hemvati Nandan Bahuguna Garhwal University, India
Pham Quoc Cuong	Ho Chi Minh City University of Technology, Vietnam
Rajiv Tewari	University of Allahabad, India
Shahzad Ashraf	Hohai University, China
Tran Huu Tam	University of Kassel, Germany
Truong Cong Doan	International School, VNU, Vietnam
Vu Tuan Anh	Industrial University of Ho Chi Minh City, Vietnam
Waralak V. Siricharoen	Silpakorn University, Thailand

Contents

Advances in AI in Computing and Communications

Advancing Online Education: An Artificial Intelligence Applied System for Monitoring and Improving Employee Engagement in Enterprise Information Systems

Nguyen Thanh Son[1], Trong Tien Hoang[2], Satyam Mishra[2] ⓘ,
Nguyen Thi Bich Thuy[3], Tran Huu Tam[4], and Cong-Doan Truong[2](✉)

[1] VNPT-Media Software Company, Hanoi, Vietnam
`sonnt.196@gmail.com`
[2] International School, Vietnam National University, Hanoi, Vietnam
`{tienht,tcdoan}@vnu.edu.vn`
[3] University of Science, Vietnam National University, Hanoi, Vietnam
`nguyenthibichthuy@hus.edu.vn`
[4] FPT University, Hanoi, Vietnam
`tamth3@fe.edu.vn`

Abstract. Online learning has gained significant popularity, but maintaining learner focus remains a challenge, especially in financial enterprise training systems. The need for training has increased with banking and finance digitalization trends, yet high learning curves and prolonged sessions often lead to distractions. This research introduces an online learning tool that monitors and quantifies learner attention in real-time. Using the MobileNet Convolutional Neural Network, we detect seven core emotions, which, combined with attention scores, form a Concentration Index (CI). Learners are then categorized as "Highly-engaged," "Normally Engaged," or "Disengaged." With 70% accuracy on training and 65% on testing, our engagement metrics provide actionable insights for educators and administrators, enhancing virtual learning and aiding in analytical problem-solving strategies.

Keywords: Online Learning · Learner Focus · Real-Time Attention Quantification · Convolutional Neural Network (CNN) · MobileNet · Emotion Detection · Concentration Index (CI)

1 Introduction

Enterprises are continuously evolving, adopting advanced technologies to improve customer experience. As a result, there's an imperative to ensure the workforce is updated with the latest knowledge to adeptly handle these innovations. Many financial institutions have adopted in-house Learning Management Systems (LMS) to foster knowledge transfer, enhance student engagement, and utilize results for career progression. Current

© ICST Institute for Computer Sciences, Social Informatics and Telecommunications Engineering 2024
Published by Springer Nature Switzerland AG 2024. All Rights Reserved
P. Cong Vinh and H. Mahfooz Ul Haque (Eds.): ICTCC 2023, LNICST 586, pp. 3–18, 2024.
https://doi.org/10.1007/978-3-031-59462-5_1

forecasts anticipate the global LMS market to grow at a rate of 23% by 2024, reaching an estimated revenue of roughly 12.48 billion [1]. However, these enterprise LMS systems are often standalone systems in the enterprise system architecture or only providing very high-level results on learning performance of the attendants.

E-learning holds the promise of personalizing learning experiences, delivering real-time feedback to educators on student performance [2]. Its initial adoption at the university level showcased its merits, where traditional full-time onsite learning was often perceived as time-consuming, whereas online methods were lauded for their flexibility and cost-efficiency [3]. Yet, e-learning poses challenges in areas like peer and educator-student interactions, prompt educator support, and sustaining attention [4]. As its popularity soars, these issues become more evident, driving our aim to innovate in emotion detection and ongoing student engagement assessment.

Various studies underscore the individual's ability to grasp cognitive processes [5, 6]. Some emphasize the creation of learning systems that discern learners' emotional states [7–9]. Other research explores integrating motivational skills in smart learning systems [10]. With evidence supporting emotion detection via facial expressions, it's been found that six unique emotions can predictably be identified with 89% accuracy [11]. While one study [12] presented in-depth results on facial expression-based emotion recognition, understanding emotions like boredom and fatigue remains under-explored. A segment of research champions the identification of confidence, frustration, and boredom in e-learning to deliver tailored feedback [13]. The value of embedding emotions in e-learning was asserted in [14]. Notwithstanding extensive studies on eye movement [15, 16] and yawn detection [17], tracking drowsiness and unusual head movement has been less addressed in e-learning contexts. Though past work has touched upon emotion recognition in e-learning, a comprehensive solution with a proof of concept has been absent.

Our study endeavors to create a comprehensive online learning platform incorporating emotion recognition. This solution encompasses an Android app fostering educator-student engagement, a desktop web interface, and robust computing units and databases for machine learning, feature storage, and data management. The aim is not only to improve in-class learning performance, but also to provide management with novel quantifiable metrics in assessing employee performance such as ability to concentrate over a long period of time, ability to learn new skills.

- Step 1: Face Recognition - The product starts by integrating the MTCNN (Multi-Task Cascaded Convolutional Neural Network) model for face recognition. This foundational step paves the way for tracking learners' facial expressions in subsequent stages.
- Step 2: Focus Classification - After successful face detection, the system utilizes the MobileNet model to determine if learners are focused. MobileNet, known for its efficient image classification prowess, is employed for this purpose.
- Step 3: Emotion Classification - The system then uses MobileNet to classify learners' emotions based on facial expressions, identifying states like happiness, sadness, surprise, among others.
- Step 4: Concentration Index Calculation - As elaborated in Sect. 2.4 of this research, a concentration index is computed to quantify engagement levels. It integrates results

from both emotion and focus evaluations to provide a holistic measure of learners' attention during e-learning.

- Step 5: Results Presentation for Educators - Lastly, the system offers a visual summary of learners' emotions, focus, and concentration indices to teachers or administrators. These real-time insights empower educators to adapt their instruction based on learners' engagement.

The product's efficiency depends on its precision in emotion recognition, focus classification, and concentration index computation. Preliminary results show a 70% success rate on the training set and 65% on the test set in detecting emotions, underscoring its potential for practical use.

2   Methodology

To accomplish the specified objective, the authors utilized the FER2013 dataset in tandem with the Multi-Task Cascaded Convolutional Neural Network (MTCNN) and MobileNet. These models' outputs were then integrated to compute the Concentration Index.

2.1   FER2013 Dataset

For retraining the MobileNet model, the FER2013 dataset [18] was selected. This dataset is apt for emotion recognition tasks executed via algorithms akin to MobileNet. It consists of grayscale facial images with pre-assigned labels. For this study, the dataset was partitioned into 28,709 training observations and 3,589 test observations (Fig. 1).

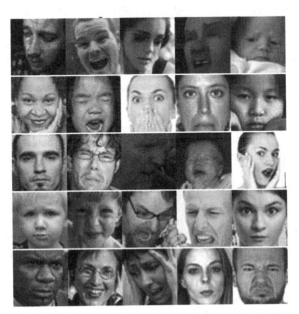

Fig. 1. A 5 × 5 collage showcasing diverse facial expressions from the FER-2013 dataset.

To address issues of limited sample size and class imbalance, the authors applied data augmentation and transfer learning techniques. Theoretically, leveraging these techniques on this dataset should bolster the overall accuracy and robustness of real-time emotion detection. Recent studies have shown that facial emotion detection tasks yield the highest accuracy when deep learning algorithms are employed. Some research even indicates enhanced accuracy with a combined dataset approach [19].

2.2 MultiTask Cascaded Convolutional Neural Network (MTCNN)

The MultiTask Cascaded Convolutional Neural Network (MTCNN) [20] is a state-of-the-art face detection technique integral to this research. MTCNN distinguishes itself by implementing a three-stage cascaded structure to optimize face detection. It commences by resizing the image across multiple scales, ensuring the detection of faces irrespective of their size.

– Proposal Network (P-network): This is the first phase, designed to roughly identify possible face regions. To achieve a comprehensive scan, the P-network uses a lower threshold which might lead to some false positives.
– Refine Network (R-network): This subsequent stage sharpens the earlier detections by refining face regions and reducing false positives. It further utilizes non-maximum suppression (NMS) to eliminate overlapping detections.
– Output Network (O-network): As the final layer, the O-network perfects the bounding box predictions, ensuring the accuracy of face detections.

One of the standout features of MTCNN is its capability to identify facial landmarks, which is invaluable for precise tasks like face alignment, further underscoring its adaptability and precision in face-related tasks. MTCNN serves as the first critical step in the pipeline of real-time emotional reaction detection. Its robustness and accuracy in face detection set the stage for subsequent models, like MobileNet, to interpret the nuanced changes in facial expressions and categorize emotional states effectively.

2.3 MobileNet

Google's MobileNet, designed with the Depthwise Separable Convolution (DSC) technique, revolutionized the field of efficient deep learning. Particularly recognized for its compactness and computational efficiency, MobileNet [21] stands out as an optimal neural network architecture for resource-limited platforms like mobile devices. The unique implementation of depth-wise separable convolutions divides the convolution process into depth-wise and point-wise layers, ensuring reduced computational overhead and fewer parameters. When applied to tasks like real-time emotion recognition using the FER-2013 dataset, MobileNet's efficiency and lightweight design make it an ideal choice, enabling fast and accurate analysis without the need for extensive computational resources.

MobileNet is specially designed to ensure efficient feature extraction while conserving computational resources. This makes it ideal for real-time applications, notably in the realm of face recognition and emotion analysis. Given the challenges of detecting student engagement in online learning scenarios, the MobileNet architecture offers a compelling balance of performance and computational efficiency for mobile devices.

The Depthwise Separable Convolution divides the convolution process into two distinct layers [22]:

Depthwise Convolution: This applies a unique filter to each individual input channel, distinguishing it from the standard convolution where filters are incorporated across all input channels. The mathematical representation for this is:

$$\text{Depthwise } (F, K) = F \times K \times K$$

where:

F is the feature map size.

K is the kernel size.

Point-wise Convolution: Utilizes a 1×1 convolution to modify the dimensionality of the combined channels.

$$\text{Pointwise } (F, M, N) = F \times F \times M \times N$$

where:

F is the feature map size.

M is the number of input channels.

N is the number of output channels.

When analyzing the computational efficiency, the total cost for Depthwise separable convolutions is given by:

$$\text{TotalCost} = (D_F \times D_F \times M \times D_K \times D_K) + (D_F \times D_F \times M \times N)$$

where:

DF is the feature map size.

M is the number of input channels.

N is the number of output channels.

DK is the kernel size.

Compared to the computational expense of a standard convolution, the reduction achieved through Depthwise Separable Convolution can be expressed as:

Standard Convolution Cost – Depthwise Separable Convolution Cost

Standard Convolution Cost

Within the MobileNet architecture, while there are up to 30 layers present, the core processes involve the following pivotal layers:

– Convolution Layer
– Depthwise Layer
– Pointwise Layer
– Softmax Layer: Primarily for classification.

Batch Normalization (BN) and ReLU: Upon contrasting the performance of a 30-layer network employing traditional convolution against a similar 30-layer network utilizing Depthwise Separable Convolution (MobileNet) on the ImageNet dataset, the insights reveal: MobileNet exhibits a marginal 1% drop in accuracy. However, there's a noteworthy reduction, approximately 90%, in the Mult-Adds and parameters, underscoring its efficiency.

In the context of our task – detecting emotional reactions in the FER-2013 dataset – this efficiency means the model can quickly process and interpret facial expressions, making it a fitting choice for real-time student engagement detection.

2.4 Concentration Index Calculation

The concentration index [23] serves as a metric to gauge students' engagement during e-class learning sessions. Derived from both emotional recognition outcomes and attention scores, this real-time calculation offers insights into a student's immediate focus and attentiveness. Building the concentration index involves two key components: the emotional recognition model and the attention score. The former leverages a pre-trained convolutional neural network [24] to discern a range of emotions, such as anger, happiness, and sadness. Concurrently, eye-tracking technology maps the student's retinal focus and gaze patterns, providing data for the attention score.

By integrating emotional and attentional metrics, the concentration index offers a nuanced view of student engagement. Educators can then categorize this engagement into three levels: high, normal, and disengaged. This comprehensive approach ensures a more accurate representation of a student's involvement in the learning process.

2.5 Proposed Model Architecture

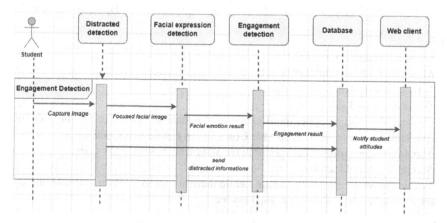

Fig. 2. Proposed Model Architecture

The proposed model architecture (Fig. 2) presents a systematic approach for real-time engagement detection in online learning settings. It adeptly merges several components—face recognition, emotion analysis, attention tracking, and the concentration index calculation—to offer a thorough insight into students' engagement dynamics.

For optimal performance and real-time responsiveness, certain tasks should be offloaded to servers with robust computational capabilities, while others should be processed at the mobile edge. Face recognition and emotion analysis, given their complexity and reliance on neural networks like MTCNN and MobileNet, would benefit from server-side processing. This would ensure high accuracy without straining the mobile device. Conversely, attention tracking, using tools like SeeSoSDK [25], and basic preprocessing tasks could be executed at the mobile edge. This division of tasks would minimize latency, particularly for operations that require immediate feedback, such as monitoring a student's gaze in real-time.

3   Results

3.1   Experiment 1: Data Augmentation Techniques

The initial experiment delves into the influence of data augmentation techniques on dataset expansion and the corresponding impact on model performance. By employing augmentation methods like horizontal flips, rotations, translations, and zoom on the training dataset [26], this experiment seeks to elucidate their role in enlarging the dataset and fortifying the model's generalization potential. Our findings shed light on how augmentation impacts the model's accuracy and its capacity to avert overfitting. While horizontal data flipping stands out as an efficient technique for data augmentation in CNNs [27], it's crucial to be mindful that for diminutive images, this method can significantly alter the image structure, potentially compromising performance (Table 1).

Table 1. ImageDataGenerator settings summary

Settings	Effect
width_shift_range = 0.15 height_shift_range = 0.15	These dictate horizontal and vertical image shifts. Considering the images are cropped to a 48x48 size centered on the face, excessive shifts might inadvertently introduce noise, potentially obscuring crucial facial features. An optimal threshold of 0.15 is established
zca_whitening	This has been disabled, given that grayscale images don't significantly benefit from this form of whitening
zoom_range = 0.15	Administers random image zooms. Any zoom constants beyond 0.15 risk distorting image proportions, possibly losing emotion-specific details
horizontal_flip = True	Activated to handle the predominance of upright faces in the dataset, this setting amplifies training diversity through mirrored image generation
shear_range = 0.15	Modifies the image by adjusting its contour angle. Maintaining a shear angle of 15 degrees ensures image proportions remain intact and complements the data augmentation strategy

In summation, the chosen augmentation settings are calibrated to balance between retaining image fidelity and emotional nuances while simultaneously enhancing training variety. Techniques like horizontal flips, rotations, translations, and zooming are tactically deployed to enrich the dataset. For example, horizontal flipping introduces mirrored image variations, mitigating any inherent orientation bias. Meanwhile, controlled manipulations through rotations, translations, and zooming bolster the model's resilience against spatial alterations. It's essential to recognize that while augmentation fosters diversification, it can also be a source of noise. Consequently, striking a balance becomes especially important and difficult. The overarching goal of Experiment 1 is to utilize these augmentation strategies to elevate MobileNet's efficacy in real-time engagement detection within online learning environments.

3.2 Experiment 2: Class Weights for Balancing Classes

Class weighting is a technique used to address class imbalances by attributing distinct weights to each class according to the number of training samples present. As delineated in the Sklearn documentation, the class weights for every class can be calculated using the formula:

$$CW = \frac{n\_samples}{n\_classes.np.bincount(y)}$$

where:

    $n\_samples$: the total number of rows in a dataset.

    $n\_classes$: the total distinct classes within the dataset.

    $np.bincount(y)$: the count of each specific class in the dataset.

The second experiment focuses on understanding the influence of class weighting on the precision of engagement detection. It encompasses the assignment of greater weights to less represented classes in line with their sample proportions. The objective is to amplify the model's responsiveness to minority classes, thus highlighting enhanced efficacy, particularly when identifying rarer emotions or engagement tiers. In challenging the predisposition towards predominant classes, the research aims for a more precise and holistic evaluation of engagement, shedding light on student dynamics during online education.

3.3 Experiment 3: Fine-Tuning MobileNet

The third experiment delves into fine-tuning the MobileNet architecture, emphasizing transfer learning for emotion recognition within online learning contexts. Utilizing the MobileNet structure pre-trained on the ImageNet dataset, a specific approach was employed for fine-tuning. In convolutional neural networks (CNNs), the latter layers discern high-level features, making them prime candidates for transfer learning [28]. Given the diminutive image size, utilizing the full extent of the MobileNet can be excessive; hence, the architecture is truncated at the 12th block. The terminal layer of the pre-trained model was discarded, paving the way for the integration of a global max-pooling layer followed by a dense prediction segment within the CNN:

- The GlobalAveragePooling2D layer amasses the distinct features of each image into a consolidated 1280-element vector.
- A dense layer is incorporated to channel these features into individual predictions for each image. A softmax activation function is paired with this dense layer, producing seven outputs to correspond with the seven identifiable emotions.
- Optimization was carried out using the categorical cross-entropy loss function paired with the Adam optimizer.

For fine-tuning, the foundational layers of the neural network were set immutable, allowing exclusive training of the terminal layer, yielding a more accurate model rendition. The applied callback functions included:

- EarlyStopping: Ceases model training if a stipulated improvement threshold isn't met over a defined epoch span.
- ReduceLROnPlateau: Curtails the learning rate when the model ceases to learn.

Training of this adapted model was conducted over the FER-2013 dataset across five epochs, as depicted in Fig. 3.

```
Epoch 1/5
449/448 [==============================] - 22s 49ms/step - loss: 0.3028 - accuracy: 0.3423 - val
_loss: 1.8122 - val_accuracy: 0.3761
Epoch 2/5
449/448 [==============================] - 22s 49ms/step - loss: 0.2968 - accuracy: 0.3656 - val
_loss: 2.1448 - val_accuracy: 0.3553
Epoch 3/5
449/448 [==============================] - 22s 50ms/step - loss: 0.2970 - accuracy: 0.3679 - val
_loss: 1.9577 - val_accuracy: 0.3892
Epoch 4/5
449/448 [==============================] - 22s 50ms/step - loss: 0.2983 - accuracy: 0.3685 - val
_loss: 2.1780 - val_accuracy: 0.3608
Epoch 5/5
449/448 [==============================] - 22s 50ms/step - loss: 0.2979 - accuracy: 0.3671 - val
_loss: 1.8160 - val_accuracy: 0.3789
```

Fig. 3. Model summation's simple fine-tuning after five epochs

Fine-tuning of the entire custom model with a learning rate: 0.0001 (Fig. 4).

```
Number of layers in the base model: 81
Model: "functional_1"

_____
Layer (type)                    Output Shape            Param #
===============================================================
input_2 (InputLayer)            [(None, 48, 48, 3)]     0
_____
mobilenet_trunc (Functional)    (None, 1, 1, 1024)      2162880
_____
global_average_pooling2d (Gl    (None, 1024)            0
_____
pred (Dense)                    (None, 7)               7175
===============================================================
Total params: 2,170,055
Trainable params: 2,152,263
Non-trainable params: 17,792
_____
```

Fig. 4. Module summarization for secondary experiments

With 44 epochs, the authors get accuracy for seven emotion categories (Fig. 5).

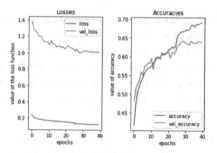

Fig. 5. Training history

3.4 Experiment 4: Analyzing Engagement Detection

The concluding experiment emphasizes the evaluation of engagement detection performance. To assess the model's precision in emotion recognition, performance metrics are calculated across each emotion category. Various visual representations, such as confusion matrices, emotion prediction visualizations, and juxtapositions of predicted versus actual labels, encapsulate the results. These graphical insights spotlight the model's proficiency and pinpoint potential areas for refinement concerning engagement level detection. Figure 6 delineates the performance metrics for the classification model. The performance is categorized for seven emotions, as follows: 0: 'Angry', 1: 'Disgust', 2: 'Fear', 3: 'Happy', 4: 'Sad', 5: 'Surprise', 6: 'Neutral'.

	precision	recall	f1-score	support
0	0.54	0.59	0.56	467
1	1.00	0.02	0.04	56
2	0.54	0.39	0.45	496
3	0.83	0.87	0.85	895
4	0.55	0.50	0.53	653
5	0.79	0.72	0.75	415
6	0.53	0.70	0.60	607
accuracy			0.64	3589
macro avg	0.68	0.54	0.54	3589
weighted avg	0.65	0.64	0.63	3589

Fig. 6. Measuring the performance of a classification model

Comparatively, our custom model showcased positive accuracy when compared against earlier models trained on the FER2013 dataset, as illustrated in Fig. 6. With a compact footprint of approximately 25 MB, the trained model is highly suitable for mobile application integrations (Fig. 7 and Table 2).

Analyzing Incorrect Predictions: The confusion matrix accentuates the model's exceptional prowess in discerning happiness, while also highlighting indicators for enhancement in other emotion categories. A confluence of factors, such as a limited dataset for certain categories and potential inconsistencies in data quality, play a part in the overall accuracy. More often than not, misclassified images bear a stronger resemblance to the predicted class than to their designated categories.

Table 2. Mislabeled cases breakdown

Category	Missed labels	Observations
Angry	238	467
Disgust	0	56
Fear	164	496
Happy	163	895
Sad	269	653
Surprise	78	415

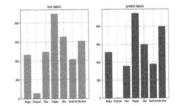

Fig. 7. Test and Predicted labels distribution comparison

3.5 System Implementation and Deployment

Designed Online Learning System Overview

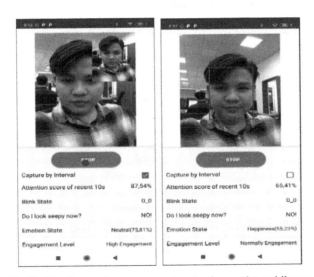

Fig. 8. Test Screen for engagement evaluation on the mobile app

This section looks into the architecture and features of the online learning system, focusing on its capability to consistently monitor student engagement and provide real-time feedback to educators. The system's core objective is to enhance the digital educational experience by fostering increased interaction and commitment between learners and educators. Our experiments target a two-part proof-of-concept system: a student-centric mobile application and an educator-centric web application, both streamlining virtual interactions.

The mobile application includes a test screen that depicts underlying operations. Over time, images of students are collected (See Fig. 8) and subsequently examined to extract metadata encompassing emotional states and engagement metrics. This metadata, once it meets specified criteria, is stored in a distant database. Post-session, educators can access this data via the web application, where visual representations, such as charts (see Fig. 9), provide insights into the session's effectiveness and students' emotional trajectories using radar charts.

Crafting a neural network from the ground up can be both resource-intensive and time-consuming, especially when constrained by a limited dataset. Such processes often stumble upon hurdles resulting in compromised accuracy. These challenges encompass issues like data size constraints and imbalances in label distribution, which curtail the model's proficiency in feature extraction from images. Good models may underperform when paired with too datasets, underscoring the crucial nature of model fine-tuning and optimal learning rate determination. As a remedy, transfer learning emerges, offering the advantage of capitalizing on pre-existing models and consistently delivering superior performance, even with data restrictions. Essentially, transfer learning repurposes insights gleaned from pre-trained models to address the task at hand. Convolutional Neural Network (CNN) layers serve as detail extractors, processing multiple granularity levels. Transfer learning harnesses these insights for enhanced performance. The architecture of transfer learning divides into:

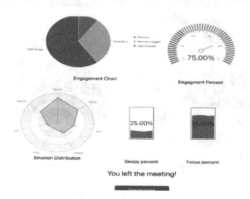

Fig. 9. Engagement metrics available after classroom session ends

- **Part 1:** The foundational network responsible for feature extraction via 2D convolutional layers. The topmost fully connected layers are omitted, assimilating this foundational network from a pre-trained model segment.
- **Part 2:** Here, fully connected layers work on data dimension reduction and compute the probability distribution for output. The primary output's unit tally mirrors the categories inherent to the classification challenge.

Comparison with Leading Approaches

The Depthwise Separable Convolution, a key feature of MobileNet, yields performance metrics on par with leading methodologies, albeit with a more compact network framework. This characteristic of MobileNet, reiterated in Tables 3, 4, & 5, demonstrates its ability in providing a lightweight model tailored for mobile device deployment [21].

Table 3. Comparing 1.0 MobileNet-224 with GoogleNet and VGG 16 on the ImageNet

Model	ImageNet Accuracy	Million Mult-Adds	Million Parameters
1.0 mobileNet-224	70.6%	569	4.2
GoogleNet	69.8%	1550	6.8
VGG 16	71.5%	15300	138

Table 4. Comparing MobileNet with Squeezenet and AlexNet

Model	ImageNet Accuracy	Million Mult-Adds	Million Parameters
0.50 mobileNet-160	60.2%	76	1.32
Squeezenet	57.5%	1700	1.25
AlexNet	57.2%	720	60

Table 5. MobileNet distilled from FaceNet

Model	1e-4 Accuracy	Million Mult-Adds	Million Parameters
FaceNet	83%	1600	7.5
1.0 MobileNet-160	79.4%	286	4.9
1.0 MobileNet-128	78.3%	185	5.5
0.75 MobileNet-128	75.2%	166	3.4
0.75 MobileNet-128	72.5%	108	3.8

3.6   Potentials for Integration with Enterprise Information System

Enterprises are continually striving to surpass their competitors, and to do so, they must harness cutting-edge technologies like machine learning, AI solutions, including NLP and sentiment extraction. Such technological advancements necessitate a modern workforce equipped with lifelong learning abilities. While these skills often lie dormant and emerge only in specific scenarios, they are challenging to measure. Despite the increasing budgets for education and training, there's a critical need for optimizing these allocations. Companies that can effectively allocate these resources gain a distinct advantage. The solution presented in this paper offers a dual advantage. First, it optimizes in-class performance by highlighting instances where learners' attention wanes, necessitating immediate intervention. Second, it allows for a continuous assessment of an individual's ability to focus and acquire new skills. This data can be incorporated into other analytic functions, facilitating the categorization of employees based on their attention span and learning capacities.

4   Conclusion

Online education has presented numerous opportunities, yet sustaining learner engagement, especially in the financial enterprise training systems, remains an imperative challenge to address. Our research introduces a pioneering online learning tool designed for real-time attention monitoring, intertwined with emotion recognition. Using the MobileNet Convolutional Neural Network, we have successfully detected seven key emotions, translating these findings into a novel Concentration Index (CI). This CI system classifies learners into distinct engagement categories, namely "Highly engaged," "Normally Engaged," and "Disengaged."

Our model's accuracy, reflecting 70% during training and 65% during testing, affirms its robustness and efficiency. By offering these quantifiable metrics, educators are empowered with real-time feedback, enabling them to customize their teaching methods accordingly. Further, the graphical outputs serve as an insightful resource for administrators, presenting an illustrative overview of learner engagement trajectories.

In essence, this study lays down a foundational framework, propelling the enhancement of interactive and immersive virtual learning environments. As we look to the horizon, we envision harnessing broader datasets for improved emotion detection, refining the CI's accuracy, and integrating innovative technologies like chatbots. A commitment to constant evolution and embracing collaborative efforts is paramount to remain attuned to the ever-shifting landscape of online education, ensuring we continually hone engagement metrics and intervention strategies.

References

1. https://emerline.com/blog/e-learning-in-banking
2. Meyen, E.L., Aust, R.J., Bui, Y.N., Isaacson, R.: Assessing and monitoring student progress in an e-learning personnel preparation environment. Teach. Educ. Spec. Educ. **25**, 187–198 (2002)
3. Guncaga, J., Lopuchova, J., Ferdianova, V., Zacek, M., Ashimov, Y.: Survey on online learning at universities of Slovakia, Czech Republic and Kazakhstan during the COVID-19 pandemic. Educ. Sci. **12**, 458 (2022)
4. Dumford, A.D., Miller, A.L.: Online learning in higher education: exploring advantages and disadvantages for engagement. J. Comput. High. Educ. **30**, 452–465 (2018)
5. Ortony, A., Clore, G.L., Collins, A.: The Cognitive structure of emotions cambridge. UK: Cambridge University Press (1988)
6. Krithika, L.B., GG, L.P.: Student emotion recognition system (SERS) for e-learning improvement based on learner concentration metric. Procedia Comput. Sci. **85**, 767–776 (2016)
7. Picard, R.W., et al.: Affective learning—a manifesto. BT Technol. J. **22**, 253–269 (2004)

8. de Vicente, A., Pain, H.: Motivation diagnosis in intelligent tutoring systems. In: Goettl, B.P., Halff, H.M., Redfield, C.L., Shute, V.J. (eds.) Intelligent tutoring systems, pp. 86–95. Springer, Heidelberg (1998). https://doi.org/10.1007/3-540-68716-5_14

9. Du Boulay, B., Luckin, R.: Modelling human teaching tactics and strategies for tutoring systems. Int. J. Artif. Intell. Educ. **12**, 235–256 (2001)

10. de Vicente, A., Pain, H.: Informing the detection of the students' motivational state: an empirical study. In: Cerri, S.A., Gouardères, G., Paraguaçu, F. (eds.) Intelligent Tutoring Systems: 6th International Conference, ITS 2002 Biarritz, France and San Sebastian, Spain, June 2–7, 2002 Proceedings, pp. 933–943. Springer, Heidelberg (2002). https://doi.org/10.1007/3-540-47987-2_93

11. Den Uyl, M., Van Kuilenburg, H.: The FaceReader: online facial expression recognition. In: Proceedings of Measuring Behavior, pp. 589–590. Citeseer (2005)

12. Happy, S., George, A., Routray, A.: A real time facial expression classification system using local binary patterns. In: 2012 4th International Conference on Intelligent Human Computer Interaction (IHCI), pp. 1–5. IEEE (2012)

13. Woolf, B., Burelson, W., Arroyo, I.: Emotional intelligence for computer tutors. In: Workshop On Modeling and Scaffolding Affective Experiences to Impact Learning at 13th International Conference on Artificial Intelligence in Education, Los Angeles, California. (2007)

14. Feidakis, M., Daradoumis, T., Caballé, S., Conesa, J.: Measuring the Impact of Emotion Awareness on e-learning Situations. In: 2013 Seventh International Conference on Complex, Intelligent, and Software Intensive Systems, pp. 391–396. IEEE (2013)

15. Startsev, M., Zemblys, R.: Evaluating eye movement event detection: a review of the state of the art. Behav. Res. Methods **55**, 1653–1714 (2023)

16. Deubel, H., Schneider, W.X.: Saccade target selection and object recognition: evidence for a common attentional mechanism. Vision. Res. **36**, 1827–1837 (1996)

17. Lu, Y., Liu, C., Chang, F., Liu, H., Huan, H.: JHPFA-Net: Joint Head Pose and Facial Action Network for Driver Yawning Detection Across Arbitrary Poses in Videos. IEEE Trans. Intell. Transp. Syst. **24**, 11850–11863 (2023)

18. FER-2013 (2013)

19. Ezerceli, Ö., Eskil, M.T.: Convolutional neural network (CNN) algorithm based facial emotion recognition (FER) system for FER-2013 dataset. In: 2022 International Conference on Electrical, Computer, Communications and Mechatronics Engineering (ICECCME), pp. 1–6. IEEE (2013)

20. Zhang, K., Zhang, Z., Li, Z., Qiao, Y.: Joint face detection and alignment using multitask cascaded convolutional networks. IEEE Signal Process. Lett. **23**, 1499–1503 (2016)

21. Howard, A.G., et al.: Mobilenets: efficient convolutional neural networks for mobile vision applications. arXiv preprint arXiv:1704.04861 (2017)

22. Chollet, F.: Xception: deep learning with depthwise separable convolutions. In: Proceedings of the IEEE Conference on Computer Vision and Pattern Recognition, pp. 1251–1258 (2017)

23. Sharma, P., et al.: Student engagement detection using emotion analysis, eye tracking and head movement with machine learning. In: Reis, A., Barroso, J., Martins, P., Jimoyiannis, A., Huang, R.-M., Henriques, R. (eds.) Technology and Innovation in Learning, Teaching and Education: Third International Conference, TECH-EDU 2022, Lisbon, Portugal, August 31–September 2, 2022, Revised Selected Papers, pp. 52–68. Springer Nature Switzerland, Cham (2022). https://doi.org/10.1007/978-3-031-22918-3_5

24. Mishra, S., Minh, C.S., Chuc, H.T., Long, T.V., Nguyen, T.T.: Automated Robot (Car) using Artificial Intelligence. In: 2021 International Seminar on Machine Learning, Optimization, and Data Science (ISMODE), pp. 319–324. IEEE (2021)

25. https://docs.seeso.io/

26. Mishra, S., Thanh, L.T.: SATMeas - object detection and measurement: canny edge detection algorithm. In: Pan, X., Jin, T., Zhang, L.-J. (eds.) Artificial Intelligence and Mobile Services – AIMS 2022: 11th International Conference, Held as Part of the Services Conference Federation, SCF 2022, Honolulu, HI, USA, December 10–14, 2022, Proceedings, pp. 91–101. Springer International Publishing, Cham (2022). https://doi.org/10.1007/978-3-031-235 04-7_7

27. Shorten, C., Khoshgoftaar, T.M.: A survey on image data augmentation for deep learning. J. Big Data **6**, 1–48 (2019)

28. Tajbakhsh, N., et al.: Convolutional neural networks for medical image analysis: full training or fine tuning? IEEE Trans. Med. Imaging **35**, 1299–1312 (2016)

Algebraic Semantics of Register Transfer Level in Synthesis of Stream Calculus-Based Computing Big Data in Livestream

Pham Van Dang[1,2,3]([⊠]) [iD], Phan Cong Vinh[1,2,3] [iD], and Nguyen Bao Khang[4] [iD]

[1] Graduate University of Science and Technology, Vietnam Academy of Science and Technology, Hanoi, Vietnam
{pvdang,pcvinh}@ntt.edu.vn

[2] Institute of Applied Mechanics and Informatics, Ho Chi Minh City, Vietnam

[3] Faculty of Information Technology, Nguyen Tat Thanh University, Ho Chi Minh City, Vietnam

[4] British International School Ho Chi Minh City, Ho Chi Minh City, Vietnam
knguyen22@bisvietnam.com

Abstract. This paper represents verification algorithms and register transfer level (RTL) specification as algebraic aspects proposed to validate the results of RTL synthesis. Major properties of this approach, the conception of an algebraic semantics-based model (ASM), to be interpreted as a Chu space, is viewed as an algebraic semantics foundation for the RTL formalization and the conception of algebraic semantics-based specification automata (ASA_{SPEC}) are given for formal correctness of the results of RTL synthesis. Approaching formal verification is focused on functional equivalence examining to define if the algebraic RTL automata (ASA_{RTL}) are equivalent to ASA_{SPEC}. To put it another way, the comparison is determined as an assessing that examines the synthesis algorithm is produced an effective RTL specification.

Keywords: Algebraic semantics · Algebraic semantics-based model (ASM) · Algebraic semantics-based specification automata (ASA_{SPEC}) · Algebraic RTL automata (ASA_{RTL}) · Big data in livestream (BDL) · Register transfer level (RTL) · Stream calculus-based computing BDL · Control step (CStep) · Functional unit (FU)

1 Introduction

In recent years, several researchers of many areas have been analyzing techniques known as partial order methods, which can obviously reduce the running time of formal validation by avoiding redundant exploration of executive scenarios [1, 4]. This paper performs development an algebraic semantics-based model (ASM) for the RTL formalization and via the algebraic semantics, proposes a formal verification approach to proving the result correctness of RTL synthesis in stream calculus-based computing BDL. To put it another way, approach of this paper is to model the behaviors using algebraic semantics as a

P. Cong Vinh and H. Mahfooz Ul Haque (Eds.): ICTCC 2023, LNICST 586, pp. 19–35, 2024.
https://doi.org/10.1007/978-3-031-59462-5_2

foundation and utilize this model to construct attracting properties of the model that should remain both at the behaviors and RTLs. After that RTL synthesis, this paper will verify the same properties continue to remain for designing the RTL. In addition, two achievable targets from this approach are accurately examining an RTL specification regarding a behavioral specification, bisimulation of two RTL synthesis results of the same algorithms.

In stream calculus-based computing big data in livestream (BDL), correctness validation is usually a hard and open problem in generally giving all researchers. It can be done via two fundamental methods to be formal verification and simulation [1–6]. In the formal verification approach, demonstrating of theorem and examining of model are considered the most fashionable techniques to show whether the design of RTL synthesized from the behavioral specification of algorithm is mathematically correct. Finding formal verification approaches to supply exact and rapid validation clearly is a so valuable goal. In the research [7], a categorical method (to be interpreted as algebraic semantics) is utilized to build a vigorous formal basic for the contextual perception model (to be interpreted as algebraic semantics-based model) so as to acquire the algebraic semantics.

This paper is structured as follows. Section 1 presents introduction and objectives of this paper. Section 2 overviews related work. Section 3 describes stream algebra and uses some fundamental operators for BDL. Section 4 specifies algebraic semantics for RTL. Section 5 describes verification algorithms for the results of RTL synthesis. Section 6 outlines conclusions and future work. Finally, there are references.

2   Related Work

Normally, a Chu space is a matrix over a set $\{0, 1\}$, to be interpreted as, an array whose entries are drawn from $\{0, 1\}$. Formally, in [8–15], a Chu space is viewed as a binary relation between two sets of events E and states S. It is written as a triple (E, S, R), in which $R : E \times S \rightarrow \{0, 1\}$ is the binary relation as a properties function of a $E \times S$ subset.

Here, E and S are examined as two generic mathematical sets. Figure 1 gives some Chu spaces examples. The E elements are symbolized by $e_0, e_1, e_2, e_3, ... e_n, 0 \leq i \leq n$ and the elements of S are symbolized by $s_0, s_1, s_2, s_3, ... s_m, 0 \leq j \leq m$.

In [2, 3, 12], they have symbolized E as the events set and S as the states set. A state is determined about an occurrence relation $R(e, s)$ which is true where the event e has happened in the state s. Therefore, each state s is an E subset holding the events that have happened in the state s. Algebraic semantics is viewed as a Chu space C specified by the triple (E, S, R), in which $E = \{e_0, e_1, e_2, e_3, ..., e_n\}, 1 \leq i \leq n$ is an events set, $S = \{s_0, s_1, s_2, s_3, ..., s_n\}, 1 \leq i \leq n$ is a states set, and $R : E \times S \rightarrow \{0, 1\}$ represents the occurrence relation, to be interpreted as, $R(e, s) = 1$ if the event e has happened in the state s and $R(e, s) = 0$, otherwise. For any $e \in E$, each state $s_i \in S = 2^E$ is determined in terms of R by $s_i = \{e | R(e, s_i) = 1\}$.

The algebraic semantics in Fig. 2 has three events, $\{e_0, e_1, e_2\}$ and seven states $\{s_0, s_1, s_2, s_3, s_4, s_5, s_6\}$, and represents a system, where any event $\in \{e_0, e_1, e_2\}$ occurs and according to data produced by event that one of the remaining two events will happen. For example, in state s_0, the event e_2 has happened; s_2 describes the state in which e_1 has happened after e_2 or e_2 has happened after e_1.

An algebraic semantics can be represented in a matrix, as a Hasse diagram or as a logical formula [16, 17]. In the matrix description, each entry pair (e, s) holds the value of the occurrence relation. Therefore, the matrix rows relate to the algebraic semantics states and the matrix columns relate to the algebraic semantics events. In a Hasse diagram, an algebraic semantics is represented by the partial order existing between the states. In the logical formula, the matrix is viewed as a truth table, the logical description $f_{\mathcal{D}}$ of the algebraic semantics $\mathcal{D}$ is determined by $f_{\mathcal{D}} = \bigvee_{0 < i < n} (\wedge\{e | R(e, s_i) = 1\}) \wedge \{\wedge \bar{e} | R(e, s_i) = 0\}$, where $n = |S|$ and $e \in E$ and $\bar{e}$ is the complement of e.

Hasse Diagram   **Matrix**

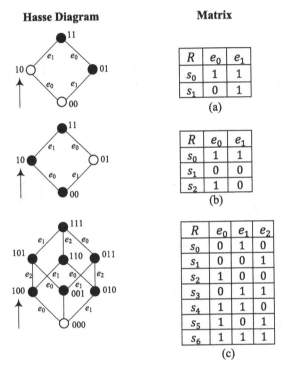

Fig. 1. Chu spaces and its descriptions by matrix (a), (b) and (c).

In which, the events $e \in E$ are seen as variables, the states $s \in S$ are seen as in terms of logical formula and the R relation defines either the variable is complemented $R(e, s_i) = 0$ or not $R(e, s_i) = 1$. Logical formula f is true for each state $s \in S$ which is allowed in the algebraic semantics. From that, we are obtained an ASM in form as follows ASM $= (E, S, R)$, where $E = \{e_0, e_1, e_2\}$ holds the set of events, $S = \{\{e_1\}, \{e_2\}, \{e_0\}, \{e_1, e_2\}, \{e_0, e_1\}, \{e_0, e_2\}, \{e_0, e_1, e_2\}\}$ holds the states set, $R(E, S)$ is the relation between event E and state S represented by the binary matrix (see Fig. 2).

Some the fundamental relations between events as follows relations of independence, precedence, conflict, and disjunctive enabling determined in [16–18] are used in this paper.

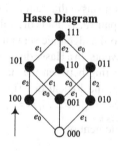

Hasse Diagram

Matrix						**Logical formula**
R	e_0	e_1	e_2			f_{ASM}
s_0	0	1	0	$\{e_1\}$		$\{\overline{e_0}, e_1, \overline{e_2}\}$
s_1	0	0	1	$\{e_2\}$		$\{\overline{e_0}, \overline{e_1}, e_2\}$
s_2	1	0	0	$\{e_0\}$		$\{e_0, \overline{e_1}, \overline{e_2}\}$
s_3	0	1	1	$\{e_1, e_2\}$		$\{\overline{e_0}, e_1, e_2\}$
s_4	1	1	0	$\{e_0, e_1\}$		$\{e_0, e_1, \overline{e_2}\}$
s_5	1	0	1	$\{e_0, e_2\}$		$\{e_0, \overline{e_1}, e_2\}$
s_6	1	1	1	$\{e_0, e_1, e_2\}$		$\{e_0, e_1, e_2\}$

Fig. 2. Algebraic semantics and its descriptions

Relation (∇): The relation of independence ($e_0 \nabla e_1$) describes the independent execution of two events e_0 and e_1 of every allowed state. To put it another way, all subsets of E are effective states. Figure 3(a) presents the algebraic semantics and its relevant logical formula.

∇	e_0	e_1	$f_\nabla =$
s_0	0	1	$\{\overline{e_0}, e_1\} +$
s_1	0	0	$\{\overline{e_0}, \overline{e_1}\} +$
s_2	1	1	$\{e_0, e_1\} +$
s_3	1	0	$\{e_0, \overline{e_1}\}$
			$= 1$

(a) Relation matrix of independence

$\prec$	e_0	e_1	$f_\prec =$
s_0	1	0	$\{e_0, \overline{e_1}\} +$
s_1	0	0	$\{\overline{e_0}, \overline{e_1}\} +$
s_2	1	1	$\{e_0, e_1\}$
			$= e_0 + \overline{e_1}$

(b) Relation matrix of precedence

den	e_0	e_1	e_2	$f_{den} =$
s_0	0	1	0	$\{\overline{e_0}, e_1, \overline{e_2}\} +$
s_1	0	0	0	$\{\overline{e_0}, \overline{e_1}, \overline{e_2}\} +$
s_2	0	1	1	$\{\overline{e_0}, e_1, e_2\} +$
s_3	0	0	1	$\{\overline{e_0}, \overline{e_1}, e_2\} +$
s_4	1	0	1	$\{e_0, \overline{e_1}, e_2\} +$
s_5	1	1	1	$\{e_0, e_1, e_2\} +$
s_6	1	1	0	$\{e_0, e_1, \overline{e_2}\} +$
				$= \overline{e_0} + e_1 + e_2$

(d) Relation matrix of disjunctive enabling

#	e_0	e_1	$f_\# =$
s_0	0	1	$\{\overline{e_0}, e_1\} +$
s_1	0	0	$\{\overline{e_0}, \overline{e_1}\} +$
s_2	1	0	$\{e_0, \overline{e_1}\}$
			$= \overline{e_0} + \overline{e_1}$

(c) Relation matrix of conflict

Fig. 3. Some fundamental relations between the events of the states in Chu space

Relation ($\prec$): The relation of precedence ($e_0 \prec e_1$) represents the event occurrence e_0 followed by the event occurrence e_1. To put it another way, this precedence relation is utilized to specify the sequential events execution. Figure 3(b) represents the algebraic semantics and its relevant logical formula.

Relation (#): The relation of conflict ($e_0 \# e_1$) describes either the e_0 event occurrence or the e_1 event occurrence. To put it another way, both the events e_0 and e_1 can never occur in e_0 same computation of the algebraic semantics. Figure 3(c) represents the algebraic semantics and its relevant logical formula.

Relation (den): The relation of disjunctive enabling den(e_0, e_1, e_2) represents the occurrence of event e_1 or e_2 enabling the occurrence of e. In addition, this relation can be used along with the relation of conflict to specify permission for events following the lines of an *if ...then...else* statement. Figure 3(d) represents the algebraic semantics and its relevant logical formula.

3 Stream Algebra for BDL

Stream algebra is represented as sets with operators. Handling the frames infinite sequences is called streams as single entities, an algebra of streams is built in two ways as in analysis, including stream differentiation and integration. In algebra, where operators and establishes identities is computed [19, 20].

The stream algebra has been proposed in [21–25] consisting of some operators such as the operators of merging, dropping, taking, zipping, splitting, copying, registering and assignment [19]. A stream σ is defined by the function in the following.

$$\sigma : \mathbb{N} \rightarrow \mathbb{A}^\omega$$

Here, $\mathbb{N} = \{0, 1, 2, 3, ...\}$ is natural numbers set and $\mathbb{A}$ is set of frames. A frame may be indicated as a framework, which holds of data types as text, image, audio, video, space, time, geometry and so on. To be interpreted as$\sigma = (\sigma(0), \sigma(1), \sigma(2), ...)$.

For formally defining stream, the stream derivative notation is used for a stream definition as follows. For every integer $n \geq 0$, with differential equation: $\left(\sigma^{(n)}\right)' = \sigma^{(n+1)}$, initial value $\sigma(0)$. The initial value of stream σ is defined namely $\sigma(0)$, and the stream derivative signified by $\sigma\prime$ and is defined by $\left(\sigma^{(n)}\right)' = \sigma^{(n+1)}$, for any integers $n \geq 0$. To put it another way, the initial value and stream derivative equivalent the head and tail of stream σ, respectively. The stream behavior σ includes two aspects, it enables for the initial value inspection $\sigma(0)$ and it can make a development to the new stream $\sigma\prime$, including the original stream from which the first element has been dropped. The initial value of $\sigma\prime$, which is $\sigma\prime(0) = \sigma(1)$, in its turn can be inspected, but note that we had to move from σ to $\sigma\prime$ first in order to do so. Now a behavioral differential equation defines a stream by specifying its initial value together with a its derivative description, which tells us how to continue.

Representing the fundamental definitions on streams that they will be used. Moreover, the authors of researches also propound a brief overview of a coinductive streams calculus [22, 25. The streams set are defined over frames set $\mathbb{A}$ by$\mathbb{A}^\omega = \{\sigma | \sigma : \mathbb{N} \rightarrow \mathbb{A}\}$. The Greek letters $\sigma, \tau, \gamma, \pi, \epsilon, ...$ are used to symbolize streams. Elements $\sigma \in \mathbb{A}^\omega$ are signified by$\sigma = (\sigma(0), \sigma(1), \sigma(2), ...)$. The stream derivate of a stream σ is $\sigma' = (\sigma(1), \sigma(2), \sigma(3), ...)$ and the initial value of σ is$\sigma(0)$. For $n \geq 0$ and$\sigma \in \mathbb{A}^\omega$, higher-order derivate is determined by $\sigma^{(0)} = \sigma$ and$\sigma^{(n+1)} = \left(\sigma^{(n)}\right)'$. This paper provides$\sigma(n) = \sigma^{(n)}(0)$.

In this paper, we use some fundamental operators for stream calculus-based computing BDL in the research [19, 20, 25] calculated in Al algorithm the following subsections.

4 Algebraic Semantics for RTL

In this paper, an algebraic semantics for an RTL specification and a verification algorithm (see Fig. 4(a)) have been developed for validating the results of RTL synthesis, using the existing concepts covered in this section.

4.1 Events Set

Definition 1 (Computation). A finite actions sequence is a computation over E events set and the computations set is symbolized by $C(E)$.

4.2 States Set

Let S be the states set. State $s \in S$ is determined by a transition relation $T(e, s_i)$, also sometimes denoted by $s_i \xrightarrow{e} s_j$, where the event $e \in E$ can make a transition from the state $s_i \in S$ to $s_j \in S$. Therefore, each state s_j is a subset of event E, holding the events that can make a transition from the s_i. To be interpreted as:

$$s_j = \left\{ e | e \in E : s_i \xrightarrow{e} s_j \right\}$$

To put it another way, the triple (E, S, T) is an algebraic semantics. For all e_i in E and s_i in S, a computation of the ASM(E, S, T) is $T = \left\{ e_1, e_2, e_3, ..., e_n : s_1 \xrightarrow{e_1} s_2, s_2 \xrightarrow{e_2} s_3, ..., s_n \xrightarrow{e_n} s_{n+1} \right\}$. From this consideration, the conception of algebraic automata is developed in the next subsections.

4.3 Algebraic Automata

Definition 2 (Algebraic automata). Algebraic automata are a triple $\mathcal{A} = (S, s_0, T)$, where S is the finite states set, s_0 is the initial state, T is a transition function from $S \times E$ into $S \bigcup \{\bot\}$.

If $T(s, e) = \bot$, no transition labelled by event e can be fired from state s. Note that $\bot$ can be considered as a sink state. A computation $T = \{e_1, e_2, e_3, ..., e_n\}$ is agreed by the automata if there exists $s_1, s_2, s_3, ..., s_n, \in S$ such that $T(s_0, e_1) = s_1, \forall 1 < i \leq n, T(s_{i-1}, e_i) = s_i$. This is symbolized by $s_0 \xrightarrow{e_1} s_1 \xrightarrow{e_2} s_2 ... s_{n-1} \xrightarrow{e_n} s_n$. If it is not the case, there exists $1 \leq k \leq n$, the states sequence such that $s_0 \xrightarrow{e_1} s_1 \xrightarrow{e_2} s_2 ... s_{k-1} \xrightarrow{e_k} \bot$.

Such a path via automata is known as the automata run over the computation T. The computations set agreed by $\mathcal{A}$ is symbolized by $C(\mathcal{A})$. The four algebraic automata of four CSteps include four states and such the four states respectively (see Fig. 4(a), 4(b) and 4(c)).

The FUs are normally built into a library representation the map between its functions and the related operators. The FUs can be implementations of single-purpose operators or multiple-purpose operators with control input signals for choosing the desired for operators [19, 20]. In Fig. 4(a), the eight single-purpose FUs are required to implement the nine operators of *split*, *take*, *zip*, *drop*, $+$, $\cdot$, $:=$, $<>$ and ■ in the following.

In Fig. 4(a), it represents RTL of AI algorithm with four CSteps. CStep 0 performs four operators as follows operators of taking, merging, splitting and copying. Then, results are stored in two registers 1 and 2. Next, CStep 1 performs three operators as follows operators of zipping, merging and dropping using values of two registers 1 and 2. Then, results are stored in two reused registers 1 and 2. CStep 2 performs a comparison using values of two registers 1 and 2 of CStep 1. Then, results are stored in reused registers 1 or 2. Finally, CStep 3 performs an assignment operator using values of two registers 1 or 2 from CStep 2, then sending result of assignment operator for output. In Fig. 4(b), it represents matrixes with four CSteps and registers respectively, in particular, representing State 0 $\left(s_0^{Se/Re}\right)$ to State 3 $\left(s_3^{Se/Re}\right)$ of CStep 0 with two registers and such CStep 1, 2 and 3 also are represented. In Fig. 4(c), it is a visual graph that describes matrixes in Fig. 4(b) representing algebraic automata for AI algorithm with four CSteps.

This paper presents now an algebraic automata product in Sect. 4.4 that permits a more complex process modularity specification. In which, each sub-process can be modelled by the algebraic automata and completeness process modeling can be acquired by computing the algebraic automata product of all sub-process represented details in the next section.

4.4 Algebraic Automata Product

This paper represents the two processes *Se* and *Re* that can be linked as in Fig. 5(a) and 5(b). Let $\mathcal{Se} = \left(S^{Se}, s_p^{Se}, T^{Se}\right)$ and $\mathcal{Re} = \left(S^{Re}, s_q^{Re}, T^{Re}\right)$ be the two algebraic automata that model the processes *Se* and *Re*, respectively. This paper defines algebraic automata product of the two processes of *Se* and *Re* as $\mathcal{Se} \times \mathcal{Re}$ in order to model the process attained by connecting *Se* to *Re*. For asynchronizing *Se* outputs with *Re* inputs so that when a data moves on between *Se* and *Re* through a register then this transfer must be occurred. This shows the determination of the *Se* and *Re* product, over the similar event set E: $\mathcal{Se} \times \mathcal{Re} = (S, s_p, T)$, in which $S = S^{Se} \times S^{Re}$, $s_p = \left(s_p^{Se} \times s_q^{Re}\right)$, where p, q are replaced for i, j, k, or l.

A transition relation T is determined in the way as follows. Let $s_i = \left(s_i^{Se} \times s_j^{Re}\right)$ be in state S and e in event E. If there exist $s_i^{Se} + 1 \in S^{Se}$ and $s_j^{Re} + 1 \in S^{Re}$ such that $T^{Se}\left(s_i^{Se}, e\right) = s_{i+1}^{Se}$ and $T^{Re}\left(s_j^{Re}, e\right) = s_{j+1}^{Re}$, we set $T\left(\left(s_i^{Se}, s_j^{Re}\right), e\right) = (s_{i+1}^{Se}, s_{j+1}^{Re})$. Otherwise, we set $T\left(\left(s_i^{Se}, s_j^{Re}\right), e\right) = \perp$.

Suppose that the output/input width *Se* is equivalent to the input/output width *Re* respectively, so these processes can be linked each other in Fig. 5, in which Fig. 5(a) is a matrix representing sixteenth states of four registers and then Fig. 5(b) is a visual graph representing RTLs of sixteenth states with four registers. Each state in $\mathcal{Se} \times \mathcal{Re}$ is a pair including a state from *Se* and a state from *Re*. The run of $\mathcal{Se} \times \mathcal{Re}$ over the agreed computation $\mathcal{T} = \{(1, 1, 0, 1)(1, 1, 1, 0)(1, 1, 1, 1)\}$ is symbolized as below:

$$\left(s_3^{Se}, s_0^{Re}\right) \xrightarrow{(1,1,0,1)} \left(s_3^{Se}, s_1^{Re}\right) \xrightarrow{(1,1,1,0)} \left(s_3^{Se}, s_2^{Re}\right) \xrightarrow{(1,1,1,1)} \left(s_3^{Se}, s_3^{Re}\right)$$

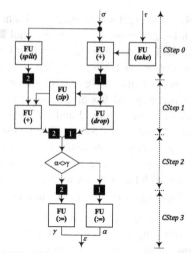

(a) Chart of RTL of Al algorithm with four CSteps along with FUs and operators

	Registers	
CStep 0	**1**	**2**
State 0 $\left(s_0^{Se/Re}\right)$	0	0
State 1 $\left(s_1^{Se/Re}\right)$	0	1
State 2 $\left(s_2^{Se/Re}\right)$	1	0
State 3 $\left(s_3^{Se/Re}\right)$	1	1

	Registers	
CStep 1	**1**	**2**
State 0 $\left(s_0^{Re/Se}\right)$	0	0
State 1 $\left(s_1^{Re/Se}\right)$	0	1
State 2 $\left(s_2^{Re/Se}\right)$	1	0
State 3 $\left(s_3^{Re/Se}\right)$	1	1

	Registers	
CStep 2	**1**	**2**
State 0 $\left(s_0^{Re/Se}\right)$	0	0
State 1 $\left(s_1^{Re/Se}\right)$	0	1

	Registers	
CStep 3	**1**	**2**
State 0 $\left(s_0^{Re/Se}\right)$	0	0
State 1 $\left(s_1^{Re/Se}\right)$	0	1

	Registers	
State 2 $\left(s_2^{Re/Se}\right)$	1	0
State 3 $\left(s_3^{Re/Se}\right)$	1	1

	Registers	
State 2 $\left(s_2^{Re/Se}\right)$	1	0
State 3 $\left(s_3^{Re/Se}\right)$	1	1

(b) Matrixes represent algebraic automata of Al algorithm with four CSteps

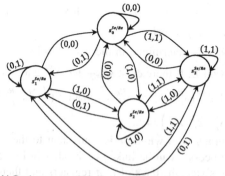

(c) Graph represents algebraic automata for Al algorithm with four CSteps

Fig. 4. The representation of algebraic automata for Al algorithm with four CSteps

$Se \times Re$	Registers			
	1	2	3	4
$s_i = \left(s_i^{Se} \times s_j^{Re}\right)$	0	0	x	y
$s_j = \left(s_j^{Se} \times s_k^{Re}\right)$	0	1	x	y
$s_k = \left(s_k^{Se} \times s_l^{Re}\right)$	1	0	x	y
$s_l = \left(s_l^{Se} \times s_i^{Re}\right)$	1	1	x	y
In which: $x, y \in \{0,1\}$ and $x \neq y$; $i, j, k, l = \overline{[0,3]} \subset \mathbb{N}^* = \mathbb{N} \cup (0)$.				

(a) This matrix represents sixteenth states of four registers.

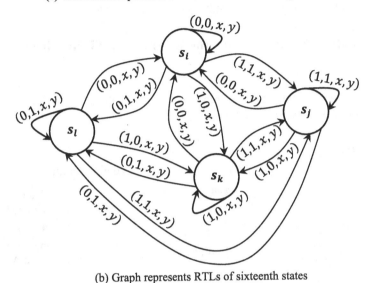

(b) Graph represents RTLs of sixteenth states

Fig. 5. Connection of the processes Se and Re and its algebraic automata product

This signifies that in the state $\left(s_3^{Se}, s_0^{Re}\right)$ on event $(1, 1, 0, 1)$, the algebraic automata product $Se \times Re$ carries out by executing Se from s_3^{Se} and in parallel, executing Re from s_0^{Re} and in parallel, and so on.

4.5 Algorithms Equivalence

Let Al and Al' be two algorithms and $\mathcal{A}$ and $\mathcal{A}'$ be their related algebraic automata. Al and Al' are equivalent $\Longleftrightarrow$ $\mathcal{C}(\mathcal{A}) = \mathcal{C}(\mathcal{A}')$. To put it another way, the algorithms Al and Al' are equal to each other if they cannot be separated by their external behaviors.

4.6 Algebraic Semantics

An algebraic semantics (known as algebraic aspects) can be explained as algebraic automata with events set E and possible states set S. Going into a state s, the algebraic automata execute some transitions over events to reach a substitute state of s. Each possible computation of the algebraic semantics relates to each run of the algebraic automata and the algebraic semantics execution specifies the algebraic automata runs set.

Algebraic automata in terms of an algebraic semantics model are represented by the events set E and the events happen to each state, to be interpreted as, the transition relation T. A further practical approach reply on relations between states is that each algebraic automata are modelled as a relations set between states and for each such relation, this paper has an algebraic semantics correspondingly. The algebraic semantics of each relation between states is viewed as an algebraic automata characteristic. Therefore, a combination of the characteristics results in the algebraic automata.

5   Verification Algorithms for the Results of RTL Synthesis

5.1   The Algorithm Steps

The verification algorithm steps are represented graphically in following Fig. 6. The algorithm steps are viewed in the following.

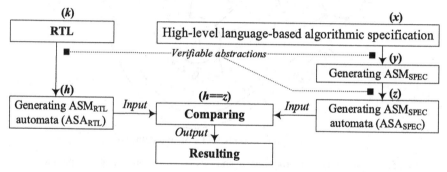

Fig. 6. An algebraic semantics-based verification algorithm for the results of RTL synthesis

5.2   High-Level Language-Based Algorithmic Specification

An appropriate high-level language-based algorithmic specification is described, this means that a program is generated in this step. A main job during this step is the actualization of the modes of various scheduling. Thus, in the very-high hardware description language example indicated in the Fig. 8, this paper has an Al algorithm with seven events associated with the Al algorithm statements, where each statement is viewed as an event.

This paper uses the udStreamsA algorithm in the [19] research to distribute its list of events for the operators of merging, dropping, taking, zipping, splitting and assignment [19] with single CStep in this algorithm to become Al algorithm below (see Fig. 7). The diverse synthesis steps of stream calculus-based computing BDL are illustrated via an example that maps input streams ($\sigma, \tau \in \mathbb{A}^{\omega}$) onto the output streams tuples ($\alpha, \gamma, \epsilon \in \mathbb{A}^{\omega}$) as defined by the algorithm specification, namely Al algorithm (Fig. 8).

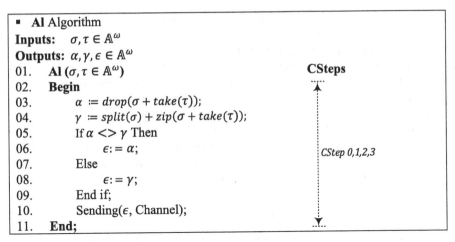

- **Al** Algorithm
Inputs: $\sigma, \tau \in \mathbb{A}^{\omega}$
Outputs: $\alpha, \gamma, \epsilon \in \mathbb{A}^{\omega}$
01.   **Al** $(\sigma, \tau \in \mathbb{A}^{\omega})$ **CSteps**
02.   **Begin**
03. $\alpha := drop(\sigma + take(\tau))$;
04. $\gamma := split(\sigma) + zip(\sigma + take(\tau))$;
05.   If $\alpha <> \gamma$ Then
06. $\epsilon := \alpha$;   CStep 0,1,2,3
07.   Else
08. $\epsilon := \gamma$;
09.   End if;
10.   Sending(ϵ, Channel);
11.   **End;**

Fig. 7. An Al algorithm for four CSteps

- **Al** Algorithm
Inputs: $\sigma, \tau, \pi \in \mathbb{A}^{\omega}$
Outputs: $\alpha, \gamma, \epsilon \in \mathbb{A}^{\omega}$
01.   **Al** $(\sigma, \tau \in \mathbb{A}^{\omega})$
02.   **Begin**   **Events**
03. $\pi := \sigma + take(\tau)$;   _____ e_0
04. $\alpha := drop(\pi)$;   _____ e_1
05. $\gamma := split(\sigma) + zip(\pi)$;   _____ e_2
06.   If $\alpha <> \gamma$ Then   _____ e_3
07. $\epsilon := \alpha$;   _____ e_4
08.   Else
09. $\epsilon := \gamma$;   _____ e_5
10.   End if;
11.   Sending(ϵ, Channel);   _____ e_6
12.   **End;**

Fig. 8. An Al algorithm and its list of events

Consider the synthesis of stream calculus-based computing BDL via the above example that computes the streams $(\sigma, \tau \in \mathbb{A}^{\omega})$ and finally mapping the streams to outputs α, γ and ϵ as determined by the Al algorithm (see Fig. 8).

5.3   Generating ASM$_{SPEC}$

The major problem is the partial order specification creation of the program statements generated in Sect. 5.2. To put it another way, this specification is utilized to show the data dependency of statements necessary for the creation of the possible algebraic semantics-based specification of the automata, namely ASA$_{SPEC}$. To fulfil this task, we need to refer to some fundamental relations between events, such as relations of independence, precedence, conflict and disjunctive enabling, as described in Sect. 2.

In approach of this paper to create ASM$_{\text{SPEC}}$, this paper utilizes the relations between events. The relations can be extracted from the system specification given in a high-level programming language as in Sect. 5.2. Let there be an AI algorithm with events set E, together with R relations between events, which were extracted from that algorithm specification in the following. In Fig. 8 (AI algorithm), the paper has seven events, where e_0 precedes e_1, e_0 precedes e_2, e_1 is independent of e_2, e_1 precedes e_3, e_2 precedes e_3, e_3 precedes e_4, e_3 precedes e_5, e_4 and e_5 are in conflict, and the execution of e_4 or e_5 enables the occurrence of e_6. The combination of these gives us the algebraic semantics for the AI algorithm above. Formally, ASM$_{\text{SPEC}}$ is described as:

$$\text{ASM}_{\text{SPEC}} = \{e_0 \prec e_1, e_0 \prec e_2, e_1 \nabla e_2, e_1 \prec e_3, e_2 \prec e_3, e_3 \prec e_4, e_3 \prec e_5, e_4 \# e_5, \text{den}(e_6, e_4, e_5)\}$$

From the list of events of AI algorithm and dependency relation between the events generated in ASM$_{\text{SPEC}}$, such algebraic automata of the ASM$_{\text{SPEC}}$ is generated (Fig. 9).

ASM$_{\text{SPEC}}$ automata (ASA$_{\text{SPEC}}$)	e_0	e_1	e_2	e_3	e_4	e_5	e_6	Logical formula (ASM$_{\text{SPEC}}$)
s_0	0	0	0	0	0	0	0	$f = f_{e_0 \prec e_1} \wedge f_{e_0 \prec e_2} \wedge f_{e_1 \nabla e_2} \wedge$
s_1	1	0	0	0	0	0	0	$f_{e_1 \prec e_3} \wedge f_{e_2 \prec e_3} \wedge f_{e_3 \prec e_4} \wedge$
s_2	1	0	1	0	0	0	0	$f_{e_3 \prec e_5} \wedge f_{e_4 \# e_5} \wedge f_{\text{den}(e_6, e_4, e_5)} =$
s_3	1	1	0	0	0	0	0	$(e_0 + \bar{e_1}) \wedge (e_0 + \bar{e_2}) \wedge 1 \wedge$
s_4	1	1	1	0	0	0	0	$(e_1 + \bar{e_3}) \wedge (e_2 + \bar{e_3}) \wedge$
s_5	1	1	1	1	0	0	0	$(e_3 + \bar{e_4}) \wedge (e_3 + \bar{e_5}) \wedge$ $(\bar{e_4} + \bar{e_5}) \wedge (\bar{e_6} + e_4 + e_5) =$
s_6	1	1	1	1	0	1	0	$\bar{e_1}\bar{e_2}\bar{e_3}\bar{e_4}\bar{e_5}\bar{e_6} + e_0\bar{e_3}\bar{e_4}\bar{e_5}\bar{e_6} + e_0 e_2 \bar{e_3}\bar{e_4}\bar{e_5}\bar{e_6}$
s_7	1	1	1	1	0	1	1	$+ e_0 e_1 \bar{e_3}\bar{e_4}\bar{e_5}\bar{e_6} + e_0 e_1 e_2 \bar{e_4}\bar{e_5}\bar{e_6} + e_0 e_1 e_2 e_3 \bar{e_4}\bar{e_6}$
s_8	1	1	1	1	1	0	0	$+ e_0 e_1 e_2 e_3 \bar{e_4} e_5 + e_0 e_1 e_2 e_3 \bar{e_5}\bar{e_6} + e_0 e_1 e_2 e_3 e_4 \bar{e_5}$
s_9	1	1	1	1	1	0	1	

Fig. 9. ASM$_{\text{SPEC}}$ automata (ASA$_{\text{SPEC}}$) of the AI algorithm

5.4 Result of RTL Synthesis

This is a result of RTL synthesis of the algorithmic behavioral specification. This result is generated from the synthesis phase and is moved to the verification phase. The RTL module [19, 26, 27] is defined by the following:

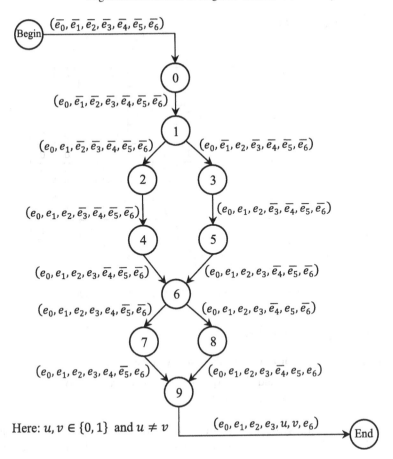

Fig. 10. RTL automata of the Al algorithm

- Processing unit that holds the declaration of the components that make up the processing unit.
- Control unit that determines the internal command sequence that must be emitted by the control unit.
- Fixed assignment that determines an operation that must be repeated every clock cycle.

The control unit is made up of steps. Each one is numbered and must be executed in a single clock unit. The Fig. 10 shows this control unit for the Al algorithm.

5.5 Generating ASA$_{RTL}$

ASA$_{RTL}$ Of this paper need to be created from the result of the RTL synthesis. Thus, from the RTL synthesis of Al algorithm, as indicated in Fig. 10, ASA$_{RTL}$ are generated in the following (see Fig. 11).

Algebraic RTL automata (ASA$_{RTL}$)	e_0	e_1	e_2	e_3	e_4	e_5	e_6
s_0	0	0	0	0	0	0	0
s_1	1	0	0	0	0	0	0
s_2	1	0	1	0	0	0	0
s_3	1	1	0	0	0	0	0
s_4	1	1	1	0	0	0	0
s_5	1	1	1	1	0	0	0
s_6	1	1	1	1	1	0	0
s_7	1	1	1	1	0	1	0
s_8	1	1	1	1	0	1	1
s_9	1	1	1	1	1	0	1
s_{10}	1	1	1	1	u	v	1
Where: $u, v \in \{0, 1\}$ and $u \neq v$							

Fig. 11. Algebraic RTL automata (ASA$_{RTL}$) of the Al algorithm

5.6 Result Comparison and Discussion

5.6.1 Result Comparison Between ASA$_{SPEC}$ and ASA$_{RTL}$

In comparing the ASA$_{SPEC}$ and ASA$_{RTL}$, to verify the correctness of a result of RTL synthesis needs to determine the following.

Definition 3 (Correctness of a result of RTL synthesis). An algebraic semantics-based result of RTL synthesis is correct iff it satisfies all the algebraic specification requirements.

Theorem 1. An algebraic semantics-based RTL synthesis result is correct iff $\mathcal{C}(RTL) = \mathcal{C}(SPEC)$ as definition 1 in Sect. 4.1. To put it another way, the computations set agreed by RTL is equivalent to the set of all computations agreed by SPEC.

Proof. For the "*if*" part, when $\mathcal{C}(RTL)$ is equivalent to $\mathcal{C}(SPEC)$, then an RTL synthesis result is correct according to definition 3. To demonstrate the "*only if*" part, this paper needs to demonstrate that if $\mathcal{C}(RTL) \neq \mathcal{C}(SPEC)$, then the result of the RTL synthesis is not correct. Therefore, there are two cases in the following.

- If $\mathcal{C}(RTL) \subset \mathcal{C}(SPEC)$ then there exists a computational requirement $\mathcal{T} \in \mathcal{C}(SPEC) \setminus \mathcal{C}(RTL)$ that is not synthesized in the RTL result. By definition 3, the result of RTL synthesis is not correct.
- If $\mathcal{C}(SPEC) \subset \mathcal{C}(RTL)$ then the specification and RTL synthesis are not equivalent. To take the consequence of this, their computing behaviors are distinctive. To put it another way, the result of RTL synthesis is not correct.

5.6.2 Discussion

The considerations above show that if the synthesis algorithm has created an effective RTL result and then comparing and contrasting are performed here as an assessing that examines whether algebraic RTL automata are equivalent to algebraic automata. Indeed, Fig. 9 and Fig. 11 show that $C(RTL) = C(SPEC)$. Therefore, the formal verification approach shows the correctness of the results of the RTL synthesis for the Al algorithm.

6 Conclusions and Future Work

This paper specified an algebraic semantics for an RTL specification and a verification algorithm developed to validate the results of RTL synthesis. Major properties of this approach, the conception of an ASM (to be interpreted as a Chu space) is considered as an algebraic semantics foundation for the RTL formalization and the conception of algebraic automata are devoted for formal correctness of the result of RTL synthesis. This formal verification approach focused on functional equivalence examining to define if the algebraic RTL automata (to be interpreted as ASA_{RTL} automata) are equivalent to algebraic specification automata (to be interpreted as ASA_{SPEC} automata). For verifying the correctness of a result of RTL synthesis, we have proved that the result using an ASM is correct iff $C(RTL) = C(SPEC)$. To put it another way, the set of all computations agreed by RTL automata (to be interpreted as ASA_{RTL} automata) is equivalent to the ones agreed by specification automata (to be interpreted as ASA_{SPEC} automata).

Furthermore, in software engineering, model-based verification (MBV) is viewed as a systematic approach to find lacks in requirements, designs or coding. MBV integrates a mathematical models form to offer an approaching logically analyzing rather than a proof of correctness strategy. MBV requires generating crucial models of the system behavior and analyzing these models based on formally representing of expected properties. Unfortunately, the specific techniques and engineering practices of applying MBV to stream calculus-based computing BDL verification have yet to be fully explored and documented. A number of challenges to the acceptance of MBV for stream calculus-based computing BDL verification have been identified, including the lack of good process support and tools for formal modeling and analysis. An essential ingredient of stream calculus is recognized as the stream bisimulation conception, which efficiently supports a stream calculus-based computing BDL approach to MBV.

References

1. Godefroid, P., Peled, D., Staskauskas, M.: Using partial-order methods in the formal validation of industrial concurrent programs. In: Presented at the Proceedings of the 1996 ACM SIGSOFT International Symposium on Software testing and analysis, San Diego, California, USA (1996)
2. Hansen, C., Kunzmann, A., Rosenstiel, W.: Verification by simulation comparison using interface synthesis. In: Proceedings Design, Automation and Test in Europe, pp. 436–443 (1998). https://doi.org/10.1109/DATE.1998.655894
3. Hansen, C., Nascimento, F.A.M.D., Rosenstiel, W.: Verifying high level synthesis results using a partial order based model. In: International High Level Design Validation and Test Workshop, San Diego, CA, USA, pp. 135–141 (1998)

4. Kordon, F., Hillah, L.M., Hulin-Hubard, F., Jezequel, L., Paviot-Adet, E.: Study of the efficiency of model checking techniques using results of the MCC from 2015 To 2019. Int. J. Softw. Tools Technol. Transfer **23**(6), 931–952 (2021). https://doi.org/10.1007/s10009-021-00615-1

5. Souri, A., Norouzi, M.: A state-of-the-art survey on formal verification of the internet of things applications. J. Serv. Sci. Res. **11**(1), 47–67 (2019). https://doi.org/10.1007/s12927-019-0003-8

6. Alur, R.: Formal verification of hybrid systems. In: Presented at the Proceedings of the ninth ACM International Conference on Embedded Software, Taipei, Taiwan (2011). https://doi.org/10.1145/2038642.2038685

7. Anh, V.T., Vinh, P.C., Cuong, P.Q.: Contextual perception in internet of mobile things: a categorical structure. Internet Things **22**, 100799 (2023). https://doi.org/10.1016/j.iot.2023.100799

8. Maruyama, Y.: Chu duality theory and coalgebraic representation of quantum symmetries. J. Pure Appl. Algebra **226**(9), 106960 (2022). https://doi.org/10.1016/j.jpaa.2021.106960

9. Myojin, S., Babaguchi, N.: A logical consideration on fraudulent email communication. Artif. Life Robot. **25**(3), 475–481 (2020). https://doi.org/10.1007/s10015-020-00597-4

10. Ivanov, L.: Automatic generation of Chu space model expressions for verification. In: 51st Midwest Symposium on Circuits and Systems, pp. 613–616 (2008). https://doi.org/10.1109/MWSCAS.2008.4616874

11. Peled, D.: Partial-Order Reduction. In: Clarke, E.M., Henzinger, T.A., Veith, H., Bloem, R. (eds.) Handbook of Model Checking, pp. 173–190. Springer International Publishing, Cham (2018). https://doi.org/10.1007/978-3-319-10575-8_6

12. Droste, M., Zhang, G.-Q.: Bifinite chu spaces. EPI Sciences Overlay Journal, lmcs:1183 - Logical Methods Comput. Sci. **6**(1) (2010). https://doi.org/10.2168/LMCS-6(1:3)2010

13. Xu-Tao, Du., Xing, C.-X., Zhou, L.-Z.: Modeling and verifying concurrent programs with finite chu spaces. J. Comput. Sci. Technol. **25**(6), 1168–1183 (2010). https://doi.org/10.1007/s11390-010-9397-y

14. Fields, C., Glazebrook, J.F.: Information flow in context-dependent hierarchical Bayesian inference. J. Exp. Theor. Artif. Intell. **34**(1), 111–142 (2022). https://doi.org/10.1080/0952813X.2020.1836034

15. Huang, F.-P., Droste, M., Zhang, G.-Q.: A monoidal category of bifinite chu spaces. Electron. Notes Theor. Comput. Sci. **212**, 285–297 (2008). https://doi.org/10.1016/j.entcs.2008.04.068

16. Buchenrieder, K.: Rapid prototyping of embedded hardware/software systems. Des. Autom. Embed. Syst. **5**(3), 215–221 (2000). https://doi.org/10.1023/A:1008950900254

17. Scheide, W., Georg, D., Helmut, K.: Using Conjoint Analysis for Software Engineering. In: CONSYSE '97 International Workshop on Conjoint Systems Engineering: ITpress Verlag, Konferenzbeitrag (1997)

18. Ulidowski, I., Phillips, I., Yuen, S.: Reversing event structures. New Gener. Comput. **36**(3), 281–306 (2018). https://doi.org/10.1007/s00354-018-0040-8

19. Van Pham, D., Phan, V.C., Nguyen, B.K.: Formally specifying and coinductive approach to verifying synthesis of stream calculus-based computing big data in livestream. Internet Things **23**, 100878 (2023). https://doi.org/10.1016/j.iot.2023.100878

20. Van Pham, D., Phan, V.C.: Overview of the stream theory-based big data in livestream. Mobile Netw. Appl. (2023). https://doi.org/10.1007/s11036-023-02180-0

21. Rutten, J.J.M.M.: Elements of stream calculus. Electron. Notes Theor. Comput. Sci. **45**, 358–423 (2001). https://doi.org/10.1016/S1571-0661(04)80972-1

22. Niqui, M., Rutten, J.J.M.M.: Stream processing coalgebraically. Sci. Comput. Program. **78**(11), 2192–2215 (2013). https://doi.org/10.1016/j.scico.2012.07.013

23. Helala, M.A., Qureshi, F.Z., Pu, K.Q.: A stream algebra for performance optimization of large scale computer vision pipelines. IEEE Trans. Pattern Anal. Mach. Intell. **44**(2), 905–923 (2022). https://doi.org/10.1109/TPAMI.2020.3015867

24. Hansen, H.H., Kupke, C., Rutten, J.J.M.M.: Stream differential equations: specification formats and solution methods. Log. Methods Comput. Sci. **13**(1) (2017). https://doi.org/10.23638/LMCS-13(1:3)2017

25. Rutten, J.J.M.M.: The Method of Coalgebra: exercises in coinduction. CWI, Amsterdam, The Netherlands, p. 261 (2019). ISBN: 978-90-6196-568-8

26. Carchiolo, V., Malgeri, M., Mangioni, G.: Hardware/software synthesis of formal specifications in codesign of embedded systems. ACM Trans. Des. Autom. Electron. Syst. **5**(3), 399–432 (2000). https://doi.org/10.1145/348019.348093

27. Bailey, B., Gajski, D.: RTL semantics and methodology. In: International Symposium on System Synthesis (IEEE Cat. No.01EX526), pp. 69–74 (2001). https://doi.org/10.1145/500001.500017

An Approach for Object Recognition in Videos for Vocabulary Extraction

Anh Bao Nguyen Le[1], Chi Bao Nguyen[1], Quoc Cuong Dang[1], Be Hai Danh[1], Huynh Nhu Le[1], Huong Hoang Luong[2], and Hai Thanh Nguyen[1(✉)]

[1] College of Information and Communication Technology, Can Tho University, Can Tho, Vietnam
nthai.cit@ctu.edu.vn
[2] FPT University, Can Tho, Vietnam

Abstract. English is the most common language globally, and it is increasingly important. English has been compiled in most online documents, information, and contents. However, with a considerable vocabulary, learning English is difficult for many people to remember. Therefore, many modern technologies have been proposed to support English learning, such as English learning technology through word-matching games to help children become excited and easily approach English from an early age. In addition, translation tools can help users look up vocabularies, antonyms, synonyms, and examples. This study presents a method to support learning English via object detection in videos, images, or even live-stream videos in real-time using deep learning architectures such as You Look Only Once (YOLO) - one of the finest families of object detection models with state-of-the-art performances. The method to obtain an mAP is 55.6 with 17GFlops. The results are vocabulary, meaning, and making sentences with that. Our method has good accuracy in data of 2786 images belonging to 59 classes.

Keywords: Vocabulary · learning English · object detection

1 Introduction

English has such an important role that society's requirements for proficiency in the English language are high. However, looking deeply into that problem, firstly, on the student's side, we may understand what the question is asking when participating in big and small exams. Secondly, for those working in professions needing to communicate fluently in English, the reality of their foreign language ability is still too, and the need to improve their vocabulary is limited, hindering their ability to meet the community's needs. Applicable in current and future work communication. Third, parents always want their children to start learning English from 3 to 4 years old, but they have a headache because they need to learn how to teach their children the basics. Therefore, it is necessary to have a method of learning English from basic to advanced.

© ICST Institute for Computer Sciences, Social Informatics and Telecommunications Engineering 2024
Published by Springer Nature Switzerland AG 2024. All Rights Reserved
P. Cong Vinh and H. Mahfooz Ul Haque (Eds.): ICTCC 2023, LNICST 586, pp. 36–51, 2024.
https://doi.org/10.1007/978-3-031-59462-5_3

As the importance of English vocabulary gradually asserts its position, the search for long-term and effective learning methods is promoted. Therefore, learning English vocabulary through pictures has become popular and strongly developed. That is also the method our team chose to research to help people improve their English vocabulary. Our brains tend to remember images and words more. Memorizing words that appear simple will make learning more exciting and not dull. At the same time, it helps to stimulate the brain, which will help us remember longer. As students majoring in information technology at Can Tho University, we are dedicated to successfully researching an Android application to learn English vocabulary through images and videos, applying AI(Artificial Intelligence) science and API(Application Programming Interface) to research, and learning additional guidance.

Because mobile apps are becoming increasingly important in our lives, this research will make vocabulary learning more enjoyable, effective, and memorable. Furthermore, users can learn for free anytime and from any location. They require a smartphone. As a result, it will contribute significantly to the advancement of education.

Furthermore, the primary research clarifies the role of information technology application in human life in general and in English learning in this article. From there, technology will serve as a bridge for Vietnamese technology to advance further by assisting people in their knowledge development. Artificial intelligence, or AI, is a branch of computer science that refers to intelligence humans have programmed to assist computers in automating intelligent human-like behaviors. In particular, artificial intelligence assists computers in absorbing human intelligence, such as image recognition, voice recognition, inference to solve problems, etc. Many people are becoming increasingly interested in the research and application of AI technology. Moreover, real-world application In the case of AI(Artificial Intelligence), image recognition, for example, uses Roboflow to label an image, select it, and label it. For example, if we train a cat image with the label "cat," the cat image will display the English word "cat" after encountering a specific image related to the voice used-a programming interface API(Application Programming Interface) for reading text, specifically vocabulary. The API is intended to enable text-to-speech functionality. An artificial intelligence-based English learning application or software was designed to assist English learners in learning vocabulary and pronunciation through intellectual activities. Since the introduction of English learning applications, the trend in learner acceptance and effective learning methods has shifted. The rapid advancement of technology allows popular learning applications to be downloaded to phones, laptops, and mobile devices on all platforms, including Android, iOS, Windows, etc.

As the importance of English vocabulary gradually increases, the search for long-term and effective learning methods is promoted. Therefore, learning English vocabulary through pictures has become popular and strongly developed. That is also the method our team chose to research to help people improve their English vocabulary. Our brains tend to remember images and words more. Memorizing words that appear simple will make learning more exciting and not dull. At the same time, it helps to stimulate the brain, which will help us remember longer. As students majoring in information technology at Can Tho University, we are dedicated to successfully researching an Android application to learn English vocabulary through images and videos, applying AI(Artificial Intelligence) science and API(Application Programming Interface) to research and learn additional guidance. Because mobile apps are becoming increasingly important, this research will make vocabulary learning more enjoyable, effective, and memorable. Furthermore, users can learn for free anytime and from any location. They require a smartphone. As a result, it can contribute significantly to the advancement of education. Furthermore, the primary research clarifies the role of information technology application in human life in general and in English learning in this article. From there, technology will serve as a bridge for Vietnamese technology to advance further by assisting people in their knowledge development. Artificial intelligence, or AI, is a branch of computer science that refers to intelligence humans have programmed to assist computers in automating intelligent human-like behaviors. In particular, artificial intelligence assists computers in absorbing human intelligence, such as image recognition, voice recognition, inference to solve problems, etc. Many people are becoming increasingly interested in the research and application of AI technology. Moreover, real-world application In the case of AI(Artificial Intelligence), image recognition, for example, uses Roboflow to label an image, select it, and label it. For example, if you train a cat image with the label "cat," the cat image will display the English word "cat" after encountering a specific image related to the voice used-a programming interface API(Application Programming Interface) for reading text, specifically vocabulary. The API is intended to enable text-to-speech functionality. An artificial intelligence-based English learning application or software was designed to assist English learners in learning vocabulary and pronunciation through intellectual activities. Since the introduction of English learning applications, the trend in learner acceptance and effective learning methods has shifted. The rapid advancement of technology allows popular learning applications to be downloaded to phones, laptops, and mobile devices on all platforms, including Android, iOS, Windows, etc. Object detection has become a massive machine-learning field in recent years. Video object detection is no exception; it is still new but increasingly important in our lives. So what is video object detection, and how important is it? Information Technology researchers and developers have decided to create Video Object Detection applications that allow machines to analyze images and detect objects. Video object detection helps reduce operational human resources, has high accuracy, continuous operation output, and is easy to monitor and operate, so it has attracted many technology industries to apply this method: number plate recognition, face recognition detection, object tracking, cars - self-driving aircraft, robotics, etc. Many prospective studies show the importance of VOD in the future being implemented in many areas such as sports (player identification and analysis of broadcast video about football [1]); medicine (detection of microscopic objects through microscopic video and analysis of sperm quality [2,3]); security (automatic gun detection [4]); space science (detecting and tracking moving objects in satellite video [5]), etc. We researched and developed a VOD in the field of education based on the benefits and importance mentioned above. It is image recognition via video conversion into English vocabulary (English vocabulary learning software). Only in the field of education, in this day and age of technology, with the explosion of the internet, is it common for students to own a phone, laptop, or another electronic device. The software is simple to install on the learner's learning device. It is critical to raise the level of education in the country to create closeness and comfort for any age group, including parents who wish to teach their children at home. It can also help people perceive technology in their daily lives more quickly. As a result, technology engineers will be inspired and driven to develop innovative and practical software.

The rest of this paper is organized as follows. In Sect. 2, the related work is introduced. In Sect. 3, the proposed fault diagnosis method is presented in detail. In Sect. 4, detailed experiments and comparisons are carried out. The summary of this paper is presented in Sect. 5.

2   Related Work

Video object detection (VOD) has gained popularity in recent years. Many studies have been conducted. Video object detection is actively studied to push detection speed and accuracy limits. The authors in [6] proposed that the method extracts a set of convolutional feature maps over the whole input image via a fully convolutional backbone network and performs region classification and bounding box regression over either sparse object proposals. The method achieved the mapping score of 78.6% at runtime of 13.0/8.6 fps on Titan X/K40, better when compared to ImageNet VID Challenge 2017 with an mAP score of 76.8% at runtime of 15.4 fps on Titan X, shows a progressive result, towards high-performance video object detection.

The authors in [7] suggested a cuboid proposal network and tubeless linking algorithm to improve the performance of detecting moving objects in videos. Experiments on the ImageNet VID dataset show that their method outperforms the static image detector and the previous state-of-the-art. In particular, their method improves results by 8.8 percent over the static image detector for fast-moving objects. Another work in [8] introduced an object query propagation (QueryProp) framework for high-performance video object detection.

They evaluated their model on ImageNet VID, which consists of 3862 training videos and 555 validation videos from 30 object categories. QueryProp propagates sparse object queries across video frames to achieve online video object detection, and no additional modules or post-processing are required. The processing speed of QueryProp can achieve 45.6 FPS while maintaining an accuracy of over 80 mAP. This novel solution enables a new framework to achieve the best performance among all online video object detection approaches and strikes a decent accuracy/speed trade-off.

The work in [9] designed the Hierarchical Video Relation Network (HVR-Net), which uses inter-video and intra-video proposal relations to improve object feature quality. They mainly evaluate their HVR-Net HVR-Net on the large-scale ImageNet VID dataset. It comprises 3862 training videos (1,122,397 frames) and 555 validation videos (176,126 frames), with bounding box annotations across 30 object categories. HVR-Net was influential and essential for video object detection.

In addition, industries such as autonomous driving, surveillance systems, drones, and robotics are increasingly driven by tremendous success in the VOD sector. For example, autonomous driving leverage video recognition, whose market is predicted to leap to $77 billion (25% of the whole automotive market) by 2035 [10], has attracted the attention of giants including Tesla[1] and Waymo[2]; surveillance systems are applied in many aspects: intelligent transportation, intelligent oil field production, and management optimization, water conservation monitoring with Advantech WebAccess automation,... [11] Along with that development, deep neural network (DNN) techniques are vulnerable to adversarial attacks. For the above reason, Themis is a software/hardware system to defend against adversarial patches for real-time robust video object detection that was recently launched [12]. Themis efficiently and accurately recovers the DNN systems from adversarial attacks with the algorithmic framework and architectural support. The results show that the proposed methodology can recover the VOD system's negative effect in real time with negligible hardware overhead.

Based on the positives regarding detection speed and accuracy, many integration studies use VOD in many practical applications. For example, the authors in [13] have researched a method that presented a fully automated pipeline for face detection, tracking using a deep convolutional neural network (CNN). In addition, a fast car detection and tracking algorithm was presented in [14] for traffic monitoring fisheye video mounted on crossroads. They used the ICIP 2020 VIP Cup dataset and adopted YOLOv5 as the object detection base model.

They studied 26 videos for training and five videos for testing, taken from a fisheye camera mounted on a pole near road intersections about 8 m above the road. Each video typically has around 1000 frames captured at 15 frames per second. Their design improves the detection rate by 17.9 pp in the night scenes and 6.2 pp for the day scenes, increasing the inference speed by nearly two times. The authors in [15] also performed a challenging task of object-based video forgery detection. They used the fast and real-time object detector You Only Look Once (YOLO) -Version 2 to automatically detect forged objects within the video with a 0.99 confidence score. A study focuses on object detection from thermal infrared images and videos of UAVs using the YOLO models once deployed in [16]. Object detection has been performed on various remote sensing platforms on spaceborne, aerial, and ground remote sensing images and videos. Results revealed that the highest mean average precision (mAP) of the person and car instances was 88.69%, the fastest detection speed achieved 50 frames per second (FPS), and the smallest model size was observed in YOLOv5-s. Recent

---

[1] https://electrek.co/2017/04/29/elon-musk-tesla-plan-level-5-full-autonomous-driving/.

[2] https://blog.waymo.com/2019/08/introducing-waymos-suite-of-custom.html.

learning-based video methods (e.g., [17–19]) typically require an extensive collection of well-annotated data for learning a new object class, making it difficult
to scale to real-world object classes in high diversity. Therefore, Few-Shot Video
Object Detection (FSVOD) was introduced in [20] with three critical contri-
butions: a large-scale video dataset FSVOD-500 comprising 500 classes with
class-balanced videos in each category for few-shot learning; a novel Tube Proposal Network (TPN) to generate high-quality video tube proposals to aggregate
feature representation for the target video object; a strategically im-proved Temporal Matching Network (TMN+) to match representative query tube features
and supports with better dis-criminative ability. Extensive experiments demonstrate that their method produces significantly better detection results on two
few-shot VOD datasets, boosting FSVOD research potential in the future.

3   Method

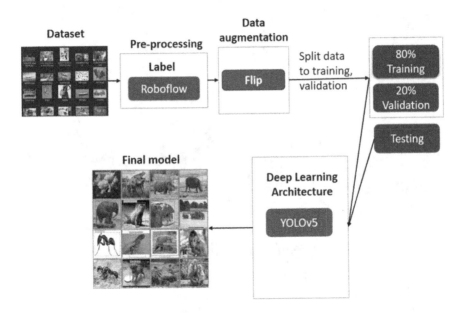

Fig. 1. The workflow for object detection in images

Figure 1 illustrates the process of forming the labeled object. The first image,
from left to right, is an image database with more than 2,500 images used to
label the correct vocabulary with the meaning of each image. The second figure,
Roboflow, is a framework with a Label Assistant feature, where labels can be
applied to objects or predictably for faster labeling. Next is using Data Augmentation with one primary method: flip. In splitting the data into 80% training and
20% validation, the testing set is not initially included in the dataset. Next is to
pass the found model through machine learning, using two main types of machine
learning architectures, YOLOv5, to classify images by taking an input image,

processing and analyzing it, and categorizing it under specific categories (Example: Butterfly, Elephant...), and finally, provide the classification and detection results.

3.1 Data Pre-processing

The image processing system's input is images taken from many different sources, including data sets on the internet and phone cameras. Image files are usually of good quality because they have gone through careful selection steps to save time and increase the quality of the process.

Fig. 2. Some examples of Labeling the pictures using Roboflow

We have collected 2786 images of 59 classes in Can Tho City, Vietnam, and some images from the internet. The number of images of each layer depends on that class's variety of shapes, colors, and shooting angles. These classes are popularly-appeared objects found in Can Tho City, Vietnam. The resolution of the image is primarily good due to careful selection.

Labeling images are carefully labeled due to regular checks to improve processing quality. Image labeling is being done on the website "Roboflow"[3] as illustrated in Fig. 2. Roboflow creates software products as a service that helps users manage image files, annotations, labels, pre-processing, data augmentations, file formats, and model training with one click. Make computer vision tasks easier.

3.2 Data Augmentation

Data augmentation is a technique used in deep learning to improve the data quality used for training, And this time, we use one data augmentation method: Flip. Flip data augmentation is called flip data augmentation by inverting entire rows and columns of image pixels horizontally. For example, in Fig. 3, the horizontal flip is performed on the input image (left side) and returns the image (right side) after flipping the entire pixel of an image.

Origin image   New image

Fig. 3. Flip data augmentation

This way, the data will be increased without adding completely new images. Using the existing image data, flip them, thereby increasing the model's accuracy. Yolov5 [21] is a product within the Yolo architecture series. This model boasts high detection accuracy and fast recognition speed, with the fastest detection speed reaching up to 140 frames per second.

3.3 Object Detection and Classification

Image classification[4] is a complex process, the accuracy of which is based on the dataset's characteristics, the complexity of the problem under analysis, and the

---

[3] https://roboflow.com.
[4] https://www.sciencedirect.com/topics/earth-and-planetary-sciences/image-classification.

appropriate of the classification algorithm. However, This process is unsuitable for this project because it cannot scan multiple objects in an image. Object detection Image classification is a complex process, the accuracy of which is based on the dataset's characteristics, the complexity of the problem under analysis, and the appropriateness of the classification algorithm. However, This process is unsuitable for this project because it cannot scan multiple objects in an image[5].

Object detection[6] is technique for indicating instances of objects in images or videos. Object detection locates each object by bounding box, and it will classify the object inside each bounding box. As such, there may be more than one object in one image. So it will be suitable for this project[7]. There are different ways to perform object detection. Popular deep learning-based approaches using YOLO v5 automatically learn to detect objects within images[8]. YOLOv5[9] is a family of object detection architectures and pre-trained models on the COCO dataset. The YOLO family of models consists of three main architectural blocks i) Backbone, ii) Neck, and iii) Head.

In our study, we use Yolov5 [21], a product within the Yolo architecture series. This model boasts high detection accuracy and fast recognition speed, with the fastest detection speed reaching up to 140 frames per second. Furthermore, the model's post-training file size is significantly smaller, nearly 90% smaller than Yolov4. This makes it well-suited for deployment on embedded devices for real-time object detection. Yolov5 comprises a total of 10 different architectures, including YOLOv5n, YOLOv5s, YOLOv5m, YOLOv5l, YOLOv5x, YOLOv5n6, YOLOv5s6, YOLOv5m6, YOLOv5l6, and YOLOv5x6.

4 Experimental Results

We collected 2786 images belonging to 59 classes. Each class has about 30 images with classes mentioned in Table 1. The classes are diversely distributed in all fields and topics. It will update more classes in any fields and topics in the future. The data is divided into two train/valid sets with a ratio of 4/1 and used five pictures per class to be a test set to evaluate the model as exhibited in Table 2. In Sect. 4.2, we train two models with and without data augmentation. The origins origin model has five classes: ant, bear, buffalo, bee, and boa. After using data augmentation shows, the ratio between the Training Set, Validation Set, and Testing Set is shown in the Table 3. In Sect. 4.3, we add two new classes, pen and lip stick, to test the model's ability to update. Each class has 50 samples. We will test the model's training process based on loss to see its ability.

---

[5] https://kikaben.com/object-detection-vs-image-classification/#chapter-1.
[6] https://www.mathworks.com/discovery/object-detection.html.
[7] https://kikaben.com/object-detection-vs-image-classification/chapter-1.
[8] https://www.mathworks.com/discovery/object-detection.html.
[9] https://github.com/ultralytics/yolov5.

Table 1. Classes in datasets

airplane	butterfly	fire hydrant	pack back	squirrel	peacock
ant	cat	fly	parking meter	starling	rabbit
bat	cheetah	frisbee	parrot	stop sign	raven
bear	chicken	giraffe	pig	suitcase	salamander
bee	cockroach	goat	sheep	tennis ball	scorpion
bench	cow	handbag	skis	tie	snake
boa	crocodile	horse	snowboard	traffic light	squid
boat	dog	iguana	soccer ball	train	stork
buffalo	eagle	monkey	sparrow	truck	hippo
bus	elephant	owl	spider	umbrella	

4.1   Environmental Settings and Metrics

Use web roboflow to label objects and Colab's GPU to run the experimental environment and train in 200 epochs (from 0–199).

Table 2. Top 10 classes with the highest numbers of samples.

Elephant = 100	Dog = 100	Horse = 100	Butterfly = 100	Chicken = 100
Pig = 87	Cat = 50	Sheep = 50	Sparrow = 50	Cow = 50

Table 3. Split the data into training, validation, and test dataset in scenario 3.

Dataset	Original samples	Data after Augmentation
Training	187	351
Validation	24	24
Test	46	46

The performance of approaches is assessed using the F1-score as revealed in Eq. 1, where TP denotes True Positive, FP denotes False Positive, and FN denotes False Negative.

$$F1 = \frac{2 * Precision * Recall}{Precision + Recall} = \frac{2 * TP}{2 * TP + FP + FN} \qquad (1)$$

4.2   Efficiency of Data Augmentation

After training two different models with the same class, one is the original model, and the model applied one way of data augmentation: flip. We compare the results of these two models below. The results of the confusion matrix of the two methods are presented in Table 4.

The accuracy of the model using and without data Augmentation is significantly different. For example, after testing with 46 different images, filtering with an accuracy of more than 60%, the model using data augmentation can recognize 42 images. In comparison, the origin model does not apply recognition of 38 images. Furthermore, most of the recognized images of the model using Data Augmentation have higher accuracy than the original model, for example, in Fig. 4. However, when examining images containing many objects, the original model can scan many objects, but the model using data augmentation is minimal, for example, in Fig. 6. This proves that data augmentation can improve the model's accuracy. The results of Precision and Recall of these two models are presented in Fig. 5. The calculation results of the two models are as follows in Table 4. The f1-score of the original model is about 94.05%, and the model using data augmentation is 94.83%. After the above comparison results, we can see that using data augmentation can improve the model's accuracy but limit its ability to recognize multiple objects in a single image.

Table 4. Confusion Matrix data without/using data augmentation

	Actual Class					
	ant	bear	bee	boa	buffalo	ACC < 60%
ant	0.92	0	0	0	0	0.08
bear	0	0.88	0	0	0	0.12
bee	0	0	0.55	0	0	0.45
boa	0	0	0	0.80	0	0.20
buffalo	0	0	0	0	0.88	0.12
	using data augmentation					
	ant	bear	bee	boa	buffalo	ACC < 60%
ant	0.92	0	0	0	0	0.08
bear	0	1	0	0	0	0
bee	0	0	0.92	0	0	0.08
boa	0	0	0	1	0	0
buffalo	0	0	0	0	0.63	0.37

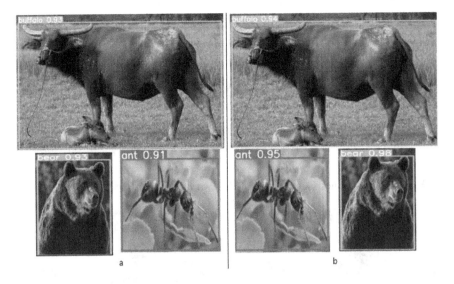

Fig. 4. Some illustration of objects recognized with bounding boxes: (a) without using data augmentation (b) using data augmentation

4.3 N-Object Detection Performance Comparison Between the Model Training Using the Architecture Starting from Scratch and the Model Starting from a Pre-trained Model Performing the Classification Tasks on the N-1 Objects

From the line charts below in Fig 7, the blue line represents training the model from the beginning. The orange line represents the training model from a previously trained model and continues to train another layer (model n+1). Comparing the object loss we see at the beginning, the orange line hits the threshold with a loss of 0.023585 but then starts to plummet, intersects and exceeds the blue line, and achieves a loss of 0.0091255. The lower the loss is, the higher the accuracy of the data and the higher the model will be, but that is the result that we have performed on the training set. Although we achieved results and saturation earlier, we are training a model from an existing model, which still has some limitations that we can see on the validation set on the correct chart. The orange line (object loss of the model) increases at the last epoch, leading to the detection of the affected object. However, because the model chosen to use is the model with the best epoch and because of the savings, If we have more time to train, then the use of the training method continues from a previous model selected to make the final product that the article is aiming for, which is the object recognition model.

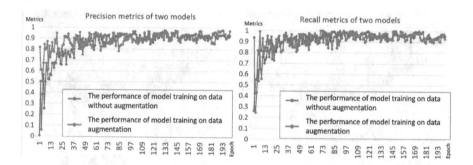

Fig. 5. Performance Comparison of the two models in the training phase

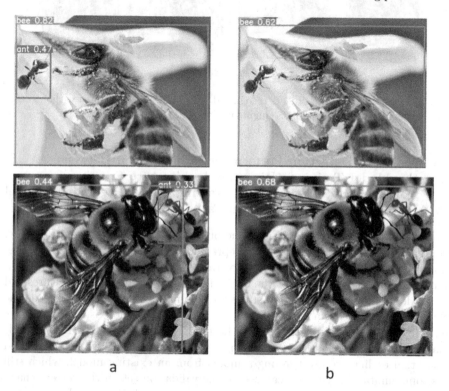

Fig. 6. Detection results on multiple objects in an image (a) without using data augmentation (b) using data augmentation

4.4 Develop an Application Using the Yolov5 Model to Support English Learning

The application will run on Android, developed in the Java programming language on Android Studio IDE. The application includes functions such as recognizing objects through images and videos to exporting a dictionary of that object, and the application also provides a dictionary function to help users look up. The dictionary has been updated with a total of 151 words, so the model will be further developed to meet the previous dictionary to be able to update new words. The application interface is as shown in Fig. 8.

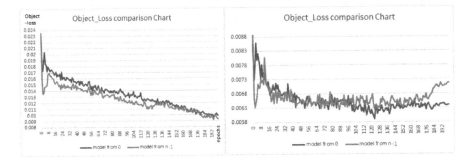

Fig. 7. Loss (y-axis) comparison through epochs (x-axis) between the model training from scratch (model from 0) and model training from a pre-trained on n-1 classes in the training set (left chart) and validation set (right chart)

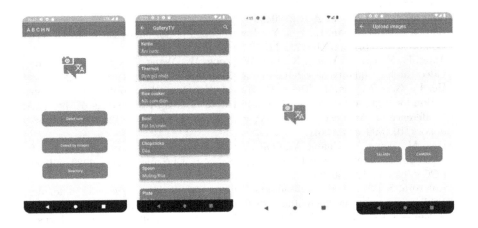

Fig. 8. Some illustrations of the application Interface

5 Conclusion

This study presented a workflow for object detection in images. We collected images from the internet and in Can Tho City, Vietnam. The data were labeled with Roboflow and then augmented by flipping original images to increase the data size for the learning. As observed from the results, the flipping techniques can help to enhance the performance and push the model to converge quickly. In addition, we also see that the model training starting from a pre-trained model can converge faster.

This work is expected to be among the first steps to developing applications for supporting learning English by vocabulary extraction. Further study can collect more data to update and add more vocabulary.

Acknowledgement. This study is funded in part by the Can Tho University, Code: THS2022-15.

References

1. Liu, H., Aderon, C., Wagon, N., Liu, H., MacCall, S., Gan, Y.: Deep learning-based automatic player identification and logging in American football videos. arXiv preprint arXiv:2204.13809 (2022)
2. Zou, S., et al.: TOD-CNN: an effective convolutional neural network for tiny object detection in sperm videos. arXiv preprint arXiv:2204.08166 (2022)
3. Zhao, W., et al.: A survey of semen quality evaluation in microscopic videos using computer assisted sperm analysis. arXiv preprint arXiv:2202.07820 (2022)
4. Gu, Y., Liao, X., Qin, X.: YouTube-GDD: a challenging gun detection dataset with rich contextual information. arXiv preprint arXiv:2203.04129 (2022)
5. Yin, Q., et al.: Detecting and tracking small and dense moving objects in satellite videos: a benchmark. IEEE Trans. Geosci. Remote Sens. **60**, 1–18 (2022). https://doi.org/10.1109/TGRS.2021.3130436
6. Zhu, X., Dai, J., Yuan, L., Wei, Y.: Towards high performance video object detection. arXiv preprint arXiv:1711.11577 (2017)
7. Tang, P., Wang, C., Wang, X., Liu, W., Zeng, W., Wang, J.: Object detection in videos by high quality object linking. arXiv preprint arXiv:1801.09823 (2018)
8. He, F., Gao, N., Jia, J., Zhao, X., Huang, K.: QueryProp: object query propagation for high-performance video object detection. In: Proceedings of the AAAI Conference on Artificial Intelligence, vol. 36, no. 1, pp. 834–842 (2022). https://doi.org/10.1609/aaai.v36i1.19965
9. Han, M., Wang, Y., Chang, X., Qiao, Y.: Mining inter-video proposal relations for video object detection (2020). https://www.ecva.net/papers/eccv_2020/papers_ECCV/papers/123660426.pdf
10. Kolarova, S.T.V., et al.: Autonomous driving (2016). https://www.ifmo.de/files/publications_content/2016/ifmo_2016_Autonomous_Driving_2035_en.pdf
11. Advantech Co., Ltd.: The future of intelligent surveillance (2012). https://advcloudfiles.advantech.com/ecatalog/MyAdvantech/MyAdvantech_No_11_eng.pdf
12. Han, H., et al.: Real-time robust video object detection system against physical-world adversarial attacks. arXiv preprint arXiv:2208.09195 (2022)
13. Schofield, D., et al.: Chimpanzee face recognition from videos in the wild using deep learning. Sci. Adv. **5**(9), eaaw0736 (2019). https://www.science.org/doi/abs/10.1126/sciadv.aaw0736
14. Ardianto, S., Hang, H.M., Cheng, W.H.: Fast vehicle detection and tracking on fisheye traffic monitoring video using CNN and bounding box propagation. arXiv preprint arXiv:2207.01183 (2022), to be published in International Conference on Image Processing (ICIP) 2022, Bordeaux, France

15. Raskar, P.S., Shah, S.K.: Real time object-based video forgery detection using YOLO (V2) (2021). https://doi.org/10.1016/j.forsciint.2021.110979
16. Jiang, C., et al.: Object detection from UAV thermal infrared images and videos using YOLO models (2022). https://doi.org/10.1016/j.jag.2022.102912
17. Torresani, G.B.L., Shi, J.: Object detection in video with spatiotemporal sampling networks (2018). https://openaccess.thecvf.com/content_ECCV_2018/papers/Gedas_Bertasius_Object_Detection_in_ECCV_2018_paper.pdf
18. Deng, H., et al.: Object guided external memory network for video object detection (2019). https://ieeexplore.ieee.org/document/9011008
19. Oh, S.W., University, Y., Lee, J.Y., Research, A., Xu, N., Research, A., Kim, S.J., University, Y.: Video object segmentation using space-time memory networks (2019). https://openaccess.thecvf.com/content_ICCV_2019/papers/Oh_Video_Object_Segmentation_Using_Space-Time_Memory_Networks_ICCV_2019_paper.pdf
20. Fan, Q., Tang, C.K., Tai, Y.W.: Few-shot video object detection (2021). https://www.researchgate.net/publication/351278547_Few-Shot_Video_Object_Detection#pf9
21. Ultralytics: Ultralytics yolov5. https://github.com/ultralytics/yolov5. Accessed 27 Sep 2023

A Self-organization Model for MAS Based on Trust

Dang Nhu Phu[ID], Phan Cong Vinh[(✉)][ID], and Nguyen Kim Quoc[ID]

Nguyen Tat Thanh University, Ho Chi Minh City 700000, Vietnam
{dnphu,pcvinh,nkquoc}@ntt.edu.vn

Abstract. This paper focuses on addressing the challenge of maintaining information coherence and robustness within a multi-agent system (MAS) that aggregates information from distributed sources, some of which may be defective intentionally or unintentionally. We propose a self-organizational approach in this context, emphasizing a systemic perspective that considers structural coupling across two levels: direct information gathering and communication. Specifically, we integrate a trust mechanism with local behavioral rules and selective environmental pressures to facilitate the emergence of two co-evolving organizations: one at the social level and the other at the spatial level. The social organization mirrors the trust relationships developed among the agents, while the spatial organization represents the deployment of agents in the environment to encourage exploration. The local behavioral rules encompass three categories: deployment rules, communication rules, and retro-action rules governing communication and deployment. We conduct simulations to experiment with the combination of these behavioral rules, observing the emergence of organizational structures and roles within the system.

Keywords: Multi-Agent System · Self-organizing · Trust · Coherence · Robustness · TrustNet · Mapping

1 Introduction

Self-organization is the inherent capacity to shift from disorder to order or to transition from suboptimal organization to an improved one [2]. When applied to information systems, self-organization signifies the system's ability to enact changes autonomously, devoid of explicit external control. The organization naturally manifests through interactions and coordination among the system's components, guided by localized rules within the system.

Illustratively, envision a swarm of potentially flawed mobile robots collaboratively mapping a hazardous terrain. These robots accumulate information from their shared environment and exchange data with other agents. Perception and communication operate within defined range limits. Conceptually, the system can be depicted as a multiagent system (MAS) wherein each agent, representing a robot, strives to construct the most precise representation of its environment by collecting information directly (e.g., through its own sensors) and indirectly (e.g., via communication with other agents). Given the

P. Cong Vinh and H. Mahfooz Ul Haque (Eds.): ICTCC 2023, LNICST 586, pp. 52–69, 2024.
https://doi.org/10.1007/978-3-031-59462-5_4

presence of defective agents, misinformation or inaccuracies regarding the environment can disrupt the system. In such a system, a significant question arises: how can we uphold the robust coherence of a multi-agent system without external control?

This paper introduces a self-organizational approach, rooted in a systemic perspective that acknowledges structural coupling between two vital components of the overall system: the direct information gathering component and the communication component. More precisely, we integrate a trust mechanism, amalgamated with local behavioral rules and environment-specific pressures, to drive the emergence of two co-evolving organizations. One operates at the social level, reflecting the trust relationships developed among the various agents. The other operates at the spatial level, mirroring the deployment of agents in the environment to stimulate exploration. The local behavioral rules encompass three categories: rules of deployment, rules of communication, and rules of retro-action, governing communication and deployment. We experiment with combining these behavioral rules in simulations to observe the emergence of organizational structures and roles within the system.

The paper is structured as follows: Sect. 2 provides an overview and contextualizes the general problem. Section 3 introduces a fundamental trust model pivotal to our self-organization model. Section 4 elaborates on our proposed model in detail. In Sect. 5, we present our experiments combining local rules to observe the emergence of self-organization and roles within the system. Finally, Sect. 6 offers a succinct conclusion and discusses potential avenues for future research.

2 General Problem Overview and Positioning

2.1 Problem Overview

The addressed issue deals with "how to maintain in a robust manner the coherence of a multi-agent system where some agents may be faulty?" It finally lands several underlying issues, namely:

- At the level of direct information collection, how to set up a mechanism which enables agents to optimize the exploration of their environment?
- At the level of communication, how to set up a mechanism which enables agents to better communicate when sharing the information about their environment?
- At the retroaction of exploration/communication, how to take into account the impact of the communication strategy on the exploration of agents in the system, and vice versa?

We propose to address these issues through a general conceptual framework in which we define local rules through a trust based mechanism. Rules are defined on respectively three levels: direct information collection level, communication level, and interaction level between these planes. By following these local rules, agents can behave to reach their goal without any outside explicit control. This also leads to the emergence of self-organization and roles in the system.

2.2 Our System Visions

Our approach is defined by the following core visions:

- A systemic perspective: The design of the entire system is envisioned to account for the interdependencies among key components, specifically the Direct Information Collecting System, Communication System, and their interactions.
- A self-organization vision: This pertains to an inherent control mechanism within the system. The system is tailored to emphasize internal mechanisms and dynamics that guide its organization, avoiding external imposition.

To operationalize these visions, we define constraints, establish local behavioral rules, and carefully balance positive and negative retroactions within our approach.

2.3 Related Works

Gleizes and colleagues [3, 6, 8] introduced a theoretical and practical approach for designing adaptive artificial software in dynamic environments. This approach is grounded in the AMAS theory and the ADELFE methodology, focusing on self-organization. However, it does not evaluate the system's overall function. The foundation of this approach lies in the AMAS theorem and ADELFE methodology, stating that for any functionally adequate system in a given environment, there exists a system with a cooperative internal medium that achieves an equivalent function. This evolving method is particularly useful when dealing with unforeseeable events in the environment.

Gershenson[7] proposed a methodology to assist engineers in designing and controlling complex systems, emphasizing the description of systems as self-organizing. Holzer et al. [9] described mathematical modeling of discrete complex systems and provided a framework for analyzing autonomy and emergence properties. Josang [10] presented an overview of attack types against trust and reputation systems, addressing research challenges in developing robust principles and mechanisms for trust and reputation systems.

Wolf and Holvoet [4, 5] proposed a comprehensive lifecycle methodology based on an industry-ready software engineering process, specifically tailored to engineer macroscopic behavior in self-organizing emergent MASs. Ye et al.'s work [14] introduced a decentralized self-organization mechanism in an agent network aimed at efficient task allocation through dynamic alterations of structural relations among agents.

Abdallah and colleagues [1, 15] developed a distributed, negotiation-based approach to dynamically form hierarchically organizational control, effectively coordinating DRL to enhance speed, quality, and convergence likelihood. Simonin and Ferber [13] presented a situated multi-agent model capable of addressing problems involving a range of agents from a few to hundreds. This approach extends the Artificial Potential Field technique. Klein and Tichy [11] proposed an approach relying on emergent fault-tolerance, where the desired behavior results from local reconfigurations of self-organizing agents.

3 Background: Trust System

In the recent years, trust and reputation became crucial issues in studying agent-based distributed autonomous systems in which software agents are faced with the uncertain behaviours of unreliable partners and need to select the most trustworthy ones to interact with. In such systems, trust among agents is one of the most important bases on which agents decide to interact with other ones. Trust is considered to be a belief that an agent has with a counterpart on honesty, reliability or reciprocativeness for some goal. Without trust, agents cannot efficiently cooperate.

Many current computational trust models are based on two factors: direct trust (linked to personal experience) and indirect trust (acquired from other agents). Our self-organization model is mainly based on a trust of this kind. In particular, we work on the trust model of Nguyen et al. [12]. We denote that:

- T_{ij} is the trust of agent i on agent j, including direct and indirect trust of i on j. The direct trust of i on j is based on the direct cooperation between i and j in the past. The indirect trust of i on j is estimated from the trust of any agent k which has cooperated with j and then shared its trust data with i.
- T_{ii} is the trust of agent i on itself.
- Each agent stores its own trust on other agents in special structures called TrustSets. When an agent j wants to cooperate with another agent k, j can estimate its trust toward k directly or indirectly, or both ways, using its TrustSet.

4 Self-organization Model

We examine a decentralized information collection system structured as a Multi-Agent System (MAS). Each agent within this system possesses the capability to explore, amass information items, and engage in communication. Information is acquired directly or indirectly through interactions with other agents. We operate under the assumption that certain agents may disrupt the system by disseminating inaccurate information, either due to flawed perceptions or conflicting interests within the community. Our model is segmented into three primary components (see Fig. 1):

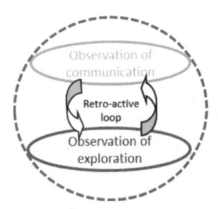

Fig. 1. System model with three parts.

1. Collective information gathering system: This encompasses the collective and direct acquisition of information, considering the overall state of available information and the proximity to the ultimate goal. Coordination of collective activities is central to this system.
2. Communication system: This facilitates exchanges between agents based on the credibility of information and the trustworthiness of the involved partner.
3. Coordination of systems: Both information gathering and communication are intricately coordinated, wherein communication guides the gathering process and vice versa.

4.1 Direct Information Collecting System

The goal of any agent in the system is to collect information. Therefore, each agent stores the explored zone which contains all visited positions by itself and agents with which it has interacted. A position is considered as visited by agent i if it is or has been inside its perception range r_i. Once an agent has visited a position, it chooses the next position to aim by considering candidate positions which are on the border of the agent's explored zone according to well known algorithms. The choice of the next position is based on the following motion rules.

Rule of Random Motion. Utilizing a random strategy, the agent selects its next position randomly from the set of available positions. This rule comes into play when an agent either has no designated position to move to or has multiple positions with equal gains.

Rule of Motion Influenced by Distance. Agents are inclined to move towards the nearest border position. Each agent calculates the shortest travel distance $D(i, X)$ from its current position to each border position X. The agent is more likely to choose a position to aim for if it has a smaller calculated distance value.

$$g_{dist}(i, X) = \frac{1}{D(i, X)} \qquad (1)$$

Rule of Motion Influenced by Quantity of Information. The quantity of information $N(i, X)$ of a specific border position is the number of data about the position X that agent i has collected. The smaller this value, the more agents tend to choose this position to visit. This is done in order to avoid the concentration of agents in the same places.

$$g_{info}(i, X) = \frac{1}{N(i, X) + 1} \qquad (2)$$

Rule of Motion Influenced by Quality of Information. We assign an information reliability metric $R(i, X)$ to each border position X, calculated based on the reliability of the information transmitters. Agents are more likely to visit positions with lower information reliability values, motivating them to verify areas with diminished reliability. This approach helps maintain coherence within the information system.

$$g_{reli}(i, X) = \frac{1}{R(i, X)} \qquad (3)$$

Rule of Motion Influenced by Other Agents

The stronger the reliability of other agents, the more likely agents are to move in their direction. In this manner, agents tend to stay in proximity to trustworthy agents and move away from less reliable ones to access dependable information. The level of attraction or repulsion between agents i and j is determined by a vector:

$$\overrightarrow{F_{ij}} = \frac{T_{ij} - 0.5}{0.5} \times \frac{\overrightarrow{V_{ij}}}{D(ij)} \tag{4}$$

where T_{ij} where T_{ij} is the trust of i on j, $\overrightarrow{V_{ij}}$ is the vector from the position of i to the position of j, and $D(i, j)$ is the distance between i and j.

Let $A_{per}(i)$ be the set of agents in the perception zone of i which have an influence on the motion of agent i. The allocated gains for each border position X influenced by these agents is:

$$g_{agent}(i, X) = \cos(\overrightarrow{F}_i, \overrightarrow{V}_{iX}) \times \left| \overrightarrow{F}_i \right| \tag{5}$$

where $\overrightarrow{F}_i = \sum_{k \in A_{per}(i)} \overrightarrow{F}_{ik}$ is the final attractive/repulsive force of i on all considered agents, $\overrightarrow{V}_{iX}$ is the vector from the position of i to the border position X. The more the force $\overrightarrow{F}_i$ is strong, or the border position X is near the force's direction (the $\cos(\overrightarrow{F}_i, \overrightarrow{V}_{iX}) \times \left| \overrightarrow{F}_i \right|$ is bigger), the more strongly this gain reinforcements the agent to move to the border position.

The gain $g(i, X)$ for border position X for agent i is the weighted combination of these four measures (after normalizing) as shown in Eq. 6.

$$g(i, X) = w_1 . \frac{g_{dist}(i,X)}{\max\limits_{Z \in P_{front}(i)} (g_{dist}(i,Z))}$$
$$+ w_2 . \frac{g_{info}(i,X)}{\max\limits_{Z \in P_{front}(i)} (g_{info}(i,Z))} + w_3 . \frac{g_{reli}(i,X)}{\max\limits_{Z \in P_{front}(i)} (g_{reli}(i,Z))} + w_4 . \frac{g_{agent}(i,X)}{\max\limits_{Z \in P_{front}(i)} (g_{agent}(i,Z))} \tag{6}$$

where $P_{front}(i)$ is the set of considered border positions for agent i; $w_1 + w_2 + w_3 + w_4 = 1$ are the positive weights. By changing the weights, the importance of each rule can be changed: The higher w_1 is, the more agent i prefers to aim the border position which is the closest to it. The higher w_2 is, the more agent i prefers to aim the border position on which it has not enough information. The higher w_3 is, the more agent i prefers to aim the most unreliable border position. The higher w_4 is, the more agent i prefers to aim the border position which brings more chances to communicate with other reliable agents.

Finally, the set of the better candidate positions to aim X_{next} is constituted by the border positions presenting the maximum gain.

$$X_{next} = X_0 : g(i, X_0) = \max\limits_{Z \in P_{front}(i)} g(i, Z) \tag{7}$$

In case of many X_0 satisfying the condition in Eq. 7, the next position to aim is randomly selected between these satisfactory positions.

4.2 Communication System

To gather information for mapping the region, agents have the capacity to directly assess the status of an area using their sensors. Moreover, they engage in communication with other agents to exchange knowledge, expediting the achievement of their objectives. Agents decide to communicate when at least one other agent is within their communication range.

The communication tendency can be considered on three levels:

- level 1: does the agent wish to communicate?
- level 2: if it wants, with which agent does it want to communicate?
- level 3: if there is a specific agent to communicate with, what information does the agent want to share with it?
- The following rules of communication answer to these questions.

Rule of General Tendency to Communication

The furthest the agent is from its aimed border position, the less the agent communicates. This rule forces the agent to reach its objective before considering communicating.

$$p(i) = \frac{D(X_{curr}, X_{next})}{D(X_{old}, X_{next})} \tag{8}$$

where $D(X_{curr}, X_{next})$ is the distance from current position X_{curr} of agent i to the selected border position X_{next}, $D(X_{old}, X_{next})$ is the distance from the old border position X_{old} of agent i (where i started to move) to the selected border position X_{next}. Intuitively, when agent i reaches its aimed border position X, this possibility is equal to 1. So the agent can communicate again. More precisely, nearer the agent comes to the aimed position, greater is the probability for it to collect reliable information on this position.

This rule answers to the question "Does the agent wish to communicate?". If the answer is yes, the next three following rules will determine with which partner the agent will communicate.

Rule of Communication Conditioned by the Reliability of the Communicating Partner.
Agents communicate in correlation with the level of trust they have in their partners. The higher the trust among agents, the more inclined they are to engage in communication.

$$p_{reli}(i, i) = T_{ij} \tag{9}$$

where T_{ij} is the trust that agent i has about agent j.

Rule of Communication Conditioned by the Duration of Disconnection. Agents tend to communicate in proportion to the duration between two consecutive communications, aiming to prevent redundant information exchange. The longer the disconnection duration between agents, the more likely they are to communicate.

$$p_{dur}(i,j) = \min\left(\frac{\Delta t_{ij}}{\underset{k \in A_{com}(i)}{\text{average}}\left(\Delta' t_{ij}\right)}, 1\right) \qquad (10)$$

where Δt_{ij} is the amount of time spent since the last communication between i and j, $\Delta' t_{ik}$ is the amount of time spent between the last two communications between i and k. $A_{com}(i)$ is set of agents having communication with i.

Rule of Communication Conditioned by the Newness of Received Information
Agents tend to communicate to agents that send new information. The newer the received data is for an agent, the more this agent tends to communicate with the sender.

$$p_{new}(i,j) = \frac{1}{2}\left(\frac{n_j}{\underset{k \in A^t_{com}(t)}{\max}(n_k)} + \frac{n_j}{n_{j'}}\right) \qquad (11)$$

where n_k is the number of new data received from agent k (including j), n'_j is the total number of data received from j. $A^t_{com}(i)$ is set of agents having communication with i at the instant t.

The combination of Eqs. (9, 10, and 11) will determine the tendency of agent i to communicate with agent j:

$$p(i,j) = w_5.p_{reli}(i,j) + w_6.p_{dur}(i,j) + w_7.p_{new}(i,j) \qquad (12)$$

where $w_5 + w_6 + w_7 = 1$ are positive weights. By changing the weights, the importance of each rule can be changed: The higher is w_5, the more agent i prefers to communicate with trustworthy partners. The higher is w_6, the more agent i prefers to communicate with long time disconnected partners. The higher is w_7, the more agent i prefers to communicate with partners that send more new data.

Once the tendency of agent i to communicate with agent j is determined, and if it wishes to, the following rules determine what information is communicated.

Rule of Communication of Direct Information. In a communication with partners, the more reliable are direct data, the more the agent tends to send them. In fact, the reliability of the direct data of an agent is computed from the trust of other agents on the agent itself. So, the more receivers trust this agent, the more the agent tends to send its direct data.

$$p(i, j, I_{dir}(i, X)) = T_{ii} \tag{13}$$

where $I_{dir}(i, X)$ is direct information of agent i about the position X, j is any receivers, T_{ii} is the trust of agent i has on himself.

Rule of Communication of Indirect Information. Similarly, the more reliable indirect data are, the more the agent tends to send them. Doing so, it contributes to the quality of the communicating system.

$$p(i, j, I_{ind}(i, X)) = reliability(I_{ind}(i, X)) \tag{14}$$

where $I_{ind}(i, X)$ is the indirect data that i has about position X, $reliability(I_{ind}(i, X))$ is the reliability of indirect data about position X that agent i received. The reliability reliability(*info*) of information *info* is calculated by the number of agents which provide the same value of *info* over the number of agents which provide information about *info*.

4.3   Self-organization in Control

As we formulate a self-organization approach encompassing two levels, we can outline a control system to interconnect these two organizational aspects and facilitate their co-evolution through self-organizing mechanisms. Consequently, the integration of the information collection system and the communication system unfolds as follows: behaviors related to collecting information are influenced by communication behaviors, and reciprocally.

Both systems are in fact very closely linked. For instance, behind rule 5 that seems only associated to the motion system, influences on the communication system can be detected. If an agent aims to go nearer to another agent, the probabiliity to communicate with it becomes greater.

Rule of Motion Reinforcement/Diversification Influenced by Accurate Information Reception. The more accurate data received from an agent are, greater is the tendency for the receiver to come closer to the transmitter. And the less accurate data received from an agent are, greater is the tendency for the receiver to go away from the transmitter

$$level_{reli}(i, j) = \frac{\sum_1^n C(I_{dir}(i, X), I_{dir}(j, X))}{n} \tag{15}$$

where n is the number of comparable data, i.e. data on the same position; $C(I_{dir}(i, X), I_{dir}(j, X))$ is the result of comparison between direct data of i about position X, and direct data of J from agent B on the same position X:

$$C(I_{dir}(i, X), I_{dir}(j, X)) = \begin{cases} 1 \, if I_{dir}(i, X) = I_{dir}(j, X) \\ -1 \, if I_{dir}(i, X) \neq I_{dir}(i, X) \end{cases} \tag{16}$$

Rule of Motion Reinforcement/Diversification Influenced by Newness of Information Exchanged

The more data received from an agent are renewed, greater is the tendency for the receiver to come closer to the transmitter. And the less data received from an agent are renewed, greater is the tendency for the receiver to go away from the transmitter

$$level_{new}(i,j) = \frac{1}{2}\left(\frac{n_j}{\max\limits_{k \in A^t_{com}(i)}(n_k)} + \frac{n_j}{n_{j'}}\right) - 0.5 \tag{17}$$

where n_k is the number of new data receipted from agent k (including j), n'_j is the total number of pieces of information receipted from j. $A^t_{com}(i)$ is set of agents having communication with agent i.

If we consider the previous rules indicating the impact of communication on motion, the attractive/repulsive force between agent i and agent j becomes:

$$\vec{F_{ij}} = \left(w_8 \cdot \frac{T_{ij} - 0.5}{0.5} + w_9 \cdot \frac{\sum_1^n C(I_{dir}(i,X), I_{dir}(j,X))}{n} + w_{10} \cdot \left(\frac{1}{2}\left(\frac{n_j}{\max\limits_{k \in A^t_{com}(i)}(n_k)} + \frac{n_j}{n_{j'}}\right) - 0.5\right)\right) \cdot \frac{\vec{V_{ij}}}{D(i,j)} \tag{18}$$

where $w_8 + w_9 + w_{10} = 1$ are the positive weights. By changing the weights, the importance of each rule can be changed: The more w_8 is high, the more agent i prefers to approach to the partners who sent reliable data in the past. The more w_9 is high, the more agent i prefers to approach to the partners who sent reliable data just in the last transmission. The more w_{10} is high, the more agent i prefers to approach to the partners who send to it more new data.

Once the attractive/repulsive force between agent i and agents in its perception zone changes, the attractive/repulsive gain for each border position also changes by the Eq. 6. In other words, this represents the influence of communication on the movement of agents.

Algorithm 1 figures in a simplified way the main engine of an agent. The order according which agent's actions are executed is: collection of data (*lines 1–2*), communication (*lines 3–26*), motion (*lines 27–49*). In the communication part, the agent first of all determines whether it communicates (*lines 3–4*). If the answer is yes, it then finds partners to communicate with (*lines 5–11*). Once the agent has found partners to communicate, it determines which data are to be sent to its partners (*lines 12–14 and 18–20*) and then sends them (*line 15 and 21*). In the motion part, the agent checks whether it is at the chosen border position. If it is not yet, it moves on to the chosen border position. Otherwise, the agent must compute the next border position to aim. In this case, the agent calculates the gain for each considered border position (*lines 28–38*), including the gain associated to distance (*line 29*), to quantity of information (*line 30*), to position's reliability (*line 31*), and to other detected agents (*lines 32–48*). The position getting the biggest overall gain is then chosen as the next border position to aim (*lines 40–46*).

Algorithm 1. Algorithm for communication and movement of agent at each step

---

1:    $X_{curr} \leftarrow$ the current position of agent i

2:    collecting of data at X_{curr}

3:    $p(i) \leftarrow \dfrac{D(X_{curr}, X_{next})}{D(X_{old}, X_{next})}$

4:    **if** $flip\big(p(i)\big) = 1$ **then**

5:      $avegare(\Delta't_i) \leftarrow$ *average of* $\Delta't_{ik}$ for all agent k which is communicated with i at the instant t

6:      **for all** agent j in communication zone of i **do**

7:        $p_{reli}(i,j) \leftarrow T_{ij}$

8:        $p_{dur}(i,j) \leftarrow min\left(\dfrac{\Delta t_{ij}}{average(\Delta't_{ik})}, 1\right)$

9:        $p_{new}(i,j) \leftarrow \dfrac{1}{2}\left(\dfrac{n_j}{max(n_k)} + \dfrac{n_j}{n_j'}\right)$

10:        $p(i,j) \leftarrow w_5 \cdot p_{reli}(i,j) + w_6 \cdot p_{dur}(i,j) + w_7 \cdot p_{new}(i,j)$

11:        **if** $flip\big(p(i,j)\big) = 1$ **then**

12:          **for all** direct data X of i **do**

13:            $p(i,j,I_{dir}(i,X)) \leftarrow T_{ij}$

14:            **if** $flip\big(p(i,j,I_{dir}(i,X))\big) = 1$ **then**

15:              send $I_{dir}(i,X)$ to agent j

16:            **end if**

17:          **end for**

18:          **for all** indirect data X of i **do**

19:            $p(i,j,I_{ind}(i,X)) \leftarrow reliability\big(I_{ind}(i,X)\big)$

20:            **if** $flip\big(p(i,j,I_{ind}(i,X))\big) = 1$ **then**

21:              send $I_{ind}(i,X)$ to agent j

22:            **end if**

23:          **end for**

24:        **end if**

25:      **end for**

26:    **end if**

27:    **if** X_{curr} is the next border position X_{next} of i **then**

28:      **for all** considered border position X of i **do**

29:        $g_{dist}(i,X) \leftarrow \dfrac{1}{D(i,X)}$

30:        $g_{info}(i,X) \leftarrow \dfrac{1}{N(i,X)+1}$

31:        $g_{reli}(i,X) \leftarrow \dfrac{1}{R(i,X)}$

32:        **for all** agent j in the perception zone of i **do**

33:          $level_{trust}(i,j) \leftarrow \dfrac{T_{ij}-0.5}{0.5}$

34:          $level_{reli}(i,j) \leftarrow \dfrac{\sum_1^n C\big(I_{dir}(i,X), I_{dir}(j,X)\big)}{n}$

35:       $$level_{new}(i,j) \leftarrow \frac{1}{2}\left(\frac{n_j}{max(n_k)} + \frac{n_j}{n'_j}\right) - 0.5$$

36:       $$\vec{F}_{ij} = \left(w_8.level_{trust}(i,j) + w_9.level_{reli}(i,j) + w_{10}.level_{new}(i,j)\right) \times \frac{\vec{V}_{ij}}{D(i,j)}$$

37:       **end for**

38:       $g_{agent}(i,X) \leftarrow \cos(\vec{F}_i, \vec{V}_{iX}) \times |\vec{F}_i|$

39:       **end for**

40:       **for all** considered border position X of i **do**

41:
$$g(i,X) = w_1.\frac{g_{dist}(i,X)}{max(g_{dist}(i,Z))} + w_2.\frac{g_{info}(i,X)}{max(g_{info}(i,Z))} + w_3.\frac{g_{reli}(i,X)}{max(g_{reli}(i,Z))}$$
$$+ w_4.\frac{g_{agent}(i,X)}{max(g_{agent}(i,Z))}$$

42:       **end for**

43:       $max(g(i,Z)) \leftarrow$ the biggest of $g(i,Z)$ for all considered border position Z of agent i

44:       **for all** considered border position X of i **do**

45:          **if** $g(i,X) = max(g(i,Z))$ **then**

46:             $X_{next} \leftarrow X$

47:          **end if**

48:       **end for**

49: **end if**

5   A Case Study: Danger Mapping

5.1   Modeling and Simulation

We demonstrate our approach through a case study termed "Danger Mapping". In this scenario, we envision a swarm of localized mobile robots patrolling an uncharted territory. The goal for each robot is to construct the most comprehensive, accurate, and dependable map of the land while utilizing minimal resources. Robots possess the capability to directly ascertain the nature of nearby zones via their sensors. Additionally, they can communicate with other robots to exchange insights regarding the environment (the map) and fellow agents (trust).

The aim of this simulation is to showcase the emergence of organizations and roles within the system. Specifically, we focus on the emergence of roles at the exploration level, the communication level, and the retroaction between these two levels.

5.2   Results

Emergence in the Exploration System

In the 400 m × 400 m GIS (Geographic Information System) environment, we constructed 200 dangerous zones and positioned 50 agents with suitable ranges. This setup ensured that agents could encounter a diverse array of other agents during the experiment, facilitating the manifestation of system emergence and roles (see Fig. 2).

Among the predictable roles that emerge in the process of self-organization, we specifically focused on one of the fundamental roles: the explorer. Using the number of detected zones as a metric for each agent, we classified an agent as an explorer if the number of zones it detected exceeded the average number of detected zones for all agents in the system.

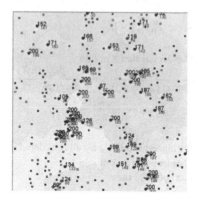

Fig. 2. Emergence in the system

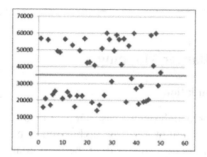

Fig. 3. Emergence of the explorer role

The results are shown in the Fig. 3 where the explorers are represented by points which are above the average line. The number of detected zones by explorers is significantly much higher than that of other ones ($M(explorer) = 52207$, $M(otherwise) = 22076$, $p < 0.001$, see Fig. 4).

Emergence in the Communication System

In order to observe emergence in the communication system, particularly the emergence of simple roles like transmitter or receiver, we introduced two indicators: the number of sent messages and the number of received messages for each agent. Therefore, an agent can be considered as a transmitter if it tends to send more messages than it receives. In the contrary, an agent can be considered as a receiver if it tends to receive more messages than it sends.

The results are shown in Fig. 5. The transmitters are represented by points which are above the middle line and the receivers are represented by points which are under the middle line. The emergence of these two roles are significant. In the role of transmitter,

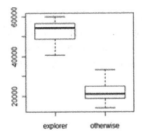

Fig. 4. Significant difference on the number of detected zones between explorer and others

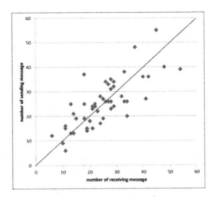

Fig. 5. Emergence of the transmitter and receiver roles

the number of sent messages is significantly higher than that of received ones ($M(sent)$ = 28.33, $M(received)$ = 22.54, $p < .04$, see Fig. 6.a). Inversely in the role of receiver, the number of received messages is significantly higher than that of sent ones ($M(sent)$ = 21.88, $M(received)$ = 28.52, $p < .02$, see Fig. 6.b).

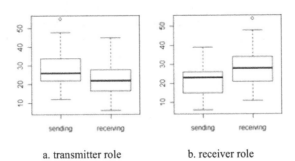

a. transmitter role   b. receiver role

Fig. 6. Significant difference on the number of sent and received messages: transmitter role 6.a, and receiver role 6.b.

Emergence in the Trust System

In order to show the emergence in the trust system, we consider two indicators: the trust of the agent on itself and the trust of the community on the agent (its reputation). The initial value of self-trust is 1.0, and that of reputation is 0.5. The more the agents trust an agent, the more the agent's reputation is increased, and vice versa. The more an agent recognizes that many agents trust it, the more its self-trust is increased, and vice versa.

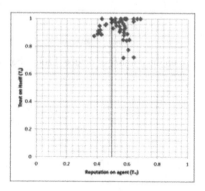

Fig. 7. Emergence of the reliable and unreliable agents

The results are shown in Fig. 7. On the reputation level, the reliable agents are represented by points on the right side of the middle vertical line, the unreliable agents are represented on the left side of the middle vertical line. The difference on the reputation between the two groups is significant ($M(reliable) = 0.576, M(unreliable) = 0.427, p < 0.001$, see Fig. 8). Unfortunately, there is no significant difference on the self-trust level between the two groups ($p > 0.7$): agents trust on themselves even if no other trusts on them. Actually, the simulation we implemented uses a number of interactions between agents that can be considered as few. Now an agent needs many negative advices to lower its self-trust and there were not enough of them. The same remark could be applied on the values of reputation that we got. They are not very far from the initial value 0.5. But they are enough for the demonstration so to distinguish between reliable and non reliable agents. The gap between the medium trust values could have been greater if the simulation could have lasted longer and offered many more transactions between agents.

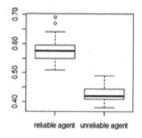

Fig. 8. Significant difference on the reputation between reliable and unreliable agents

Emergence in the Exploration/Communication System

In order to observe emergence in the exploration/communication system, we launch two scenarios:

- The first scenario uses ($w_1 = w_2 = w_3 = 0.3$, and $w_4 = 0.1$). We expect that in this scenario, agents tend to explore their environment rather than communicate. We call this scenario as the exploration scenario.
- The second scenario uses ($w_1 = w_2 = w_3 = 0.1$, and $w_4 = 0.7$). We expect that in this scenario, agents tend to communicate rather than explore their environment. We call this scenario as the communication scenario.

In these scenarios, we use two indicators: the number of sent/received messages, and the number of detected zones for each agent.

Unsurprisingly, there are significant differences in both indicators which are measured in two scenarios. The number of detected zones in the first scenario is significantly higher than in the second one ($M(exploration) = 48102$, $M(comunication) = 42459$, $p < 0.04$, Fig. 9.a). Inversely, the number of sent/received messages in the first scenario is significantly lower than in the second one ($M(exploration) = 30.34$, $M(communication) = 35.78$, $p < .05$, Fig. 9.b). This results fulfill our expectations in the using of weights (w_1, w_2, w_3, w_4) in Eq. 6 to regulate the emergence.

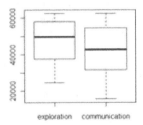 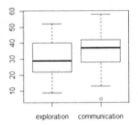

a. The number of detected zones   b. The number of exchanged messages

Fig. 9. Significant difference on the number of detected zones 9.a, and the number of sent/received messages 9.b between two scenarios

6 Conclusion

This paper introduces a self-organizational approach tailored for a multi-agent system, particularly one that operates in a disturbed state, utilized for distributed information collection. The approach adopts a systemic perspective, emphasizing a structural interconnection between two crucial levels: direct information gathering and communication. Specifically, a trust mechanism is integrated with localized behavior rules and environmental selective pressure, facilitating the emergence of two co-evolving organizations-social and spatial. The social organization mirrors the trust-based relationships developed among the diverse agents, while the spatial organization delineates the strategic deployment of agents in the environment to enhance inter-agent communication.

The local behavior rules encompass three primary categories: deployment rules, communication rules, and rules governing the interaction between communication and deployment. Our simulations experiment with a combination of these behavior rules to observe the emergence of organizations and distinct roles within the system. The outcomes demonstrate the emergence of a well-organized system and the delineation of roles across different levels: explorers in the direct data collection, transmitters and receivers at the communication level, and agents categorized as reliable or unreliable in the context of trust. Identifying the emergence of intricate roles that intersect the exploration and communication levels is an avenue for our future research endeavors.

References

1. Abdallah, S., Lesser, V.: Multiagent reinforcement learning and self-organization in a network of agents. In: AAMAS 2007: Proceedings of the 6th International Joint Conference on Autonomous Agents and Multiagent Systems, pp. 1–8. ACM, New York (2007)
2. Ashby, W.: Principles of the self-organizing dynamic system. J. Gen. Psychol. **37**(2), 125–128 (1947)
3. Capera, D., Georgé, J.-P., Gleizes, M.-P., Glize, P.: The AMAS theory for complex problem solving based on self-organizing cooperative agents. In: Proceedings of the Twelfth International Workshop on Enabling Technologies: Infrastructure for Collaborative Enterprises, WETICE 2003, pp. 383–288. IEEE Computer Society, Washington, DC (2003)
4. De Wolf, T., Holvoet, T.: Emergence and self-organisation: a statement of similarities and differences. In: Lecture Notes in Artificial Intelligence, pp. 96–110. Springer, Heidelberg (2004)
5. De Wolf, T., Holvoet, T.: Towards a methodology for engineering self-organising emergent systems. Self-Organiz. Autonomic Inf. **135**, 18–34 (2005)
6. Di Marzo Serugendo, G., Gleizes, M.-P., Karageorgos, A.: Self-organization in multi-agent systems. Knowl. Eng. Rev. **20**, 165–189 (2005)
7. Gershenson, C.: Design and control of self-organizing systems (2007)
8. Gleizes, M.P., Camps, V., Glize, P.: A theory of emergent computation based on cooperative Self-Organization for adaptive artificial systems. In: 4th European Congress of Systems Science (1999)
9. Holzer, R., de Meer, H., Bettstetter, C.: On autonomy and emergence in self-organizing systems. In: Hummel, K.A., Sterbenz, J.P.G. (eds.) IWSOS 2008. LNCS, vol. 5343, pp. 157–169. Springer, Heidelberg (2008). https://doi.org/10.1007/978-3-540-92157-8_14
10. Jøsang, A.: Robustness of trust and reputation systems. In: Fourth IEEE International Conference on Self-Adaptive and Self-Organizing Systems, SASO 2010, Budapest, Hungary, 27–28 September 2010, Workshops Proceedings, pp. 159–165. IEEE Computer Society (2010)
11. Klein, F., Tichy, M.: Building reliable systems based on self-organizing multi-agent systems. In: Proceedings of the 2006 International Workshop on Software Engineering for Large-Scale Multi-agent Systems, SELMAS 2006, pp. 51–58. ACM, New York (2006)
12. Nguyen Vu, Q.A., Hassas, S., Armetta, F., Gaudou, B., Canal, R.: Combining trust and self-organization for robust maintaining of information coherence in disturbed MAS. In: Proceedings of SASO 2011: 5th IEEE International Conference on Self-Adaptive and Self-Organizing Systems. IEEE Computer Society Conference Publishing Services (CPS), Ann Arbor (2011)
13. Simonin, O., Ferber, J.: Un mod'ele multi-agent de résolution collective de problèmes situeés multi-échelles. In: JFSMA 2003, RSTI/hors série (2003)

14. Ye, D., Zhang, M., Sutanto, D.: Self-organisation in an agent network via learning. In: Proceedings of the 9th International Conference on Autonomous Agents and Multiagent Systems, AAMAS 2010, vol. 1, pp. 1495–1496. International Foundation for Autonomous Agents and Multiagent Systems, Richland (2010)
15. Zhang, C., Lesser, V.R., Abdallah, S.: Self-organization for coordinating decentralized reinforcement learning. In: van der Hoek, W., Kaminka, G.A., Lespérance, Y., Luck, M., Sen, S. (eds.) AAMAS, pp. 739–746. IFAAMAS (2010)

A Business Process and Data Modelling Approach to Enhance Cyber Security in Smart Cities

Josef Horalek [iD], Tereza Otcenaskova [iD], Vladimir Sobeslav[(✉)] [iD], and Petr Tucnik [iD]

Faculty of Management and Informatics, University of Hradec Kralove, Hradec Kralove, Czech Republic
{josef.horalek,tereza.otcenaskova,vladimir.sobeslav, petr.tucnik}@uhk.cz

Abstract. The term Smart City represents a strategic concept for a city or region that involves the use of modern technologies to influence the quality of life in the city. At the technological level, a wide range of IoT devices are used, which are interconnected through modern low-latency networks to enable the creation of intelligent applications with added value for their users. However, this relatively simple and noble idea represents a wide range of technologies and approaches, making the idea of ensuring Cyber Security in Smart Cities difficult. When implementing any technology in an organization, the processes, assets, and people that bring the technology to life, are crucial. The aim of this paper is to analyze the key capabilities, frameworks and standards that would facilitate and support the possibility of developing Smart Cities. The first part of the article introduces the issue of Cyber Security and Smart Cities. Subsequently, the key approaches for ensuring security in creating Smart Cities are analyzed. The final part presents the BPMN-SC data model based on business process model notation and key security standards while incorporating the specifics of Smart Cities.

Keywords: BPMN-SC Model · Business Process Modelling · Cyber Security · ISO 27001 · Smart Cities

1 Introduction

The term Smart City, which has become increasingly popular in recent years, refers to cities that use technologies to deliver services and solve problems that occur in the city. Essentially, a Smart City aims to optimize city functions, promote economic growth, and improve the quality of life of its citizens by using a variety of modern technologies, data collections and smart applications [16]. Thus, it is expected to make smarter, more efficient, and accessible services for citizens while ensuring the Cyber Security of modern technologies. There are many definitions that describe what Smart Cities are, but the key issue is that they encompass a wide range of technologies, smart devices, specialized protocols, utilization of mobile networks and Internet, cloud services, application development, big data processing issues and many more. According to the Berkley Center

© ICST Institute for Computer Sciences, Social Informatics and Telecommunications Engineering 2024
Published by Springer Nature Switzerland AG 2024. All Rights Reserved
P. Cong Vinh and H. Mahfooz Ul Haque (Eds.): ICTCC 2023, LNICST 586, pp. 70–84, 2024.
https://doi.org/10.1007/978-3-031-59462-5_5

for Long-Term Cyber Security (CLTC) and their survey of The Cybersecurity Risks of Smart City Technologies [1], the Internet of Things (IoT) and other smart technologies which are being used in Smart Cites are posing greater risks in aggregate than other technologies. Local officials and authorities should therefore consider whether cyber risks outweigh the potential gains of technology adoption on a case-by-case basis. Moreover, they should exercise particular caution when technologies are both vulnerable in technical terms and constitute attractive targets to capable potential attackers because the impacts of an attack are likely to be great. Deloitte [7] in their report 'Making smart cities cybersecure' defines three key factors that influence the cyber risk in Smart Cities.

1. Convergence between Information Technology (IT) and Operational Technology (OT) infrastructures on the boundary of the physical and cyber world. This represents for example the challenges and different views for the utilization of IoT sensors and actuators in physical and cyber environments.
2. Interoperability representing the coexistence band of frequent interactions between legacy and smart systems and platforms including the on-premise and cloud solutions.
3. Integration and comingling of services across domains through IoT and digital technologies.

It is important to mention that Smart Cities are far from being just about Information and Communication Technologies (ICT) but include a range of non-technological perspectives. People are key players, and in case of Smart Cities, it is mainly people who provide services to citizens. The legislative framework and the establishment of rules under which smart services are provided are also very important. Strategic planning at the city and regional level is also an integral part of this, to provide the means to realize community and policy objectives. The following Fig. 1 presents the key components of a sustainable Smart City, according to the European Innovation Partnership on Smart Cities and Communities research center [17].

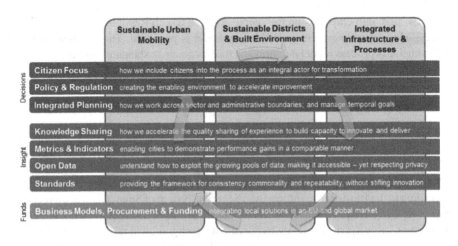

Fig. 1. Concept of Sustainable Smart City [26]

An integral part of the Smart City concept is also data, which can be divided into sensitive data and open data. Sensitive data in the public administration domain include mainly personal data, which are protected by legislation, in the European Union (EU) for example by GDPR act [30]. Open data, on the other hand, represents data that are a sign of public sector transparency and provide citizens with a possibility to control the functioning state apparatus. Furthermore, these comprise also data freely available to citizens as a service [22]. According to the EU initiative and the Operational Implementation Plan for Smart Cities, the following key recommendations are essential [19]:

- Consistent use of standards, protocols and generic data formats that enable and support interoperability between different systems, avoid lock-in of specific out-doors and promote competition in the solutions developed.
- Ensuring access to third-party data (with full protection of personal data and trade secrets), thus creating support for the development and improvement of new applications.
- Leveraging existing infrastructures and enabling their unrestricted reuse for different purposes.

Apparently, the concept of Smart Cities covers a very broad spectrum of IT or OT technologies including energy, transportation, healthcare, and many others. The integration of next generation mobile networks or the use of the cloud to provide smart services to citizens - using open but also very sensitive data - opens new challenges in cyber security of Smart Cities. Given the widespread popularity of modern technologies, the question is not if, but how to protect services and data in Smart Cities. As already mentioned, a Smart City is far from being just about technology, but mainly about the people and processes in a city or region that shape the key services provided to citizens to improve their quality of life. The question is how to link these relatively separate principles into one homogeneous approach for enhancing the security of Smart Cities. The key to the successful implementation of the Smart Cities concept is to identify the specific needs and domains that characterize this area. Based on the domain model of use in the EU and with emphasis on the specifics in the Czech Republic [29], the Business Process Model for Smart Cities (BPM-SC) model is proposed. The BPM-SC is based on the business process model notation and the key security standards while considering the specifics of Smart Cities.

2 Related Works

The previous section highlighted the wide range of ICT that are used in the Smart City concept. However, it is not only technologies but also organizations, people, rules, processes, or data that together shape the smart services for citizens. Currently, a lot of technological approaches, standards, frameworks, methods, or technologies exist [10]. According to the Research on Information Security System of Smart City Based on Information Security Requirements [25], there are three important requirements the create information security: management requirements, technological requirements and lastly the construction and operation requirements. To fulfil the technological requirements in the area of Smart Cities, European Union Agency prof Cybersecurity (ENISA) recommends the use of security baselines [14]. As stated above, there is also a variety of security standards which can help to ensure security from the organizational perspective. Smart Cities and Smart Regions are represented also by the people who provide the service to citizens, rules and laws, processes, data, and their interconnection. To ensure the security of complex organizations, it is very important to uncover the actors, entities, analyze the processes, data utilization and their interconnection to see the organization in a systematical and holistic way. For these purposes, the utilization of Business Process Modeling and Ontologies in various research and applications in this area occurs, for example [4, 9, 12, 24, 31]. From the above-mentioned reasons, the following approaches with respect to Smart City were selected.

2.1 Security Control Baselines

The first important and often used approach to enhance cyber security is the use of security baselines as a methodological support. This approach is mainly used when implementing IT/OT technologies for organizations of all sizes. According to NIST [8], it is mainly a set of information security controls that has been established through information security strategic planning activities to address one or more specified security categorizations. Security baselining is the process of capturing a point in time understanding of the current system security configuration. Establishing an easy means for capturing the current system security configuration can be extremely helpful in responding to a potential security incident [5, 13].

Security baselines do not cover the entire process of ensuring cyber security in an organization because they do not examine the organization in detail as a complex system that is defined by individual entities, their relationships or by defining the sensitivity of the data that are generated in such a system. Rather, they are about implementing best practices to enhance system security at the technology level. As we have already mentioned, smart technologies and their effective deployment make it possible to transform an ordinary city or region into a smart one. In the Smart City concept, it is advisable to use a security foundation defined by the manufacturer or a security strategy or best practices for the implementation of technologies. According to [18], technology systems and the use of security foundations can be categorized as follows:

- Physical environment security - prevent physical devices from being accessed or damaged under unauthorized conditions, to ensure the security of hardware devices.
- Network transmission security - mainly the establishment of cross network authentication and encryption mechanism between heterogeneous transmission networks, to prevent the security risks of cross isomerism network and enhance the transmission efficiency of information across the network.
- Host system security - in Smart City refers to the host security technology challenge in cloud computing environment and also the on-premise technologies related with the local installed IT/OT technologies which are deployed in the region or Smart City.
- Data resources security - large amount of collection, filtering and integration of business data and meticulous business analysis and association rules mining, enterprises or related data management departments can perceive their own network security situation.

- Application services security - The security of application services is mainly to consider the security increase, reinforcement, and transformation of the application systems, and to provide a unified support platform for the security protection functions of the cloud computing center and the region.

2.2 Security Standards and Frameworks

In the domain of standards and regulations for the domain of cyber security, there are two leading organizations, namely Cybersercurity and Infrastructure Security Agency (CISA) for United States area, and ENISA for the states in EU. CISA is an organization established by the US Department of Homeland Security and ENISA was established by order of the European Parliament and the Council of Europe (management is appointed by the Council). Both agencies provide recommendations, tools, and support for improvement of cybernetic security of organizations and states.

The main difference is geographical and legislative context in which they function. CISA has competencies to do inspections and audit critical infrastructure while ENISA is an independent body of EU Council and has no authority to enforce its recommendations or certify products and services. For technical standards and frameworks, CISA uses NIST. NIST, among other activities, defines NIST Cybersecurity Framework. ENISA uses the international standard ISO/IEC 27001 as a framework for defining requirements and procedures, which set out the requirements for establishing, implementing, maintaining and continuously improving an Information Security Management System (ISMS) and serves as an audit control framework. ISO/IEC 27002 provides detailed additional guidelines for application and control of security standards. The importance of agency ENISE increased with the implementation of Directive (EU) 2022/2555 of the European Parliament and of the council on measures for a high common level of cyber security across the Union, amending Regulation (EU) No. 910/2014 and Directive (EU) 2018/1972, and repealing Directive (EU) 2016/1148 (NIS 2 Directive) [8].

NIS2 is legislation of EU in the area of cybernetic security and follows the original directive of NIS from 2016 which strengthens legal measures for increasing the overall level of cyber security in EU by stating: readiness of member states, risk management requirements, and incident reporting for subjects providing important or basic services, cooperation, and co-ordination between member states and EU, sanctions, and supervision. The directive also extends the range of entities that must comply with cyber security rules to other areas such as energy, transport, healthcare and digital infrastructure. NIS2 Directive also allows member states to impose fines on subjects up to 10 million EUR or 2% of worldwide turnover for previous fiscal year (depending on which one of those is higher) if they violate measures for cyber security risks control and/or obligations for cyber security incidents reporting. NIS2 Directive also assigns the set of new tasks to ENISA, for example development and maintenance of European registry of vulnerabilities which will contain information about known SW/HW vulnerabilities and recommendations for their handling. The Secretariat of the European Cyber Crisis Contact Organisation Network (CyCLONe), which will coordinate responses to large-scale cross-border cyber incidents or crises, also provides support to Member States in implementing and complying with the European Commission's zero-tolerance requirements in their national legal systems. CyCLONe is using its expertise in the field of cyber security, in particular for entities providing essential or basic services in the context of NIS2 Directive, and supporting the harmonization of risk management and incident reporting requirements for entities ensuring essential or basic services in the context of NIS2 Directive.

Based on the aforementioned, it is obvious that both CISA and ENISA define general frameworks. In case of ENISA, these are to be implemented into national legislation of EU member states and through regional administration manage their control and enforcement. Both agencies create process and technical frameworks which ease the implementation, control and monitoring for affected organizations. The practice shows that the individual measures allowing achievement of proper cyber security levels are similar and defined on the basis of ISO/IEC 27001:2013 and NIST Cybersecurity Framework (CSF) at the same time. This proves their high rate of mutual similarity.

2.3 Ontological Engineering

There are various approaches to data modelling relating to cyber security. Among others, the ontology-based approaches help to identify the vulnerabilities [20]. Various ontological frameworks can be implemented too [18, 20, 27, 28]. Mozzaquarto et al. [18] emphasize that IoT being used in Smart Cities is facing many cybersecurity challenges and attacks. To eliminate these issues, they propose the improvements resulting from the ontological analysis identifying the ontology-based cybersecurity framework. This framework reflects the model-driven methodology considering the organizational processes as well as monitoring and ensuring the adaptation of the environment. Salnitri et al. [23] prove the ontology usage through the combination of BPMN-Query language and the Reference Model of Information Assurance & Security (RMIAS) comprising the high-level security ontology as a baseline. De Nicola and Villani [6] introduce various types of Smart City ontologies and justify their relevance for crisis management including numerous aspects of security. Moreover, in pursuit to increase system's security capability, Chergui and Benslimane [3] use the BPMN extension based on complete cyber security ontology for modelling of the security requirements. The abovementioned efforts might be umbrellaed by Unified Cyber Ontology (UCO) which represents „foundation for standardized information representation across the cyber security domain/ecosystem" [11]. This concept together with Cyber-investigation Analysis Standard Expression (CASE) provide significant community-developed and community-recognized tool for interoperability and cyber investigation. It helps to create flexible as well as explicit data models. The ontological approaches ensure particular advantages such as:

- misinterpretation and ambiguity elimination
- consistency and possibility to reuse the concepts and structures
- portability among domains and technologies
- integrity of representation [2, 11]

2.4 Business and Data Modelling

Business environment and its processes can be modelled by various tools. In connection to data which represent from the security perspective one of the most critical assets, the very efficient tool is BPMN (Business Process Model and Notation) [21, 23]. BPMN is a standardized modelling tool and defines three types of diagrams: (i) collaboration diagram, (ii) conversation diagram, and (iii) choreography. The most frequently used is collaboration diagram which also contains the most important semantic elements. It allows modelling of business process workflows and possible interactions with external entities via B2B, B2C, B2G etc. relationships.

In the context of data modeling, BPMN distinguishes between (smaller) data objects with potential indication of input/output semantics, and data stores, used for larger databases. An interesting phenomenon when modeling work with data artifacts is that almost every activity can be connected to some kind of data objects. It is therefore important to choose an appropriate level of abstraction to keep diagrams transparent and comprehensive. Data objects are more frequently used in workflows and therefore will be mainly addressed in this sub-section.

The data objects are perceived as static entities in BPMN. While there obviously are changes being made, which can be indicated by input/output indicators when needed, data object internal state itself is encapsulated. The change is described by properly named activities (tasks or sub-processes), connected to the respective data objects. Internal dynamics of data objects is not being represented and security-related attributes of data, that can be very important, require use of some form of specialized BPMN extension for the security domain. This is discussed in more detail in sub-Sect. 3.2 of this paper.

While there are some limitations in BPMN when modelling data dynamics, notation allows us to identify process owners by use of elements of pools and lanes. The "pool" usually refers to larger part of the organization or some external entity, "lanes" identify individual actors whose responsibilities are processes shown within the respective lane. As the workflow is under way (which can be imagined as a movement of imaginary token through the diagram), the model reader can see clearly how the responsibility is shared between individual actors. From the cyber security point of view, this is quite advantageous, since the roles and responsibilities of individual users can be more easily identified, and access control mechanisms and strategies adjusted as needed.

The identification of process owners is also related to data objects security [15]. The diagram captures who owns the process working with data object and such actor also bears responsibility for the data object safety. Moreover, processes can be influenced by occurrence of events (of internal or external origin) or messages from external entities such as during B2B communication. Specialized "message flow" connector element is used here to capture B2B interactions and can hold information about the communication in its description. However, more detailed attributes related to data object safety again require the use of specialized BPMN extension, see sub-Sect. 3.2.

3   Business Process and Data Model Approach for Smart Cities

This chapter refers to the Smart Cities Domain and based on this introduces the BPMN metamodel extension with security-related elements. Moreover, the data type categorization including the measures to protect them.

3.1 Smart Cities Domain Model in the Czech Republic and Smart Cities Specifics

For the description of the current state-of-the-art of the domain model for Smart Cities in the Czech Republic, mostly general scientific methods were used. First, the available materials, especially academic articles, norms, laws, and standards, were reviewed. On the basis of this review and the analysis of national documentation, the domain model of Smart Cities in the Czech Republic was developed and published [29] (Fig. 2).

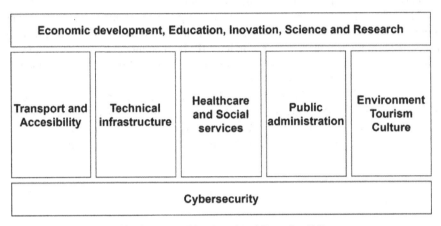

Fig. 2. Smart City Functional Domains [29]

This model is generally accepted by the professional public as a conceptual domain model of Smart Cities in the Czech Republic. Based on it, the Business Process Model representing basic data flows and process relationships was created. This model is supported by requirements for cyber security according to NIS2 requirements, respectively to the implementation of requirements from ISO/IEC 27001. The basic principle is that in individual functional domains security requirements are implemented. These are perceived as a process of control according to PDCA (Plan, Do, Check, Act). This is implemented not only to the domain model as a whole but also in the context of individual domains. This process approach allows us to fulfill criteria of ISO/IEC 27001 and especially areas of Appendix A of this standard, namely A.6 Organization of information security, A.7 Human resource security, A.8 Asset management, A.17 Information security aspects of business continuity management, and A.18 Compliance with requirements. Other criteria, mostly of technical nature, are influenced by the processes and technologies specific for the specific domain.

3.2 A Proposal of Abstract BPM-SC Based on Smart City Domain Model

One of the effective approaches to design, re-engineer, analyze, or understand internal functioning of the organization is BPMN (Business Process Model and Notation) analysis. In its standard version, it allows capturing of process workflows, especially in the most frequently used collaboration diagram. For the security-related issues, other BPMN diagrams, namely conversation diagram and choreography diagram, have only limited value since most semantics is provided by elements in collaboration diagram. Moreover, the standard notation is enhanced by the extension of graphical elements to capture aspects specific for the security domain.

The review of research papers done in this area shows that security extensions content to BPMN metamodel quite vary, depending mainly on the level of detail preferred by individual authors. Particular differences include the work with data-related artifacts, roles and permissions given to individual actors and process owners, and representation of security requirements/goals. The used terminology - or rather simply naming - of individual extension components also vary, making the situation somehow less transparent. There are security standards/norms that can be used as a basis for identification of security components for incorporation into BPMN metamodel [3, 21, 23, 32]. In this case, the most relevant standard for EU context is ISO/IEC 27001 (and related standards) describing information security and management.

The BPMN core elements are shown in Fig. 3. From the security perspective, especially two groups of elements are important more than the others: participants and data artifacts. The former is used for identification of actors with the responsibility for processes, the latter should be protected by properly set security management strategy.

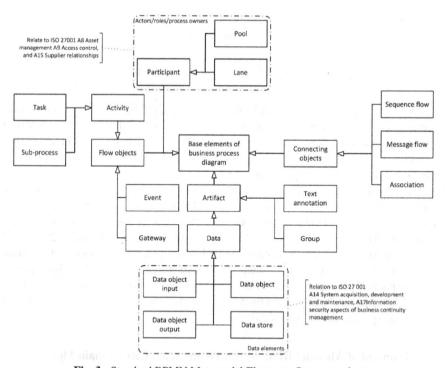

Fig. 3. Standard BPMN Metamodel Elements. Source: authors.

The proposed BPMN extension which considers the requirements of ISO/IEC 27001 standard is shown in Fig. 3. The security data model based on the BPMN metamodel standard, intended for the Smart City area and applicable to defined functional domains, was designed with regard to the fulfillment of process and technical measures not specified in NIS2. These fulfil the recommendations of Annex A of ISO 2700 standard, which serve as a basic security framework. A fundamental principle of cyber security is the determination of the assets value. Critical assets in Smart City domain are represented mainly by data and information creating the data sets. One of the most used principles for determining the data assets value is based on the confidentiality, integrity, availability (CIA) triad. The specific classification of sub-parameters is determined by the asset manager. Generally, the usage of the evaluation scale containing an even number of values can only be only recommended. Even though such scale would eliminate the "middle"/neutral values. In the proposed security data model, these are gray-colored items entered into the security goal section.

After evaluating particular data sets, it is necessary to determine their type. With regard to the focus of the security data model on Smart City, an analysis of occurring data types was carried out, especially during the designing of Smart City functional domains model [29]. Consequently, these data types were categorized. This resulted in five-point data scale of data types.

1. Public data – represented by publicly available data, e.g. in the data portals of the authorities ready for end processors/users. This category requires necessarily to keep the corresponding integrity.
2. Sensitive - represented typically by sensitive data appearing especially during their creation and processing. These are not intended for publication or before their publication, it is necessary to set rules and technologies for their protection, not only at the level of integrity, but also at the confidentiality level.
3. Confidential – this is non-public data subject to higher protection than Sensitive data. These include e.g. information about organizations established by the government, such as financial statements or internal methodologies. None of this data could have an impact in areas of financial, reputational, or also security risks.
4. Critical – this category includes data from the field of energy management, internal IT systems, financial and accounting systems, etc. Here, special emphasis is put on preserving their integrity, confidentiality, but especially availability, as this type of data also helps to regulate partial services of the entire Smart City environmental system.
5. Regulatory – these data with the highest protection, which is given not only by cyber security requirements, but also by other relevant legislative acts such as the GDPR regulation, the protection of healthcare systems, etc. Breach of the security of this information has legal consequences in the form of financial fines/reimbursements, restriction of the activity of the provided service or loss of license.

In order to fulfill security measures, it is necessary to implement appropriate technical measures based on technology-oriented measures resulting from recommendations of ISO 27001. This means setting of the appropriate level according to A.10 Cryptography. When implementing the cryptography protection, it is necessary to consider the data storage length with regard to the estimated the impenetrability of sub-algorithms. It is also critical to implement means and technologies for A.9.4 System and application access control, which form the basic security measures to ensure data confidentiality. An integral but sometimes underestimated are measures guaranteeing A.11 Physical and environmental security. This is not only a centrally controlled system of physical access to the spaces where data is stored, but also to the spaces, where the data is created and managed. It is also necessary to set appropriate measures to secure personal computing systems where data is found in the form of PCs, laptops, mobile phones, tablets, but also external storage media. With regard to the use of the proposed model for the Smart City area, which is based on data communications, it is both logical and necessary step to mention the measures in the area of A.13 Communications security. The aim is to ensure an adequate level of integrity and availability of data assets. This is a measure based on the security of the layers of the TCP/IP architecture both in the area of MAN, LAN and WAN networks. All these measures must be tested before their deployment, but also within their life cycle, using appropriate test data. Therefore, the requirements from A.14.3 Test data are also included in this category. All technical orientation measures would be inefficient if the incident management system according to A.16 Information security incident management was not implemented. Without this measure, security is blind and does not allow effective response to potential security incidents. All of the beforementioned technical-oriented security measures have a wide range of specific implementations, which provide fulfilment of several described parts within one technological solution. Nevertheless, only as a whole, they form an effective technological assurance of cyber security over classified data.

After the evaluation and classification of data sets, it is absolutely to determine the authorization for operations with these data from the security point of view. The CRUD (Create, Read, Update, Delete) approach used in UML modeling represents a suitable model for data type determination. To manage these operations, it is necessary to set up organizationally oriented measures based on the ISO 27001 standard, among which A.8 Asset management and A.9 Access control are. Their aim is to establish, enforce, check and adjust access to data assets. During this process, it is absolutely necessary to use the principle of minimal corrections established on the basis of user roles and groups, including the introduction of more level approval of authorizations above standard access. Furthermore, a group of measures A.14 System acquisition, development and maintenance, A.15 Supplier relationships and A.17 Information security aspects of business continuity management should be deployed. There are all connected with the determination of penetrations and principles for maintaining the continuity of activities, which is often affected by supply chains, system development and maintenance. Establishing these rules, considering the access to data, is one of the most important components for ensuring the integrity and confidentiality of data, its classification and value. It is a complex security solution based on precisely defined organizational measures and process management, which are followed by technological solutions.

The security data model introduced above, based on the BPMN metamodel standard, thus provides a unique connection among the standard measures listed in ISO 27001, the process concept of their implementation and process control of an organization or complex of organizations from the point of view of data sets. It represents a unique model that enables the security manager to provide a process view for the company's board of directors and at the same time a data-oriented view for the system specialists responsible for the selection and implementation of necessary technologies (Fig. 4).

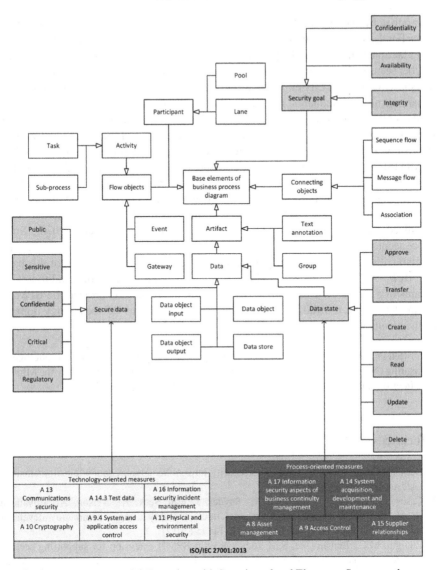

Fig. 4. BPMN Metamodel Extension with Security-related Elements. Source: authors.

4   Conclusion

The use of modern technologies, ubiquitous high-speed networks and smart applications is leading to the gradual adoption of the Smart City concept. As it was analyzed in this paper, the concept of Smart Cities not only represent a wide range of technologies, but also people and organizations, that provide services to citizens, play a very important role. The Smart City concept with the characteristic use of a broad spectrum of technologies, integration of processes and uncovering the interconnections, represents essentially a complex system that is not easy to secure because the standard e-government services are enriched by OT technologies, sensor networks, cloud solutions, open data and many others. For the above reasons, the aim of this paper was to analyze the key approaches that would facilitate and support the possibility of developing Smart Cities with an emphasis on cyber security. In each part of the article, a key approaches that can be used to enhance the security of a Smart City or region were presented. These included security baselines, relevant norms and standards, ontologies, but also business process modelling. BPMN approach allows to see the cyber security in a holistic way and describe the Smart City or region as a complex system that needs to be decomposed into individual entities, establishing their relations, and defining data assets that need to be protected. Within the ARTISEC project (see the Acknowledgement), which is focused on the creation of a data model with an emphasis on the use of artificial intelligence for cyber security, an abstract data model, meta-model respectively, was created. This meta-model is based on the extension of the BPMN notation with the specifications of the internationally recognized security standard ISO27001, while considering the specifics of the Smart City concept. These specifics are based on the model of functional domains and the use of Smart Cities in EU, particularly in the Czech Republic. The key output of this paper is the BPM-SC data model that can be implemented in the specific areas and functional domains of a Smart City. As a future work within the ARTISEC project, the BPM-SC data model will be utilized on selected e-government/IT and OT technology domains and the results will be verified.

Acknowledgement. The financial support of the project "Application of Artificial Intelligence for Ensuring Cyber Security in Smart City" (ARTISEC), n. VJ02010016, granted by the Ministry of the Interior of the Czech Republic is gratefully acknowledged.

References

1. Berkeley Center for Long-Term Cybersecurity. https://cltc.berkeley.edu/publication/smart-cit ies/. Accessed 31 Mar 2023
2. Casey, E., Barnum, S., Griffith, R., Snyder, J., van Beek, H., Nelson, A.: Advancing coordinated cyber-investigations and tool interoperability using a community developed specification language. Digit. Investig. **22**, 14–45 (2017)
3. Chergui, M.E., Benslimane, S.M. (eds.) A valid BPMN extension for supporting security requirements based on cyber security ontology. In: 8th International Conference on Model and Data Engineering (MEDI), Marrakesh, Morocco (2018)
4. Computer Security Resource Center. https://csrc.nist.gov/publications/detail/sp/800-53b/ final. Accessed 31 Mar 2023
5. Conrad, E., Misenar, S., Feldman, J.: Chapter 8 - domain 7: security operations (e.g., foundational concepts, investigations, incident management, disaster recovery). In: Conrad, E., Misenar, S., Feldman, J. (eds.) CISSP Study Guide. 3rd edn. Syngress, Boston, pp. 347–428 (2016)
6. De Nicola, A., Villani, M.L.: Smart City Ontologies and Their Applications: A Systematic Literature Review. Sustainability **13**(10), 5578 (2021)
7. Deloitte. https://www2.deloitte.com/content/dam/Deloitte/de/Documents/risk/Report_mak ing_smart_cities_cyber_secure.pdf. Accessed 31 Mar 2023

8. Directive (EU) 2022/2555 of the European Parliament and of the Council of 14 December 2022 on measures for a high common level of cybersecurity across the Union, amending Regulation (EU) No 910/2014 and Directive (EU) 2018/1972, and repealing Directive (EU) 2016/1148 (NIS 2 Directive) (Text with EEA relevance) (2022)

9. Dong, N., Zhao, J., Yuan, L., Kong, Y.: Research on information security system of smart city based on information security requirements. J. Phys. Conf. Ser. **1069**, 012040 (2018)

10. European Union Agency for Cybersecurity (ENISA). https://www.enisa.europa.eu/publicati ons/baseline-security-recommendations-for-iot. Accessed 31 Mar 2023

11. Unified Cyberontology. https://unifiedcyberontology.org. Accessed 31 Mar 2023

12. ISO/IEC 27001: Information technology - Security techniques - Information security management systems – Requirements (2013)

13. ISO/IEC 27002: Information technology — Security techniques — Code of practice for information security management. International Organization for Standardization (2013)

14. Kaspersky Daily. https://www.kaspersky.com/blog/cybersecurity-ontology/40404/. Accessed 31 Mar 2023

15. Kokolakis, S., Demopoulos, A., Kiountouzis, E.: The use of business process modelling in information systems security analysis and design. Inf. Manag. Comput. Secur. **8**, 107–116 (2000)

16. Manville, C., Kotterink, G.B.: Mapping Smart Cities in the EU. EPRS: European Parliamentary Research Service, Belgium (2014)

17. Maschio, I.: European Innovation Partnership on Smart Cities and Communities. European Comission (2023)

18. Mozzaquatro, B., Agostinho, C., Goncalves, D., Martins, J., Jardim-Goncalves, R.: An ontology-based cybersecurity framework for the Internet of Things. Sensors **18**(9), 3053 (2018)

19. Open Data. https://opendata.gov.cz/informace:kontext:smart-city. Accessed 31 Mar 2023

20. Pastuszuk, J., Burek, P., Ksiezopolski, B. (eds.) Cybersecurity ontology for dynamic analysis of IT systems. In: 25th KES International Conference on Knowledge-Based and Intelligent Information & Engineering Systems (KES), Szczecin, Poland (2021)

21. Rodriguez, A., Fernández-Medina, E., Piattini, M.: A BPMN extension for the modeling of security requirements in business processes. IEICE Trans. Inform. Syst. **E90-D**(4), 745–752 (2007)

22. Massink, R., Manville GCJCJMJKPRKTALMW, C., Bas, K.: Mapping Smart Cities in the EU. European Parliamentary Research Service (2014)

23. Salnitri, M., Dalpiaz, F., Giorgini, P.: Designing secure business processes with SecBPMN. Softw. Syst. Model. **16**(3), 737–757 (2017)

24. San Martín, L., Rodríguez, A., Caro, A., Velásquez, I.: Obtaining secure business process models from an enterprise architecture considering security requirements. Bus. Process Manage. J. **28**(1), 150–177 (2022)

25. Silicon Labs. https://pages.silabs.com/rs/634-SLU-379/images/Preparing_for_Next-Gen_ Cyber_Attacks_on_IoT.pdf. Accessed 31 Mar 2023

26. Staalduinen van, W., Bond R., Dantas, C., Jegundo, A.L.: Smart Age Friendly Cities, Age Friendly Smart Cities. European Comission, Futurium (2022)

27. Syed, R.: Cybersecurity vulnerability management: a conceptual ontology and cyber intelligence alert system. Inf. Manage. **57**(6), 103334 (2020)

28. Temple, W.G., Wu, Y., Cheh, C., Li, Y., Chen, B., Kalbarczyk, Z.T., et al.: CyberSAGE: the cyber security argument graph evaluation tool. Empir. Softw. Eng. **28**(1), 18 (2022)

29. Urbanik, P., Horalek, J.: Design of the Smart City Domain Concept in the Czech Republic, pp. 803–814. Hradec Economic Days, University of Hradec Kralove (2023)

30. Vojkovic, G.: Will the GDPR slow down development of smart cities?. In: IEEE 2018 41st InternationalConvention on Information and Communication Technology, Electronics and Microelectronics (MIPRO), Opatja, Croatia, pp. 1295–1297 (2018)
31. Wang, Z., Zhu, H., Liu, P., Sun, L.: Social engineering in cybersecurity: a domain ontology and knowledge graph application examples. Cybersecurity 4(1), 1–21 (2021)
32. Zareen, S., Akram, A., Khan, S.A.: Security requirements engineering framework with BPMN 2.0.2 extension model for development of information systems. Appl. Sci. 10(14), 4981 (2020)

Possibilities of Using Fuzz Testing in Smart Cities Applications

Lubomir Almer⬥, Josef Horalek⬥, and Tomas Svoboda^(✉) ⬥

Faculty of Management and Informatics, University of Hradec Kralove, Hradec Kralove,
Czech Republic
{lubomir.almer,josef.horalek,tomas.svoboda}@uhk.cz

Abstract. In recent years, technological advances in various fields of human activity have enabled the development of smart city applications that can help improve life in modern cities. In order to validate that the functional requirements of the applications are met and, above all, to ensure security and resilience against vulnerabilities and constantly evolving cyber threats, it is imperative that these applications are adequately tested before being put into operation. The aim of this paper is to present an analysis of the use of fuzz testing to test the stability, correctness and security of applications and information systems that are applicable in the smart city domain. The paper presents an analysis of the possibilities of using different types of fuzz testing and maps the different fuzz testing tools that are applicable in implementation projects in different areas of smart cities. Furthermore, a testing method for the use of fuzz testing is proposed and presented. This method is then validated using a set of proposed tests and outputs for a selected project.

Keywords: testing · fuzz testing · application security · information systems · security · smart cities · smart application

1 Smart Cities Application Testing

In the last more than a decade, the smart city concept has spread worldwide and influences the design of city strategies regardless of their geographical location, population and existing models and processes for providing services to residents [1]. The concept of smart cities is based on the principle of using modern ICT services, including the areas of IoT and cloud computing. The use of modern information technologies and applications brings several problems and challenges, which are analyzed in the article Privacy in the Smart City-Applications, Technologies, Challenges, and Solutions [2]. These are challenges related to ensuring cybersecurity of applications and technologies in smart cities and comprehensive protection of data based on their confidentiality or sensitivity [3]. Globally, the number and severity of cyber-attacks have been increasing in recent years, and they no longer target only IT technologies, but increasingly also industrial and OT technologies [4]. It cannot be assumed that cyber-attacks will not also target

P. Cong Vinh and H. Mahfooz Ul Haque (Eds.): ICTCC 2023, LNICST 586, pp. 85–97, 2024.
https://doi.org/10.1007/978-3-031-59462-5_6

smart city applications and solutions in the future, and it is therefore imperative to address the issue of having adequate or designing new methods and approaches on how to implement adequate protection for smart city applications and IT solutions [5]. The basic requirements for cybersecurity of applications in smart cities are the issues of ensuring secure software development and its adequate testing before putting it into production operation to ensure software quality [6].

2 Related Work

Cybersecurity Curriculum Design: A Survey [7] addresses the issue of effective software quality assurance with emphasis on the necessary involvement of the programmers of these applications in particular, who can ensure an adequate level of application security through properly chosen techniques and design patterns. Application programmers are complemented by the article Processes, Systems & Tests: Defining Contextual Equivalences. [8] to include application testers who are responsible for the actual testing of the application, i.e., proving that the required functionality is consistent with the software specification. The idea of software quality assurance in smart cities is addressed in the paper Testing Strategies for Smart Cities applications [9], where approaches and documented testing strategies in smart cities are analyzed. These include testing via test-bed, testing in the lab and testing on a simulator. However, the authors state that unit tests can also be used for application testing. A similar perspective on testing is then presented in The Campus as a Smart City: University of Málaga Environmental, Learning, and Research Approaches [10]. A specific approach to application-specific testing, based on testing for the smart traffic control domain through unit tests of smart city applications, is presented by the authors of the article Design and Implementation of a Smart Traffic Signal Control System for Smart City Applications [11]. A new approach to application testing using fuzz testing (fuzzing) for information and cybersecurity assurance, with an emphasis on detecting application vulnerabilities in smart cities and reducing the testing time, is presented in the paper Integrating Fuzz Testing into the Cybersecurity Validation Strategy [12]. A similar approach is then presented in [13], which considers fuzz testing as part of application robustness and stability validation. Fuzzing is a testing technique for finding vulnerabilities in software applications by sending unexpected input data to target systems and applications and then monitoring the results [14]. It is an automatic or semi-automatic process that involves sending and repeatedly manipulating data to an application [15]. Fuzzers can be broadly classified into two categories: mutation-based fuzzers and generation-based fuzzers. Mutation-based fuzzers apply mutations to existing data samples to create a test space. Generation-based fuzzers create test cases from scratch by modeling the target protocol or file format.

2.1 Fuzz Testing Types

Blackbox Fuzzing: This is a technique where the fuzzer has no information about the internal state and implementation of the application. The application is a black box - it has only inputs and outputs visible. Test files are inserted on the application input. Fuzzer monitors the output and behavior of the program. Blackbox fuzzing is not used to find specific vulnerabilities but is used to identify conditions that create exceptions in the code and cause the target application to crash [16]. In other words, it is used to find unknown and undiscovered vulnerabilities. Blackbox testing not only allows the emulation of the view of cyber attackers but is an essential tool when the source code of an application is not available.

Whitebox Fuzzing: White box fuzzers analyze the internal structure of a program and learn to monitor and maximize code coverage or extreme value testing with each successive execution. White box fuzzers typically use adaptive algorithms and intelligent instrumentation during fuzz testing, which makes them more efficient and accurate in detecting vulnerabilities [17].

Greybox Fuzzing: A fuzzer takes a lightweight approach to test generation. This approach effectively reveals vulnerabilities and weaknesses. Greybox fuzzers randomly mutate program inputs to execute new paths. However, this makes it difficult to cover code that is guarded by tight controls [18].

2.2 Fuzz Testing Phases

Fuzzing testing consists of the following phases [19, 20]:

1. **Target identification** - an optional phase used only by potential attackers. Testers already have their target identified.
2. **Input identification** - the goal is to analyze and describe the area for a possible attack. Exis-sues many forms of inputs to the application: network, files, registries, environment variables, command line commands, and more. There are several tools that can be used to identify inputs. These include Command Line Arguments, Environment Variables (ShareFuzz), Web Applications (WebFuzz), File Formats (FileFuzz), Network Protocols (SPIKE), and many others.
3. **Fuzz Data Generation** - The purpose of the fuzzer is to test for vulnerabilities that are accessible through inputs in the application. Therefore, the fuzzer must generate test data that should delineate the target input space, which can then be passed to the target application's input. Test data can either be generated before testing, or more often iteratively generated on demand at the beginning of each test suite. A general approach to fuzz testing is to iteratively provide test instances to the target and monitoring the response. If, during testing, a test case is found to have caused an application failure, the combination of the specific test case and information about the nature of the failure it caused constitutes a defect report. Defect reports can be considered as the final output of fuzz testing for forwarding to developers [13].
4. **Exception Monitoring** - The generation and execution of test data that trigger manifestations of software defects must be detected. This is achieved by using an oracle, a generic term for a software component that monitors a target and reports a failure or exception. An oracle can take the form of a simple check, or it can be a debugger running on the target that monitors for exceptions and collects detailed logging information [13].

5. **Determining exploitability** - Once defects on the application are identified, it is necessary to process this report and forward it to the developers for fixing. The tester can also investigate the defects in question and determine the level of exploitability risk.

2.3 Testing Environment and Methodology

To demonstrate this procedure, a web application with a microservice architecture will be tested. JAVA 8 was chosen for the backend of this application, the frontend is rendered in Coffee script, Oracle database is used for data. This is an application that is used in practice for banking system. Partial fuzzers will be applied to the above application to scan the application. For testing purposes, a test environment was set up and the following activities were performed:

- Identification of entry points.
- Generation/creation of random data.
- Running Fuzz testing.
- Analysis of testing outputs.
- Repeating fuzz tests if necessary.

2.4 Fuzz Test Design

There will be white-box testing, as the tested application is known, and the source code is available. The goal is to verify the functionality of the application and find any undetected bugs. During fuzz testing, several types of responses to requests sent by fuzzers can be encountered. These responses are shown in Table 1.

Table 1. Response code descriptions.

Code	Description
200	Successful response - server to process request
204	Successful response without content, with header only
301	Permanent redirection to the URL specified in the response header
302	Request was received and redirected to another URL
303	Redirection to a new URL, usually a POST request
401	Unauthorized access
403	URL was not recognized
405	The method used (GET, POST, PUT, DELETE) is not allowed
500	Server did not process the request

The tested application contains a set of forms that could contain potential errors. It is also designed to scan URLs and hidden folders that could be exploited by an attacker. Cookies will also be fuzzed.

3 Fuzz Testing Outputs

This chapter describes the individual tests and their outputs. The tests include form, URL, cookie, and hidden page and folder tests. Since this was a known application, the first phase of testing (target identification) was skipped and only the following phases were implemented in the testing.

3.1 Fuzz Testing - Forms

The wfuzz tool will be used to test the forms. An internet banking application is identified as the target. After the necessary installation of python, pycurl and colorama modules the tool can be run. First, it is necessary to get through the authorization. This can be done using several methods, such as invoking curl with a POST request and providing login credentials. Then the focus can be on the forms themselves. In the case of this test, the forms for changing the username, submitting a transaction, and changing the password will be fuzzied.

Test A: Changing Your Username

- *Input identification*: text input in the form - field for username.
- *Data generation*: created dictionary usernames.txt, which contains non-valid values.
- *Running the test*:

```
Wfuzz -c -z file,wordlist/general/usernames.txt -d
"alias=FUZZ" url_adresa
```

- *Test result*: the result shows an attempt to redirect. In this case it is a redirect to the authorization component and then the request is processed on the server. The result of this test cannot be considered completely valid. Due to the security of the application, the final tests had to be done manually (Fig. 1).

Test B: Sending the Transaction

- *Identification of inputs:* form inputs for beneficiary account, variable symbol, part ku and message.
- *Data generation:* a dictionary bankccounts.txt was created for the beneficiary accounts, varsymbols.txt for the variable symbol and amount.txt for the amount. The character length t-testing for the message will only take place in a command where a disproportionately long character string is entered.

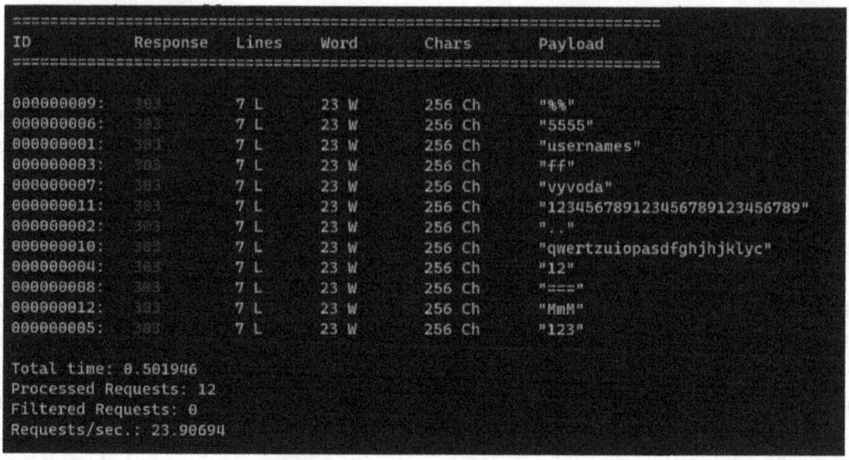

Fig. 1. Fuzzing output for username changes.

- *Running the test:*

```
wfuzz -f output.txt -c -z file,wordlist/gen-
eral/bankaccounts.txt -z file,wordlist/gen-
eral/varsymbols.txt -z file,wordlist/gen-
eral/amount.txt -d "accountNumberCreditIn-
put=FUZZ&bankCodeCredit=0100&variableSymbol=FUZ2Z&a
mount=FUZ3Z&textarea=longlongtexttextextetxtextetxt
etextetxtettxtettxfttextextextextextextextetxe-
txtextetxetxtextetxtetxtetxtext" Url_adress
```

- *Test result:* in this case it is a redirect to the authorization component and then the request is processed on the server (Fig. 2).

Test C: Change Password

- *Identification of inputs:* input for new password and input for re-entering this password.
- *Data generation:* a dictionary passwords.txt was created to change the password when the password violates the mentioned conditions.
- *Running the test:*

```
wfuzz -f outputPasswords.txt -c -z file,word-
list/general/passwords.txt -d "currentPass-
word=Heslo123&newPassword=FUZZ&reNewPassword=FUZZ"
```

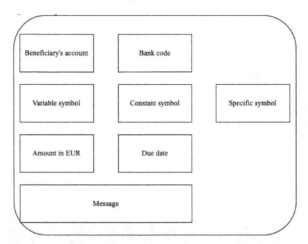

Fig. 2. Transaction form

- *Evaluation of results:* wfuzz seems to be a very useful tool for form fuzzing, but there are some limitations. If the application is already deployed and includes an authorization component for successful form submission, the test results cannot be considered. At this point, it is already much more convenient to take advantage of the implemented automated tests and test the extreme values of the forms. It is more advisable to use wfuzz during initial development, when testers can generate dictionaries with extreme values (Fig. 3).

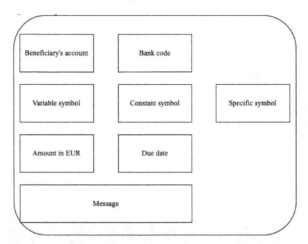

Fig. 3. Fuzzing result for password change

3.2 Fuzz Testing – URL

URL fuzzing was also performed using the wfuzz tool. The target application this time was the operator console, which does not have two-factor authentication.

- *Input identification*: URL of the operator console.
- *Data generation*: default dictionary common.txt, containing keywords.
- *Running test A:* in the first step, the link was fuzzed before authentication.

```
Wfuzz - z file,wordlist/general/common.txt --hc
404,403 url_adresa/FUZZ
```

- *Test results A*: the result for this test is 3 potentially exploitable addresses:

  - https://url_adresa/client
  - https://url_adresa/css
  - https://url_adresa/js

However, the keyword addresses have been checked and are redirects that are subsequently blocked due to insufficient permissions (Fig. 4).

Fig. 4. Fuzzing URL – test A

- *Running test B*: next, the test focused on URL discovery after authorization to the apli-cache. Before the actual test, it is necessary to find out the valid sessionid of the logged in user and then use it.

```
Wfuzz -z file,wordlist/general/common.txt --hc
404,403 -b "sessionid=566d78ce-998f-458f-a0cd-ee-
bec0bb4f8b" url_adresa/FUZZ
```

- *Test result B*: in this case no potential address for abuse was detected (Fig. 5).

Fig. 5. Fuzzing URL for authorization

3.3 Fuzz Testing – Cookies

The wfuzz tool will again be used for testing cookies. The tool contains a default wordlist that contains the generated values.

- *Input identification:* Application URL
- *Data generation:* default dictionary common.txt, containing keywords
- *Running the test*:

```
wfuzz   -z   file,wordlist/general/common.txt   -b
"cookie=FUZZ" url_adresa
```

- *Test result:* when used on the app, the answer 200 can be seen. So the server answered the call. Valid cookies values were found, but other factors such as https encryption and cookie expiration time need to be taken into account (Fig. 6).

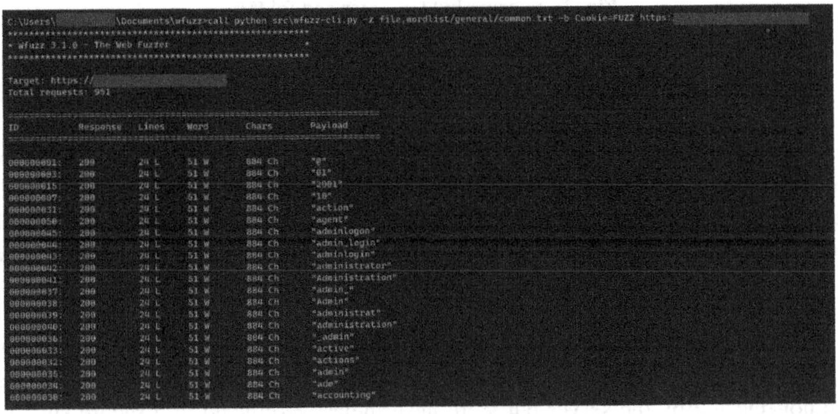

Fig. 6. Fuzzing cookies

3.4 Fuzz Testing - Hidden Pages and Folders

The ffuf tool was chosen for this type of testing and is easy to install. It works by generating requests from the dictionary.

- *Input identification*: application URL
- *Data generation*: dictionary admin-panel, which can be found from the attachments.
- *Running the test*: ffuf   -c   -w   admin-panels.txt -u url_adresa
- *Test results*: two potential vulnerabilities were found in this case. It should be noted that this is a 302 status. The pages were then manually scanned and both were redirected to the default 404 page (Fig. 7).

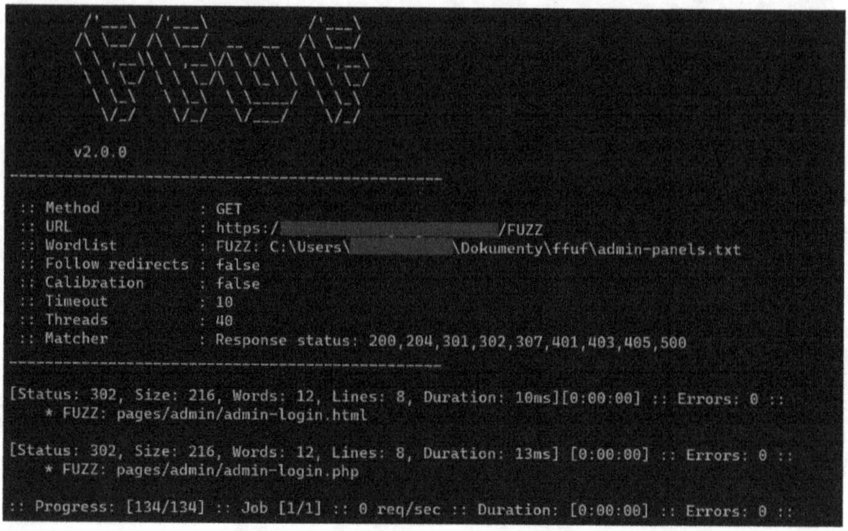

Fig. 7. Fuzzing hidden pages and folders

4 Outputs Analysis

In the first set of tests, forms were validated using the fuzz tool. The setup of the tool is timesaving and the commands are intuitive. The tool also includes a set of already-generated dictionaries that can be used. In testing, it was necessary to get through the initial authentication and then fuzz the forms. However, the forms are secured by an additional authorization component. Therefore, they had to be retested with automated tests and manually.

URL testing was done with fuzz on an Internet banking operator application where there is no need to go through two-factor authentication. Testing revealed 3 sites that were not rejected by the server but were nevertheless redirected to a secure site. The sites found were verified and the error was ruled out.

URL testing is more specific to black box testing to scan for vulnerabilities. For URL testing, it would be more appropriate to use specialized penetration testing tools such as OWASP ZAP. The cookie test revealed interesting results, where any value can be inserted into cookies. Here, however, HTTPS encryption must be considered.

For tests of differently generated request headers, the tool is efficient and can detect non-valid inputs that pass within a short while. In combination with the Burp Suite tool, which is used in security testing and can be used to send requests with modified headers, it is possible to identify errors in the headers. The fun tool was used in testing hidden folders. The tool can be put into operation very quickly and testing can begin. However, it offers very similar capabilities to fuzz and does not contain basically generated dictionaries. This test revealed two potential hidden pages, which were immediately investigated. However, the links have redirect to a 404 page and there is no way to get anywhere through them. Again, it would be more efficient to use a dedicated scan tool to scan the folders. The dictionaries generated in this case cannot be sufficient to cover all sites and it would be more appropriate to scan instead of fuzzing (Table 2).

Table 2. Summary of testing results.

TEST	RESULT
TEST OF FORMS A	Critical error not detected
FORMS TEST B	Critical error not detected
FORMS TEST C	Critical error not detected
URL TEST	Critical error not detected
COOKIES TEST	Low priority finding
HIDDEN FOLDERS TEST	Critical error not detected

Fuzz testing a web application for Internet banking is very specific and many tools cannot be applied to it. Introducing new technologies would also have negative impacts on the funding of the whole project. Since the critical bug was not observed, it would be difficult to justify the decision on fuzzes. The non-discovery of a critical bug may also be related to the fact that the application has been deployed in live operation for several years and is regularly tested by penetration testing and security experts. Testing the web application using fuzzes revealed many pitfalls and pitfalls. From a project management perspective, deploying fuzz tools can be very time-consuming, and from the customer's side, deploying these types of tests can be pointless due to finances. Quality fuzz tests require skilled professionals and a lot of time to select the right tools, install and create special tests. However, some basic fuzzing and input generation can be used during development itself before the application is deployed into live operation. There are many tools for fuzz testing, but their use is very specific. Many of them are limited to one particular language or only generate data. Using them in the development process is useful, but there's no need to spend hours unnecessarily inventing the same tests. Fuzzing is also an essential part of software security.

Conclusion

This paper presents approaches and techniques for using fuzzy testing to accelerate application development and deployment. The current era calls for the rapid and dynamic development of client applications, where the speed and surpassing of development often go against the fuzziness of the developed applications both at the back end and front end. In this respect, the application support of Smart City projects is no exception, where applications form the user interface for end users to the Smart City outputs. The chosen tests were deployed on backend applications where security is one of the most important components and the presented tests have unambiguously demonstrated the effectiveness of fuzzy tests even on such critical applications. We are convinced that the extension of the fuzzy test suite to applications, not only in the area of Smart City-related products but in general all applications used.

Acknowledgment. The financial support of the project "Application of Artificial Intelligence for Ensuring Cyber Security in Smart City" (ARTISEC), n. VJ02010016, granted by the Ministry of the Interior of the Czech Republic is gratefully acknowledged.

References

1. Manville, C., Cochrane G., Kotterink, B.: Mapping Smart Cities in the EU. EPRS: European Parliamentary Research Service, Belgium (2014). CID: 20.500.12592/0scs9f. https://policy commons.net/artifacts/1339578/mapping-smart-cities-in-the-eu/1949353/. Accessed 10 Oct 2022

2. Eckhoff, D., Wagner, I.: Privacy in the smart city—applications, technologies, challenges, and solutions. IEEE Commun. Surv. Tut. **20**(1), 489–516 (2018). ISSN 1553-877X. https://doi.org/10.1109/COMST.2017.2748998. Accessed 16 Jun 2023

3. Alamer, M., Almaiah, M.A.: Cybersecurity in smart city: a systematic mapping study. In: 2021 International Conference on Information Technology (ICIT), 14 July 2021. IEEE (2021). ISBN 978-1-6654-2870-5. https://doi.org/10.1109/ICIT52682.2021.9491123. Accessed 16 Jun 2023

4. Hero, A., et al.: Statistics and data science for cybersecurity. Harvard Data Sci. Rev. **5**(1) (2023). https://doi.org/10.1162/99608f92.a42024d0. Accessed 16 Jun 2023

5. Chen, D., Wawrzynski, P., Lv, Z.: Cyber security in smart cities: a review of deep learning-based applications and case studies. Sustain. Cities Soc. **66** (2021). ISSN 22106707. https://doi.org/10.1016/j.scs.2020.102655. Accessed 16 Jun 2023

6. Lim, C., Cho, G.-H., Kim, J.: Understanding the linkages of smart-city technologies and applications: key lessons from a text mining approach and a call for future research. Technol. Forecast. Soc. Change **170** (2021). ISSN 00401625. https://doi.org/10.1016/j.techfore.2021.120893. Accessed 16 Jun 2023

7. Mouheb, D., Abbas, S., Merabti, M.: Cybersecurity curriculum design: a survey. In: Pan, Z., Cheok, A.D., Müller, W., Zhang, M., El Rhalibi, A., Kifayat, K. (eds.) Transactions on Edutainment XV. LNCS, vol. 11345, pp. 93–107. Springer, Heidelberg (2019). https://doi.org/10.1007/978-3-662-59351-6_9 Accessed 16 Jun 2023

8. Aubert, C., Varacca, D.: Processes, systems & tests: defining contextual equivalences. Electron. Proc. Theoret. Comput. Sci. **347**, 1–21 (2021). ISSN 2075-2180. https://doi.org/10.4204/EPTCS.347.1. Accessed 16 Jun 2023

9. Costa, A., Teixeira, L.: Testing strategies for smart cities applications. In: Proceedings of the III Brazilian Symposium on Systematic and Automated Software Testing, 17 September 2018, pp. 20–28. ACM, New York (2018). ISBN 9781450365550. https://doi.org/10.1145/3266003.3266005. Accessed 16 Jun 2023

10. Fortes, S., et al.: The campus as a smart city: University of Málaga environmental, learning, and research approaches. Sensors **19**(6) (2019). ISSN 1424-8220. https://doi.org/10.3390/s19061349. Accessed 16 Jun 2023

11. Lee, W.-H., Chiu, C.-Y.: Design and implementation of a smart traffic signal control system for smart city applications. Sensors **20**(2) (2020). ISSN 1424-8220. https://doi.org/10.3390/s20020508. Accessed 16 Jun 2023

12. Vinzenz, N., Oka, D.K.: Integrating fuzz testing into the cybersecurity validation strategy. In: Proceedings of the SAE WCX Digital Summit, 06 April 2021. https://doi.org/10.4271/2021-01-0139. Accessed 16 Jun 2023

13. Lämmel, P., Tcholtchev, N., Schieferdecker, I.: Enhancing cloud based data platforms for smart cities with authentication and authorization features. In: Companion Proceedings of the 10th International Conference on Utility and Cloud Computing, 05 Dec 2017, pp. 167–172. ACM, New York (2017). ISBN 9781450351959. https://doi.org/10.1145/3147234.314 8087. Accessed 16 Jun 2023

14. Rodriguez, L.G.A., Batista, D.M.: Resource-intensive fuzzing for MQTT brokers: state of the art, performance evaluation, and open issues. IEEE Netw. Lett. **5**(2), 100–104 (2023). ISSN 2576-3156. https://doi.org/10.1109/LNET.2023.3263556. Accessed 16 Jun 2023

15. Hernández Ramos, S., Villalba, M.T., Lacuesta, R.: MQTT security: a novel fuzzing approach. Wirel. Commun. Mob. Comput. **2018**, 1–11 (2018). ISSN 1530-8669. https://doi.org/10.1155/2018/8261746. Accessed 16 Jun 2023

16. Wüstholz, V., Christakis, M.: Harvey: a greybox fuzzer for smart contracts. In: Proceedings of the 28th ACM Joint Meeting on European Software Engineering Conference and Symposium on the Foundations of Software Engineering, 08 November 2020, pp. 1398–1409. ACM, New York (2020). ISBN 9781450370431. https://doi.org/10.1145/3368089.3417064. Accessed 16 Jun 2023

17. Godefroid, P.: Fuzzing. Commun. ACM **63**(2), 70–76 (2020). ISSN 0001-0782. https://doi.org/10.1145/3363824. Accessed 16 Jun 2023

18. Pham, V.-T., Bohme, M., Roychoudhury, A.: AFLNET: a greybox fuzzer for network protocols. In: 2020 IEEE 13th International Conference on Software Testing, Validation and Verification (ICST), pp. 460–465. IEEE (2020). ISBN 978-1-7281-5778-8. https://doi.org/10.1109/ICST46399.2020.00062. Accessed 16 Jun 2023

19. Eceiza, M., Flores, J.L., Iturbe, M.: Fuzzing the Internet of Things: a review on the techniques and challenges for efficient vulnerability discovery in embedded systems. IEEE IoT J. **8**(13), 10390–10411 (2021). ISSN 2327-4662. https://doi.org/10.1109/JIOT.2021.3056179. Accessed 16 Jun 2023

20. Beaman, C., Redbourne, M., Mummery, J.D., Hakak, S.: Fuzzing vulnerability discovery techniques: survey, challenges and future directions. Comput. Secur. **120** (2022). ISSN 01674048. https://doi.org/10.1016/j.cose.2022.102813. Accessed 16 Jun 2023

Unified Smart City Domain Model for Central Europe

Tomas Svoboda$^{(\boxtimes)}$ (ID), Lubomir Almer (ID), Patrik Urbanik (ID), Vladimir Sobeslav (ID), and Josef Horalek (ID)

Faculty of Informatics and Management, University of Hradec Kralove, Hradec Kralove, Czech Republic
{tomas.svoboda,lubomir.almer,patrik.urbanik,vladimir.sobeslav, josef.horalek}@uhk.cz

Abstract. In recent years, the concept and implementation of smart cities has become an important topic at the level of countries, regions and cities. However, it is currently not clearly defined what all areas are part of a smart city, or what functional domains a smart city addresses. The aim of this paper is to analyse the current state of smart city concepts in the world and then to identify the functional domains that define the areas belonging to a smart city. This analysis represents an input to propose a further model of functional domains for Central Europe. The relevance of the model is verified by comparing the identified functional domains with existing regional and national smart city strategies in the Czech Republic.

Keywords: Smart city model · smart energy · smart infrastructure · smart transportation · smart healthcare · analysis · functional domains · cybersecurity

1 Introduction

Over more than the last decade, the smart city label has spread across the globe, influencing city strategies regardless of their size. The concept of smart city has also been introduced as a strategy [1] encompassing modern urban environments with an emphasis on the effective use of modern information and communication technologies (ICT) especially to enhance their competitiveness [2]. In order to face the growing problems related with the urban areas development, which are analyzed in detail [3], and their agglomerations, responsible governmental units, local businesses, non-profit organizations and other actors must make a concerted and managed effort to solve these problems [4].

In order to effectively solve the problems associated with the implementation of smart cities, it is essential to involve the target group itself, i.e. the citizens living in these cities and their social activities in the form of non-profit organizations, etc., so that the idea of smart cities associated with the implementation of modern intelligent ICT systems as it is presented in their articles [5, 6]. The smart city idea itself is not new, but the first references can be found as early as 1993 [7], where various investments in

© ICST Institute for Computer Sciences, Social Informatics and Telecommunications Engineering 2024
Published by Springer Nature Switzerland AG 2024. All Rights Reserved
P. Cong Vinh and H. Mahfooz Ul Haque (Eds.): ICTCC 2023, LNICST 586, pp. 98–110, 2024.
https://doi.org/10.1007/978-3-031-59462-5_7

telecommunications in Singapore are documented and represent the role they have in the production and distribution processes that define Singapore [7] as a "smart city".

It is therefore clear that the smart city issue has been addressed for many years and that selected parts of the smart city concept have been implemented in various ways. However, it is necessary to answer together with the authors of the article smart city and Value Creation [8] the question of what all smart city is, or what functional domains the smart city area includes, as we can agree with the authors that there is no recognized definition of a smart city so far and some cities that call themselves smart are completely lacking a strategic vision of their smart future. The question is how to approach this issue holistically and identify the different functional domains of a smart city. In order to identify the functional domains that are part of a smart city, the decision has been made to construct a unified and all-encompassing model by analyzing the findings derived from previously conducted reviews.

The first step to find a coherent and unified model of functional domains is to analyze the conclusions of the already developed reviews. The second step is to verify the degree of applicability of the proposed model in current smart city strategies in the Czech Republic and to generalize this model for use in Central Europe.

2   Related Work

2.1   Functional Smart City Domains

The search for a definition of the meaning of a smart city is addressed in the Systematic Literature Review [10], with an emphasis on the search for an answer whether smart City is included in specific urban strategies promoted by government strategies or whether they face specific urban problems without a comprehensive framework. What all can be included in smart city strategies remains unclear and often vague which is also based on the analysis published in the article Smart Cities: Definitions, Dimensions, Performance, and Initiatives [11], which aims to clarify the meaning of the word "smart" in the context of cities through an approach based on an in-depth review of relevant studies as well as official documents of international institutions.

A new perspective based on defining smart city domains of interest is then provided by the Literature Review [12], based on a literature review, with the aim of discovering and classifying the different schools of thought, universities and research centres as well as companies that deal with the smart city domain, and discovering alternative, models, architectures, approaches and frameworks.

A similar approach is presented in [13], which analyses more than a hundred sources with a focus on providing a data-driven view of smart city architectures and the key technologies that enable their implementation. However, despite the dozens of published papers on smart city, there is no major shift in finding a coherent smart city model, which is also the case of Camero A. and Alba E. [14], who in 2019 mapped in detail the targeted use of modern ICT technologies in the smart grid. Despite the non-perfection or even the absence of a single comprehensive smart city model, there are a number of sub-project implementations around the world, where the challenges arising from the interdependence of the different smart city domains have to be addressed, involving significant political, technical and socio-economic challenges for the designers, integrators and organisations involved in the management of these new entities. This is the area addressed in the study [15], which focuses on security, privacy and risk in smart cities, highlighting information security threats and challenges to smart city infrastructure in the area of data management and processing. The study analyses many of these challenges, offers a synthesis of relevant key literature and develops a framework for smart city interaction.

2.2 Architecture Models

The approach of Lombardi, et al. [18] focused on generic models and architectures that describe the main smart city characteristics, and also approaches which can result to improve its smartness. Primarily, this involves defining and quantifying strategic visions for cities. A different approach is then presented by Dameri [19], who uses the following basic components to define a smart city: people, land, infrastructure and government (Fig. 1).

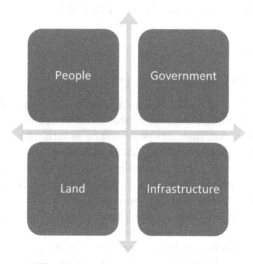

Fig. 1. The core city components [19]

Land is the geographical area in which a city is located. Infrastructure includes transport facilities, etc. People includes all citizens, not just residents. Government includes the city authorities whose task is to manage the administration of the city. From a smart city perspective, according to [20, 21], it is necessary to include the main aspects of a smart city, which are efficiency, environmental friendliness and innovation.

The general goal of smart cities is to improve the quality of everyday life of citizens, who are often unaware that the city or government is designing, implementing and operating smart solutions, as they are not involved in defining smart city priorities and projects on the quality of life [22]. Thus, cities create strategies and visions, but their outputs are not sufficiently communicated to citizens. Palumbo and Cosseta underscore the pivotal role of individuals in the concept of a smart city [22]. In their focus on social innovation, they assert that social and open innovation are crucial for generating fresh ideas associated with smart cities. Another intriguing perspective on generating public value in a smart city is outlined by [23] in their conceptual model. In this context, the author highlights that creating value and ensuring citizen benefits in a smart city necessitate active participation in research activities, the implementation of policy commitments, citizen engagement, and financial support from the private sector for individual smart city initiatives, along with the provision of tangible technical solutions. It is indisputable, therefore, that the overarching objective of smart cities is to enhance both the overall quality of the city and the quality of life within it. While these two aspects are not synonymous, they are intricately interconnected, primarily through specific smart projects [24, 25].

The intelligence of a city itself encompasses various dimensions. Giffinger [26], a highly cited author, identifies six distinct dimensions of a smart city, as illustrated in Fig. 2. Employing this framework to categorize specific smart projects and construct an evaluation framework poses challenges, particularly due to the interrelated or overlapping nature of these different dimensions.

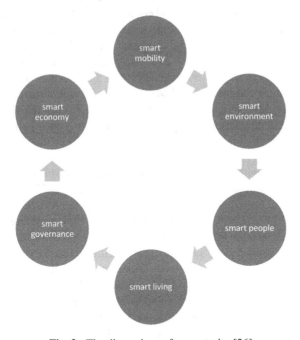

Fig. 2. The dimensions of a smart city [26].

Hence, employing a framework proves to be a more effective approach, grounded in the fundamental smart city components, comprising a diverse range of projects aimed at enhancing either the city's quality of life or the city itself. This enhancement is gauged through a set of KPI', reflective of the distinct benefits emanating from each project. Consequently, articulating and quantifying the manifold advantages brought about by an individual project is a more streamlined approach [27].

Individual projects serve as instrumental tools for the implementation of a smart city. These projects ought to possess specific attributes, particularly leveraging advanced technological solutions, aligning with both environmental and economic considerations. A multitude of smart projects often concentrate on specific domains such as energy efficiency in buildings, greenhouse gas emission reduction, widespread broadband adoption, delivery of e-services, mobile government, and more. However, it becomes increasingly crucial not only to furnish technical solutions to urban challenges but also to integrate each project into a comprehensive overarching smart framework [28].

2.3 Smart City Strategies Around the World

Agenda 21 serves as the foundational document outlining a development plan for the 21st century, impacting not only individual countries but the entire world. Also, it plays a substantial role in shaping the contemporary manifestation of the smart city perspective in the Czech Republic. [29]. It was approved at the United Nations (UN) Conference on Environment and Development in Rio de Janeiro in 1992 and is considered one of the basic long-term strategic plans for sustainable development, which is applicable both at the global level and at the level of individual countries and administrative regions. Particularly relevant for the implementation of the plan in individual territories is Chapter 28: Local Government Initiatives to Promote Agenda 21, in the section on Empowering Important and Relevant Groups, which calls on the relevant public authorities in each territory to adopt the plan as their own agenda [30]. Consequently, the Czech Republic initiated a development program named MA21 [31], overseen directly by the Ministry of the Environment. MA21 functions as a practical tool, translating the tenets of sustainable development into actionable measures tailored for municipalities and regions. Its purpose is to guarantee a high and good well-being and ecological conditions in a designated area.

In direct continuity with Agenda 21, other global plans have been developed. Among these, the pivotal document is the Millennium Declaration [32], primarily centered around 8 Millennium Development Goals. Subsequent to the Millennium Declaration, the present UN worldwide initiative is the Agenda 2030 [33], outlining 17 Sustainable Development Goals, spanning the years 2015 to 2030.

This principle extends to documents dedicated to supporting the smart city endeavor, aligning seamlessly with the SDGs. The inception of this initiative within the EU traces back to Europe 2020 or the Digital Agenda—a decade-long strategy geared towards fostering intelligent and sustainable development. Stemming from this framework, a sector-specific initiative named Smart Cities and Communities was inaugurated in 2011, concentrating primarily on industrial aspects. In 2012, The European Innovation Partnership on Smart Cities and Communities was established, imparting a foundational structure to the Smart Cities concept (Smart Cities Methodology, 2018).

2.4 Smart City Strategies in the Czech Republic

The Czech Republic has pledged to fulfill the objectives outlined in the 2030 Agenda, leading to the establishment of the Strategic Framework Czech Republic 2030 [34]. This document, emerging as a result of this commitment, serves as the cornerstone for the smart city initiative in the Czech Republic. Issued by the Office of the Government of the Czech Republic, it stands as a comprehensive strategic development framework upon which various sub-national and regional documents/strategies derive their foundation. It is the basis for the Regional Development Strategy 2021+ [35], which, based on the above-mentioned framework document, sets out the objectives at the national level for the period of years 2021–2027 (seven years). The SRR21+ explicitly outlines its primary objective as pinpointing a tailored approach aligned with the need of individual regions. It aims to identify specific interventions to foster a balance in competitiveness among regions while concurrently fostering sustainable development within each specific region.

The Innovation Strategy of the Czech Republic for the period 2019–2023 [36] stands out as another pivotal document. It serves as a strategic blueprint for the Czech Republic's approach to research, development, and innovations, aspiring to position the country among the most innovative within the EU. Within this framework, the strategy also unveiled a fresh brand: "Cech Republic: The country for the future", being presented at the international level.

In accordance with the Smart Cities Concept and under the influence of all the above-mentioned documents, at the turn of 2020–2021 new development and Smart Strategies started to emerge in individual regions of the Czech Republic with a view to the following years, most often to 2027. However, there is currently no analysis that confirms that the respective regional strategies contain functional domains that are truly relevant for the smart city area.

3   Identification and Analysis of Functional Domains

3.1   Processing Methods

In the description of the current state of the problem, mainly general scientific methods were used. First of all, a search of available materials was used, especially documents in electronic form, norms, laws, standards and articles from the Internet. The literature search helped to provide an up-to-date view of the issue under study. Among the general methods, analysis, synthesis, comparison, induction and deduction were also used. Analysis was used in the context of objectifying and clarifying the various aspects and relationships under study within the Smart Cities concept. Synthesis was used to summarize the findings. Comparison was used mainly in the context of comparing the different aspects under investigation. In-duction and deduction was used to establish the relationships between the different aspects. The collected documents underwent categorization based on the entity responsible for their publication: public institution, university, or private company. Their content underwent additional scrutiny employing the methods, as well as through the lens of Nam and Pardo's smart city model [16] (see Fig. 3). This model was selected for analysis as it delineates a smart city framework across three dimensions: technology, institutions, and people.

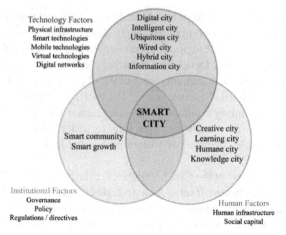

Fig. 3. Smart city core components [16]

The following outlines the steps in the conducted analysis of the current state of the art solutions for addressing smart city challenges. This analysis aimed to identify the functional domains of the smart city model withing the broader context of the scientific community and the overarching concept of a smart city. For the systematic analysis, the PRISMA approach [17] was used, the specific use of which is illustrated in the process diagram Fig. 4.

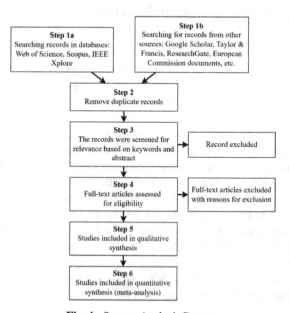

Fig. 4. System Analysis Process

3.2 Input Data

The input data were articles indexed in the Web of Science, Scopus and IEEE Xplore databases, supplemented by articles from Google scholar, Taylor & Francis, Research-Gate and documents published by the European Commission and national smart city strategies. At the same time, the time criterion was chosen that the articles were no older than five years, i.e. from 2017 to 2022. The following keywords were used for the analysis, linked to the search strings:

- smart city &

  o energy; smart energy; smart grid smart city; smart building; smart street; smart light-ning; energy management; smart streetlight; IoT smart city; 5G smart city; smart governance; e-government; smart city governance; e-governance; smart govern-ment; collaborative governance; internet of things; social networks; machine learn-ing; air pollution; internet of health things; unmanned aerial vehicles; smart gov-ernment; smart waste management; disabled people; fire fighters; unmanned aerial vehicles; police; communication; e-health; education; smart education; Innovation; smart city education; smart people; knowledge economy; smart urbanism; smart cit-izenship; entrepreneurship, citizen education; research; schools; science; start-ups; security; air quality; water meter; electricity meter; culture; tourism; image detec-tion; Image processing; outdoor parking; parking detection; smart cities; traffic engineering; improving; parking; availability; prediction.

3.3 Analysis Results

The analysis was divided into sub-phases. In the first phase, 307 articles were selected on the basis of the above criteria, which were then selected, and duplicates were removed in the second phase. This resulted in 268 articles that were referred for further analysis. In the third phase, abstract analysis was performed to eliminate selection bias based on the search strings from the above keywords.

After this analysis, 54 articles were excluded. This relatively high number can be attributed to the extensive combination of keywords. Thus, a total of 214 articles were subjected to the fourth stage. In this phase, a full text analysis was conducted to analyze and thematically categorize the articles into groups to define the resulting functional domains of the smart city model from a quantitative perspective, while simultaneously implementing a qualitative view of the articles with an emphasis on their contribution and innovativeness. This phase of analysis resulted in 159 detailed ana-lysed articles that were used to create the smart city functional domain model.

The examination of the articles led to the recognition of five vertical functional domains that represents the fundamental areas of interest in the context of a smart city. These are Transportation and accessibility, Technical infrastructure, Healthcare and Social services, Public administration and Environment, Tourism, Culture. These are supplemented by two overarching horizontal domains, specifically Education, identified as pivotal through the analysis and Cybersecurity. Both domains strongly support and influence the design in all other domains. It can be deduced that these domains are crucial for all forthcoming implementations and, as such, should be accorded special attention (Fig. 5).

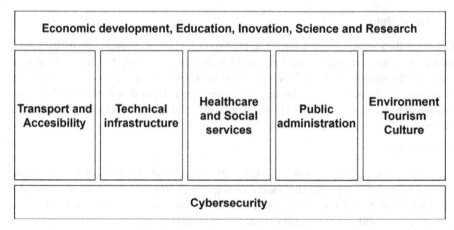

Fig. 5. Smart city application domains

Furthermore, an analysis was conducted to determine whether individual regions actively engage in the implementation of the SMART concept within their territories, and if this concept is integrated into their respective development strategies for the current period (Table 1).

Table 1. Regions and abbreviations

Region name	Abbreviation	Region name	Abbreviation
Central Bohemia Region	CB	Pardubice Region	PA
South Bohemia Region	SB	Vysočina Region	VY
Ústí Region	ÚS	South Moravia Region	SM
Karlovy Vary Region	KV	Olomouc Region	OL
Liberec Region	LB	Moravia-Silesia Region	MS
Hradec Králové Region	HK	Zlín Region	ZL
Capital City of Prague	PR	Plzeň Region	PL

The proposed model is retrospectively evaluated by comparing it with the strategies of individual regions to assess its relevance (Table 2).

Seven of the fourteen regions analysed have developed a separate strategy oriented towards the implementation of the Smart concept. The opposite is true for the Plzeň Region, where the latest version of the regional strategy is 2014 +, which is also reflected in the results in the table above.

The number of priority areas (PAs) in the documents ranges from four (specifically the Pardubice Region), to ten (the Central Bohemian Region), with six and seven PAs having the largest representation. From the nomenclature and the articulation of specific domains in the certain regions, the impact of the Czech Smart Cities Concept is evident. These regions have augmented the concept with elements that are characteristic

Table 2. Application domains in region strategies. (✓ included ✗ Not included ~ Partly included)

/ Regions Domains	CB	SB	ÚS	KV	LB	HK	PR	PA	VY	SM	OL	MS	ZL	PL
Economic development, Education, Innovation, Science and Research	✓	✓	✓	✓	✓	✓	✓	✓	✓	✓	✓	✓	✓	✗
Transportation and accessibility	✓	✓	~	✓	✓	✓	✓	✓	✓	✓	✓	✓	✓	✗
Technical infrastructure	✓	✓	✓	✓	✓	✓	✓	✓	✓	~	✓	✓	✓	✗
Healthcare and social services	✓	✓	✓	✓	✓	✓	✓	✓	✓	✓	✓	✓	✓	✓
Public administration	~	~	~	✓	✓	✓	✓	✓	✓	✓	✓	~	✓	✗
Environment, Tourism, Culture	✓	✓	✓	✓	✓	✓	✓	✓	✓	✓	✓	✓	✓	✗
Cybersecurity	✗	✗	✗	✓	✗	✗	~	✗	✗	✗	✗	✗	✓	✗

and unique to them, such as the inclusion of spa-related considerations in the Karlovy Vary Region. In contrast, some regions adhered to the conventional smart city domains outlined in the study "Mapping Smart Cities in the EU" [40], published by the European Parliament. Drawing from a similar analysis across the European cities, this study defined six fundamental smart city domains: (1) Smart Governance, (2) Smart Economy, (3) Smart Mobility, (4) Smart Environment, (5) Smart People and (6) Smart Living. The structure of Priority Areas (PAs) in the strategies of the Zlín and Liberec regions closely aligns with this conceptual framework. While other regions have taken diverse approaches in formulating their PAs, they still address all key thematic areas, albeit sometimes in the form of specific objectives. Notably, education, science, research, and innovation were consistently represented in all regional strategies, reflecting the influence of the previously mentioned Innovation Strategy, particularly the RIS3 strategy, which places a specific focus on these areas. The individual regions adapt this strategy in their own regional innovation strategies to meet their specific requirements. This underscores the significance of this domain and reinforces the assertion in the Innovation Strategy that education, science, research, and innovation play a pivotal role in realizing all 17 Sustainable Development Goals (SDGs).

4 Conclusion

The issue of smart city has been addressed for many years, and selected parts of the smart city concept have been implemented in various ways. Based on a detailed analysis of relevant scientific articles, a total of seven functional domains have been identified, which represent key areas for the fulfilment of the added value of the implementation of the smart city concept and its applicability for the improvement of the life of inhabitants and the design of a functional model of the smart city. The relevance of the model was further verified in detail in the individual smart city strategies in the Czech Republic, confirming the relevance of these domains and their solutions in the current smart city strategies in the Czech Republic. Approaches to smart city implementation within the Central European countries also largely reflect the identified functional domains. The proposed model is therefore fully applicable also in Central European countries. A current key topic in the smart city area that needs to be addressed in further research is the area of cyber security. Cybersecurity brings key requirements for ensuring security within all other functional domains of the proposed model, but is currently not sufficiently addressed in smart city strategies. Based on the adopted Directive (EU) 2022/2555 of the European Parliament and of the Council of 14 December 2022 on measures for a high common level of cybersecurity across the Union, amending Regulation (EU) No 910/2014 and Directive (EU) 2018/1972, and repealing Directive (EU) 2016/1148 (NIS 2 Directive), it can be expected that local governments will be designated as obliged entities under this Directive and thus will have to ensure the implementation of information and cybersecurity requirements also within the smart city framework. Therefore, the identification of vulnerabilities in smart city systems and the process of addressing them, including ensuring compliance with NIS2, becomes a key focus for further research in this area.

Acknowledgement. The financial support of the project "Application of Artificial Intelligence for Ensuring Cyber Security in Smart City", No. VJ02010016, granted by the Ministry of the Interior of the Czech Republic is gratefully acknowledged.

References

1. Manville, C., Kotterink, B.: Mapping Smart Cities in the EU, EPRS: European Parliamentary Research Service. Belgium (2014). https://policycommons.net /artifacts/1339578/mapping-smart-cities-in-the-eu/1949353/on10Oct2022.CID: 20.500.12592/0scs9f
2. Caragliu, A., Del Bo, C., Nijkamp, P.: Smart cities in Europe. J. Urban Technol. **18**(2), 65–82 (2011). https://doi.org/10.1080/10630732.2011.601117
3. SMART, EU-China; COOPERATION, Green City. Comparative study of smart cities in Europe and China. Current Chinese Economic Report Series, Springer (2014)
4. Nam, T., Pardo, T.A.: Conceptualizing smart city with dimensions of technology, people, and institutions. In: Proceedings of the 12th Annual International Digital Government Research Conference on Digital Government Innovation in Challenging Times - dg.o '11, New York, USA, pp. 282–291, ACM Press (2011). https://doi.org/10.1145/2037556.2037602

5. Monfaredzadeh, T., Krueger, R.: Investigating social factors of sustainability in a Smart City. Proc. Eng. **118**, 1112–1118 (2015). https://doi.org/10.1016/j.proeng.2015.08.452

6. Anthopoulos, L.G.: The Rise of the Smart City. In: Understanding Smart Cities: A Tool for Smart Government or an Industrial Trick? PAIT, vol. 22, pp. 5–45. Springer, Cham (2017). https://doi.org/10.1007/978-3-319-57015-0_2

7. Heng, T.M., Low L.: The intelligent city: Singapore achieving the next lap. Technol. Anal. Strat. Manage. **5**(2). ISSN **187–202**, 0953–7325 (1993). https://doi.org/10.1080/095373293 08524129

8. Dameri, R.P., Rosenthal-Sabroux, C.: Smart City and Value Creation. In: Dameri, R.P., Rosenthal-Sabroux, C. (eds.) Smart City. PI, pp. 1–12. Springer, Cham (2014). https://doi.org/10.1007/978-3-319-06160-3_1

9. Angelidou, M.: Smart city policies: a spatial approach. Cities **41**, S3–S11 (2014). https://doi.org/10.1016/j.cities.2014.06.007

10. Cocchia, A.: Smart and Digital City: A Systematic Literature Review. In: Dameri, R.P., Rosenthal-Sabroux, C. (eds.) Smart City: How to Create Public and Economic Value with High Technology in Urban Space, pp. 13–43. Springer International Publishing, Cham (2014). https://doi.org/10.1007/978-3-319-06160-3_2

11. Albino, V., Berardi, U., Dangelico, R.M.: Smart cities: definitions, dimensions, performance, and initiatives. J. Urban Technol. **22**(1), 3–21 (2015). https://doi.org/10.1080/10630732.2014. 942092

12. Anthopoulos, L.G.: Understanding the Smart City Domain: A Literature Review. In: Rodríguez-Bolívar, M.P. (ed.) Transforming City Governments for Successful Smart Cities, pp. 9–21. Springer International Publishing, Cham (2015). https://doi.org/10.1007/978-3-319-03167-5_2

13. Yin, C., Xiong, Z., Chen, H., et al.: A literature survey on smart cities. Sci. China Inf. Sci. **58**, 1–18 (2015). https://doi.org/10.1007/s11432-015-5397-4

14. Camero, A., Alba, E.: Smart City and information technology: A review, Cities, Volume 93. ISSN **84–94**, 0264–2751 (2019). https://doi.org/10.1016/j.cities.2019.04.014

15. Ismagilova, E., Hughes, L., Rana, N.P., et al.: Security, privacy and risks within smart cities: literature review and development of a smart city interaction framework. Inf. Syst. Front. **24**, 393–414 (2022). https://doi.org/10.1007/s10796-020-10044-1

16. Nam, T., Pardo, T.A.: Conceptualizing smart city with dimensions of technology, people, and institutions. In: Proceedings of the 12th Annual International Digital Government Research Conference: Digital Government Innovation in Challenging Times, (pp. 282–291). ACM (Jun 2011)

17. PRISMA: TRANSPARENT REPORTING of SYSTEMATIC REVIEWS and META-ANALYSES [online]. PRISMA, 2021 [cit. 2022–10–11]. https://www.prisma-statement.org//

18. Lombardi, P., Giordano, S., Farouh, H., Yousef, W.: Modelling the smart city performance. Innov.: Europ. J. Social Sci. Res. **25**(2), 137–149 (2012)

19. Dameri, R.P.: Comparing smart and digital city: Initiatives and strategies in Amsterdam and Genoa. Are they digital or smart? In: Dameri, R.P., Sabroux, C., (Eds.), Smart city. How to create public and economic value with high technology in urban space, (pp. 45–88) (2014). Springer International

20. Alawadhi, S., et al.: Building understanding of smart city initiatives. In: Electronic Government, pp. 40–53. Springer, Berlin Heidelberg (2012)

21. Carli, R., Dotoli, M., Pellegrino, R., Ranieri, L.: Measuring and managing the smartness of cities: a framework for classifying performance indicators. In: 2013 IEEE International Conference on Systems, Man, and Cybernetics (SMC), (pp. 1288–1293) (2013, October). IEEE

22. Baccarne, B., Mechant, P., Schuurman, D.: Empowered cities? An analysis of the structure and generated value of the smart City Ghent. In: Dameri, R.P., Rosenthal-Sabroux, C. (eds.) Smart City. PI, pp. 157–182. Springer, Cham (2014). https://doi.org/10.1007/978-3-319-061 60-3_8

23. Cossetta, A., Palumbo, M.: The co-production of social innovation: The case of living lab. In: Dameri, R.P., Rosenthal-Sabroux, C. (eds.) Smart City: How to Create Public and Economic Value with High Technology in Urban Space, pp. 221–235. Springer International Publishing, Cham (2014). https://doi.org/10.1007/978-3-319-06160-3_11

24. Al-Hader, M., Rodzi, A., Sharif, A. R., Ahmad, N.: Smart city components architecture. In: Computational Intelligence, modelling and simulation, 2009. CSSim'09. International Conference, (pp. 93–97). IEEE (2009)

25. Glaeser, E.L., Berry, C.R.: Why are smart places getting smarter. Rappaport Institute/Taubman Center Policy Brief, 2 (2006)

26. Giffinger, R., et al.: Smart cities: Ranking of European medium-sized cities. Vienna, Austria: Centre of Regional Science (SRF), Vienna University of Technology (2007)

27. Van den Bergh, J., Viaene, S.: Key challenges for the smart city: turning ambition into reality. In: System Sciences (HICSS), 2015 48th Hawaii International Conference on, (pp. 2385–2394). IEEE (Jan 2015)

28. Anthopoulos, L.G., Fitsilis, P.: Understanding smart city business models: a comparison. In: Proceedings of the 24th International Conference on World Wide Web Companion, (pp. 529–534). International World Wide Web Conferences Steering Committee (May 2015)

29. United Nations Conference on Environment and Development. Agenda 21, Rio Declaration, Forest Principles. United Nations (1992). https://sustainabledevelopment.un.org/outcomedo cuments/agenda21

30. CENIA: Historie a mezinárodní kontext Agenda 21. CENIA and MŽP ČR (2017). https:// ma21.cenia.cz/cs-cz/úvod/proveřejnost/historieamezinárodníkontext.aspx

31. Místní Agenda 21: CENIA and MŽP ČR (2006). https://www.mzp.cz/cz/mistni_agenda_21

32. United Nations Millennium Declaration. [United Nations Human Rights]. United Nations (2000, September 8). https://www.ohchr.org/en/instruments-mechanisms/instruments/uni ted-nations-millennium-declaration

33. Transforming our World: The 2030 Agenda for Sustainable Development. United Nations (2015). https://sdgs.un.org/publications/transforming-our-world-2030-agenda-sustai nable-development-17981

34. Kárníková, A. (Ed.): Strategický rámec Česká republika 2030. Úřad vlády České republiky, Odbor pro udržitelný rozvoj (2017). www.cr2030.cz

35. Strategie regionálního rozvoje ČR 2021+. MMR ČR (2019). https://mmr.cz/cs/microsites/uze mni-dimenze/regionalni-rozvoj/strategie-regionalniho-rozvoje-cr-2021

36. Havlíček, K.: Inovační strategie České republiky 2019–2030. Rada pro výzkum, vývoj a inovace (2019). https://www.vyzkum.cz/FrontClanek.aspx?idsekce=866015

37. Národní výzkumná a inovační strategie pro inteligetní specializaci České republiky 2021–2027. (2021). Ministerstvo průmyslu a obchodu. https://www.mpo.cz/cz/podnikani/ris3-str ategie/

38. European Commission. (2019). A European Green Deal. European Commission. https://ec.europa.eu/info/strategy/priorities-2019-2024/european-green-deal_en

39. MMR ČR. Koncepce Smart Cities. Ministerstvo pro místní rozvoj (2021). https://mmr.cz/cs/ microsites/sc/metodiky/koncepce-smart-cities

40. Manville, C., Cave, M., Pederson, T., Liebe, W., Kotterink, M.: Mapping Smart Cities in the EU. European Parliament (2014). https://www.europarl.europa.eu/RegData/etudes/etu des/join/2014/507480/IPOL-ITRE_ET(2014)507480_EN.pdf

Applying AI and Ontologies to the Covid Pandemic

Waralak Vongdoiwang Siricharoen[✉]

Faculty of Information and Communication Technology, Silpakorn University Nonthaburi,
Pak Kret 11120, Thailand
siricharoen_w2@su.ac.th

Abstract. The application of Artificial Intelligence (AI) and ontologies to the COVID-19 pandemic has been an active area of research and development. AI techniques such as machine learning, computer vision, and natural language processing have been used to analyze vast amounts of data generated by the pandemic, such as medical records, scientific literature, and social media posts. Ontologies, on the other hand, provide a structured representation of knowledge, which can be used to standardize data and facilitate data integration, enabling more efficient and effective data analysis.

Keywords: AI · Ontologies · Covid · Sematic Web

1 Introduction

The COVID-19 pandemic has shown us the importance of ontologies in disease control and prevention. By understanding the relationships between different concepts, we can better design systems and processes to respond to fast-changing circumstances. In this post, we'll explore how ontologies can be used in the context of a pandemic, and some of the challenges involved. We will also look at how the use of ontologies might change in the future as we learn more about diseases like COVID-19 (Kachaoui et al., 2020). an ontology related to the COVID-19 pandemic might represent the various entities involved in the pandemic, such as viruses, diseases, symptoms, and treatments, as well as the relationships between these entities. For example, an ontology might represent the fact that the COVID-19 virus is a type of coronavirus, and that it can cause symptoms such as fever, cough, and difficulty breathing. This information could then be used by computer systems to provide more intelligent services related to the pandemic, such as personalized advice or recommendations for preventing and treating the virus (Oyelad and Ezugwu, 2020). AI has been used in various ways to help stop the spread of covid-19. Some examples of AI-powered tools that have been used to help stop the spread of the virus include (Dhatterwal et al., 2021; Mcheick et al., 2022):

- AI-powered algorithms that can analyze large amounts of data, such as medical records and surveillance footage, to help identify potential outbreaks and track the spread of the virus.

P. Cong Vinh and H. Mahfooz Ul Haque (Eds.): ICTCC 2023, LNICST 586, pp. 111–121, 2024.
https://doi.org/10.1007/978-3-031-59462-5_8

- AI-powered tools that can analyze medical images, such as CT scans and X-rays, to help doctors diagnose diseases more accurately and quickly.
- AI-powered chatbots and virtual assistants that can provide information and support to people who are self-isolating or have questions about the virus.
- AI-powered systems can assist with contact tracing, which involves identifying people who may have come into contact with someone who has tested positive for the virus, in order to prevent further transmission.

Overall, these AI-powered tools can help in the fight against covid-19 by providing doctors and public health officials with valuable tools and insights that can help improve diagnosis, treatment, and containment efforts.

2 AI and Ontologies

AI and ontologies are related in that ontologies are often used to provide a structured and organized framework for representing knowledge and information, which can then be used by AI systems to improve their performance. An ontology is a formal representation of a set of concepts within a domain, and the relationships between those concepts. It provides a common vocabulary that can be shared and understood by humans and machines, which enables them to communicate and reason about a particular domain (Lin et al., 2021).

For example, an ontology for the domain of medicine could define concepts such as diseases, symptoms, treatments, and so on, as well as the relationships between them. This ontology could then be used by an AI system to help it understand and reason about medical knowledge and data. For instance, the AI system could use the ontology to classify and diagnose diseases, or to recommend treatments based on a patient's symptoms. In this way, ontologies can provide a critical foundation for AI systems to operate effectively and make more accurate decisions.

AI is not a part of ontologies, but rather ontologies are used to provide a structured and organized framework for representing knowledge and information that can be used by AI systems. An ontology is a formal representation of a set of concepts within a domain, and the relationships between those concepts. It provides a common vocabulary that can be shared and understood by humans and machines, which enables them to communicate and reason about a particular domain (Schneider and Šimkus, 2020).

AI, on the other hand, refers to the ability of machines to perform tasks that typically require human intelligence, such as learning, problem-solving, and decision-making. AI systems can use ontologies as a source of structured and organized knowledge and information, which can help them to better understand and reason about a particular domain. However, AI is not a part of ontologies in the same way that, for example, the wheels are a part of a car. Instead, ontologies and AI are separate but related fields, with ontologies providing a useful tool for AI systems to operate more effectively (Groza, 2020).

In the context of the Co-vid pandemic, ontologies are being developed and applied in order to improve our understanding of the disease and its Spread. In particular, ontologies can be used to represent different aspects of the pandemic, including the symptoms, transmission routes, epidemiology and treatment options. By doing so, ontologies can provide a common language for researchers to share and query data about the pandemic (Sherimon et al., 2020). Additionally, they can be used to support decision-making by identifying gaps in knowledge or areas where further research is needed (Fig. 1).

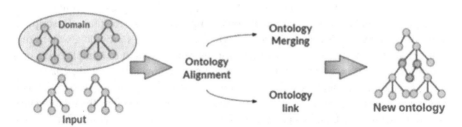

Fig. 1. Example of Methodology of creation of COVID-19 Pandemic ontology.
(Source: https://www.ncbi.nlm.nih.gov/core/lw/2.0/html/tileshop_pmc/tileshop_pmc_inline.
html?title=Click%20on%20image%20to%20zoom&p=PMC3&id=8677430_gr3_lrg.jpg).

One of an ontology being used in the context of Co-vid is the Semantic Web for Health Care and Life Sciences (SWHL) ontology. The SWHL ontology is a modular ontology that can be used to represent different aspects of health care, including diseases, treatments and clinical trials. The ontology has been used to represent data from the Co-vid Open Research Dataset (CORD-19), a dataset of scientific papers about the pandemic. By representing this data in an ontology, it becomes possible to query the dataset in order to answer specific questions about the pandemic. For example, the SWHL ontology can be used to find all papers that mention a particular symptom or transmission route.

The use of ontologies in the context of Co-vid highlights some of the advantages of using this approach. In particular, ontologies can provide a way to share and query data that is spread across different sources. Additionally, they can support decision-making by identifying gaps in knowledge or areas where further research is needed. However, there are also some challenges associated with using ontologies in this context. In particular, developing an ontology that accurately represents the domain of interest can be a challenging task.

Ontologies have been used in a number of ways to support the study and understanding of the COVID-19 pandemic. One example is the use of ontologies to represent the various entities involved in the pandemic (Sonntag, 2020), such as viruses, diseases, symptoms, and treatments, as well as the relationships between these entities. This can help to organize and structure large amounts of data and information related to the pandemic and can make it easier for computer systems to process and reason with that information.

Additionally, ontologies can be used to represent the various types of data that are relevant to the study of the pandemic, such as genetic sequences, clinical records, and epidemiological data, and can provide a common framework for representing and linking these data types. This can facilitate the integration and analysis of data from multiple sources and can support the development of more effective and efficient algorithms for studying the pandemic. Overall, the use of ontologies can help to improve our under-standing of the COVID-19 pandemic and can support the development of more effective response strategies.

There are many different ontology languages that could be used to represent informa-tion related to the COVID-19 pandemic. Some examples of languages that could be used for this purpose include OWL (Web Ontology Language), RDF (Resource Description Framework), and OWL-S (OWL for Services). These languages provide a way to rep-resent ontologies on the web, which allows for the representation of complex concepts and relationships in a way that can be understood by machines (Patel et al., 2021).

These languages could be used to represent the various entities involved in the pan-demic, such as viruses, diseases, symptoms, and treatments, as well as the relationships between these entities (Dutta and DeBellis, 2020). This information could then be used by computer systems to provide more intelligent services related to the pandemic, such as personalized advice or recommendations for preventing and treating the virus (El Bolock et al., 2021). Ultimately, the choice of ontology language will depend on the specific requirements and goals of the system, as well as the domain in which it will be used.

3   Covid Knowledge Representative

Human coronaviruses are responsible for a succession of severe epidemics that have negatively impacted global public health. China's citizens are in danger as a consequence of this development, which precipitated the current scenario. The inability of computers to analyse deconstructed and non-interoperable information hinders computer-assisted reasoning, the cornerstone of artificial intelligence.

It is thought that a lack of bioinformatics tools that can rapidly combine and evaluate a large range of data and information is one of the key challenges to the creation of effective anti-coronavirus treatments. Openness and interoperability of ontologies are fundamental needs when it comes to data integration and sharing. The construction of good ontologies that were appropriate for expressing such themes at the time needed more than the formation of taxonomies alone. This required the commencement of the collection of diverse data (He, 2022).

This creation of the ontology 'CIDO,' which was ridiculed as the community-driven source of the illness and which demonstrated the independent links relations with dif-ferent hierarchies with the development of the illness process in a patient is due to the patient's infection with the virus (Saba et al., 2022). By modelling and visualis-ing the host-coronavirus interaction pathways, it might be feasible to develop effective treatments and vaccines.

With the use of the Ontofox software, the subbranches of these ontologies including the mapped medications and their associated characteristics were extracted. Coronavirus vaccinations are modelled, represented, and analysed with Vaccine Ontology (CIDO). It is conceivable to apply CIDO in conjunction with VO to facilitate the extraction of gene-gene interactions linked with vaccines from published studies (He et al., 2020). The Coronavirus Infectious Disease Ontology (CIDO) is a community-based ontology that supports coronavirus disease knowledge and data standardization, integration, sharing, and analysis(He et al., 2020) (Fig. 2).

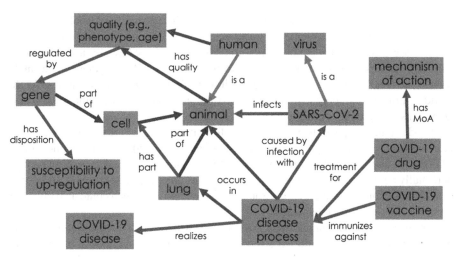

Fig. 2. The design pattern of CIDO for logically representing and linking different components related to a coronavirus disease, e.g., COVID-19.
(Source: https://media.springernature.com/lw685/springer-static/image/art%3A10.1038%2Fs 41597-020-0523-6/MediaObjects/41597_2020_523_Fig1_HTML.png?as=webp).

This standard may be used to assess data from clinical and fundamental research, as well as to correlate the sickness phenotype and transmission data with the underlying mechanisms that were discussed in the prior aims. We foresee the development and deployment of ground-breaking computational and statistical approaches and tools that will support basic research of processes as well as translational applications such as the prediction of drugs and vaccinations (Liu et al., 2021).

However, there is still much work to be done in terms of understanding the full extent of the Co-vid pandemic and how it is affecting different parts of the world. However, the use of ontologies is an important step in ensuring that the latest information is properly represented and can be used to improve the response to the pandemic.

4   Ontologies Application for Covid-19

Organizations are turning to ontologies to help them manage the COVID-19 pandemic. An ontology is a knowledge representation that uses a formal vocabulary to describe relationships between concepts. This can be used to represent information about the pandemic, such as the symptoms of the disease, the transmission methods, and the treatments.

The use of ontologies allows different organizations to share information about COVID-19. This is because ontologies provide a common vocabulary that can be used by computers to interpret the data. This way, organizations can exchange information about COVID-19 without needing to agree on every individual piece of data.

Ontologies can also be used to support decision-making during the pandemic. By representing different pieces of information in a formal way, ontologies can help decision-makers see the big picture and identify potential solutions. For example, an ontology could be used to represent the different types of data that are needed to make a decision about whether or not to implement a lockdown (Kesgavarzi and Ghaffary, 2022).

The use of ontologies is not limited to COVID-19. They have been used in other domains, such as healthcare and finance. However, the COVID-19 pandemic has highlighted the need for better ways of sharing information between organizations. As the world continues to grapple with the pandemic, ontologies will play an important role in helping us manage the crisis (Wang and He, 2021).

In addition, it appears that combining information from various sources can be an effective method for the purposes of analysis and visualisation of the application to COVID-19, as it is necessary to investigate the various factors and aspects that could potentially alter the patterns of mutations, as well as other aspects such as RNA expressions, productions and functions of protein, and metabolism, which could also influence the clinical outcomes (Hwerbi, 2020).

An example is the comprehension of protein, which might be the important component and foundation for the AI's representation and reasoning, since it acts as the essential basis for the aspect. Moreover, the development of the algorithms and tools on the interperable ontologies would also help to increase the efficacy of AI learning machine technology (Wang and He, 2021), as the performance has been influenced by the collection of large amounts of omics data and knowledge, which demonstrates that the application can be used to model, standardise, and integrate into the experiment and clinical anti-covid-19 medications.

In addition, for the paradigm ship, it is essential to comprehend the foundation of the ontology theories and frameworks by presenting precision omics, which may be the impact aspect, in order to complete the correct application process.

Applying AI and ontology to the COVID-19 epidemic can provide several benefits and is considered necessary for various reasons. Here are some key points that illustrate why it's essential:

1. **Data Management and Analysis:** The COVID-19 pandemic has generated an enormous amount of data, including infection rates, genomic sequences, clinical data, and more. AI can help manage and analyze this data more efficiently than traditional methods. Ontologies can structure and categorize the data, making it easier to understand and use.
2. **Early Detection and Prediction:** AI can be used to develop predictive models that help identify potential outbreaks and hotspots early. Machine learning algorithms can analyze historical data to forecast the spread of the virus, allowing authorities to take preventive measures in advance.
3. **Drug Discovery and Vaccine Development:** AI and machine learning are being used to expedite drug discovery and vaccine development processes. These technologies can analyze molecular structures and identify potential candidates for treatments or vaccines, significantly accelerating research efforts.
4. **Resource Allocation:** During a pandemic, resources like hospital beds, ventilators, and medical personnel become crucial. AI can help optimize resource allocation by predicting the demand for healthcare services in different regions, ensuring that resources are distributed efficiently.

5. **Contact Tracing:** Contact tracing is vital in controlling the spread of the virus. AI-powered contact tracing apps can identify potential exposures more quickly and accurately than manual methods, helping health authorities contain outbreaks.
6. **Public Health Policy:** AI can assist policymakers by simulating various scenarios and their potential outcomes. This helps in making data-driven decisions about lockdowns, social distancing measures, and vaccination strategies.
7. **Research Assistance:** Ontologies can help researchers categorize and understand the vast amount of scientific literature related to COVID-19. This can facilitate knowledge discovery and collaboration among scientists.
8. **Real-time Monitoring:** AI systems can continuously monitor data streams and news sources to provide real-time updates on the pandemic's status. This information can be invaluable for both the public and healthcare professionals.
9. **Personalized Healthcare:** AI can analyze patient data to provide personalized treatment recommendations, helping healthcare providers tailor care to individual needs and improve outcomes.
10. **Public Awareness and Communication:** AI-powered chatbots and virtual assistants can provide accurate information to the public, combat misinformation, and answer common questions about COVID-19, promoting public health awareness.

In summary, applying AI and ontology to the COVID-19 epidemic is necessary because it can significantly enhance our ability to manage and respond to the crisis effectively. These technologies enable better data management, analysis, prediction, and decision-making, ultimately helping to save lives and mitigate the impact of the pandemic.

The advantages and disadvantages of applying AI and ontologies to the COVID-19 pandemic:

Advantages:

1. **Efficient Data Management**: AI and ontologies can efficiently categorize and manage the vast amount of data related to COVID-19, making it easier for researchers and healthcare professionals to access and utilize this information.
2. **Data Analysis and Insights**: AI can analyze complex datasets to extract valuable insights, such as predicting disease spread patterns, identifying potential treatment options, and assessing the impact of public health interventions.
3. **Early Detection**: AI-powered models can detect potential outbreaks and hotspots early, enabling timely response measures to contain the virus's spread.
4. **Drug Discovery and Vaccine Development**: AI accelerates the drug discovery process by analyzing vast molecular datasets and predicting potential candidates for treatments and vaccines.
5. **Resource Allocation**: AI helps optimize the allocation of healthcare resources, ensuring that medical facilities have the necessary equipment and staff to respond to the pandemic effectively.
6. **Contact Tracing**: AI-driven contact tracing apps can identify potential exposures quickly and accurately, helping to break the chain of transmission.
7. **Public Health Policy**: AI models can simulate different scenarios, aiding policymakers in making informed decisions about public health measures and vaccination strategies.

8. **Real-time Monitoring**: AI can continuously monitor data sources, providing up-to-date information to healthcare professionals and the public, which is crucial for informed decision-making.
9. **Research Assistance**: Ontologies help researchers categorize and understand scientific literature, facilitating knowledge sharing and collaboration among scientists.
10. **Personalized Healthcare**: AI enables personalized treatment recommendations based on patient data, improving healthcare outcomes.

Disadvantages:

1. **Data Privacy Concerns**: The use of AI for contact tracing and data analysis may raise concerns about data privacy and surveillance, leading to potential privacy breaches and misuse of personal information.
2. **Data Quality**: AI models heavily rely on the quality of data. Inaccurate or biased data can lead to flawed predictions and recommendations.
3. **Ethical Concerns**There can be ethical dilemmas, such as deciding who should have access to potentially life-saving treatments and vaccines when resources are limited.
4. **Algorithm Bias**: AI models may exhibit bias, which can result in unequal outcomes for different populations, exacerbating healthcare disparities.
5. **Complexity and Cost**: Implementing AI and ontologies requires significant resources, including infrastructure, expertise, and funding, which may not be readily available in all regions.
6. **Dependency on Technology**: Overreliance on AI could lead to a lack of human expertise and decision-making, which is essential in complex situations.
7. **Misinformation**: AI can be used to spread misinformation and false narratives, making it crucial to verify information from credible sources.
8. **Regulatory Challenges**: Regulating AI in healthcare and pandemic response can be challenging, as the technology evolves rapidly, and there may be a lack of clear guidelines.
9. **Limited Generalization**: AI models may not generalize well across different regions or situations, making it necessary to adapt them for local contexts.

In conclusion, while applying AI and ontologies to the COVID-19 pandemic offers significant advantages in terms of data analysis, early detection, and resource allocation, it also raises important concerns related to privacy, bias, ethics, and the potential for misuse. A balanced approach that addresses these challenges while leveraging the benefits of AI is crucial for effective pandemic response.

The specific applications of AI and ontology to the COVID-19 pandemic:

1. Early Detection and Prediction:

- **AI Models for Early Warning**: AI algorithms can analyze various data sources, including social media, hospital admissions, and travel patterns, to detect early signs of outbreaks or unusual disease activity.
- **Ontologies for Data Standardization**: Ontologies can standardize data related to symptoms, cases, and geographical locations, making it easier to detect trends and anomalies.

2. Contact Tracing and Monitoring:

- **AI-Powered Contact Tracing**: AI can enhance contact tracing efforts by processing large datasets, identifying potential contacts, and tracking transmission chains.
- **Ontologies for Contact Data**: Ontologies can structure contact data, ensuring consistency and interoperability between contact tracing systems.

3. Drug Discovery and Treatment:

- **Drug Repurposing**: AI can analyze existing drug databases and scientific literature to identify existing drugs that could be repurposed for COVID-19 treatment.
- **Ontologies for Drug Data**: Ontologies can organize drug-related data, facilitating the discovery of potential treatments and their mechanisms of action.

4. Vaccine Development:

- **AI-Driven Vaccine Design**: AI algorithms can help design new vaccines by predicting antigen structures and optimizing vaccine candidates.
- **Ontologies for Vaccine Data**: Ontologies can standardize vaccine-related information, aiding in the development and distribution of vaccines.

5. Healthcare Resource Allocation:

- **Resource Optimization**: AI can predict the demand for medical resources, such as ventilators and ICU beds, and recommend allocation strategies.
- **Ontologies for Resource Data**: Ontologies can structure data on healthcare facilities and resources, ensuring efficient allocation.

6. Public Health Policy and Decision Support:

- **Scenario Simulation**: AI models can simulate different pandemic scenarios, helping policymakers evaluate the impact of various interventions.
- **Ontologies for Policy Data**: Ontologies can categorize policies and interventions for better decision-making.

7. Real-time Monitoring and Alerts:

- **AI-Powered Dashboards**: AI can create real-time dashboards that provide up-to-date information on COVID-19 cases, hospitalizations, and vaccine distribution.
- **Ontologies for Data Integration**: Ontologies can integrate data from diverse sources, ensuring comprehensive monitoring.

8. Research and Literature Review:

- **Literature Mining**: AI can analyze scientific literature to extract relevant information, trends, and potential research gaps.
- **Ontologies for Scientific Data**: Ontologies can categorize research findings and concepts for better collaboration among researchers.

9. Personalized Healthcare:

- **Patient Risk Assessment**: AI can assess individual patient risks based on medical history and demographics, aiding in treatment decisions.

- **Ontologies for Healthcare Data**: Ontologies can standardize patient data for personalized healthcare applications.

These applications highlight how AI and ontologies can be instrumental in various aspects of the COVID-19 pandemic, from early detection and contact tracing to drug discovery, vaccine development, resource allocation, policy-making, real-time monitoring, and personalized healthcare. Implementing these technologies effectively can contribute to better pandemic management and response.

5 Conclusion

As the world races to find a cure for the Co-vid pandemic, ontologies are being applied in ways that could help speed up the process. By understanding the relationships between the different concepts related to the disease, researchers can more quickly identify potential treatments and cures. The application of ontologies in this context is still in its early stages but has great potential to help us better understand and fight this global threat.

AI has been used in various ways to help stop the spread of covid-19. For example, AI-powered tools can be used to analyze medical images, such as CT scans and X-rays, to help doctors diagnose the disease more accurately and quickly. AI-powered algorithms can also be used to analyze large amounts of data, such as medical records and surveillance footage, to help identify potential outbreaks and track the spread of the virus.

Additionally, AI-powered chatbots and virtual assistants can help provide information and support to people who are self-isolating or have questions about the virus. Overall, AI can help in the fight against covid-19 by providing doctors and public health officials with valuable tools and insights that can help improve diagnosis, treatment, and containment efforts. Instead, ontologies and AI are separate but related fields, with ontologies providing a useful tool for AI systems to operate more effectively.

References

Dhatterwal, J.S., Kaswan, K.S., Preety, K.: Intelligent agent based case base reasoning systems build knowledge representation in COVID-19 analysis of recovery of infectious patients. Medical Virol.: Pathogenesis Disease Contr. 185–209 (2021). https://doi.org/10.1007/978-981-15-7317-0_10

Dutta, B., DeBellis, M.: Codo: an ontology for collection and analysis of covid-19 data. In: Proceedings of the 12th International Joint Conference on Knowledge Discovery, Knowledge Engineering and Knowledge Management (2020). https://doi.org/10.5220/0010112500760085

El Bolock, A., Abdennadher, S., Herbert, C.: An ontology-based framework for psychological monitoring in education during the COVID-19 pandemic. Front. Psychol. **12**, 673586 (2021). https://doi.org/10.3389/fpsyg.2021.673586

Groza, A.: Detecting fake news using machine learning and reasoning in description logics. IEEE Workshop Complex. Eng. (COMPENG) **2022**, 1–16 (2020). https://doi.org/10.1109/compeng50184.2022.9905431

He, Y.: Development and applications of interoperable biomedical ontologies for Integrative data and knowledge representation and multiscale modeling in systems medicine. Methods Mol. Biol. 233–244 (2022). https://doi.org/10.1007/978-1-0716-2265-0_12

He, Y., et al.: A comprehensive update on CIDO: the community-based coronavirus infectious disease ontology. J. Biomed. Semantics **13**(1), (2022). https://doi.org/10.1186/s13326-022-00279-z

He, Y., et al.: Cido, a community-based ontology for coronavirus disease knowledge and data integration, sharing, and analysis. Sci. Data **7**(1), 181 (2020). https://doi.org/10.1038/s41597-020-0523-6

Hwerbi, K.: Ontology-based chatbot for disaster management: use case coronavirus. Comput. Sci. J. 1–79 (2020)

Kachaoui, J., Larioui, J., Belangour, A.: Towards an ontology proposal model in Data Lake for real-time covid-19 cases prevention. Int. J. Online Biomed. Eng. (IJOE) **16**(09), 123 (2020). https://doi.org/10.3991/ijoe.v16i09.15325

Keshavarzi, M., Ghaffary, H.R.: An ontology-driven framework for knowledge representation of digital extortion attacks. Comput. Hum. Behav.. Hum. Behav. **139**, 107 (2023). https://doi.org/10.1016/j.chb.2022.107520

Lin, A.Y., Yamagata, Y., Duncan, W.D., Carmody, L.C., Kushida, T.: A community effort for COVID-19 ontology harmonization. In: CEUR Workshop, pp. 1–6 (2021)

Liu, Y., et al.: Ontological modeling and analysis of experimentally or clinically verified drugs against coronavirus infection. Sci. Data **8**(1), 16 (2021). https://doi.org/10.1038/s41597-021-00799-w

Mcheick, H., Nasser, Y., Al Wardani, F., Msheik, B.: Design covid-19 ontology: a healthcare and safety perspective. Lect. Notes Comput. Sci.Comput. Sci. 141–153, (2022). https://doi.org/10.1007/978-3-031-09593-1_11

Oyelade, O.N., Ezugwu, A.E.: Covid19: a natural language processing and ontology oriented temporal case-based framework for early detection and diagnosis of novel coronavirus (2020). https://doi.org/10.20944/preprints202005.0171.v2

Patel, A., Debnath, N.C., Mishra, A.K., Jain, S.: Covid19-IBO: A covid-19 impact on Indian banking ontology along with an efficient schema matching approach. N. Gener. Comput.Gener. Comput. **39**(3–4), 647–676 (2021). https://doi.org/10.1007/s00354-021-00136-0

Saba, D., Hadidi, A., Cheikhrouhou, O., Hamdi, M., Hamam, H.: Development of an ontology-based solution to reduce the spread of viruses. Appl. Sci. **12**(22), 11839 (2022). https://doi.org/10.3390/app122211839

Schneider, T., Šimkus, M.: Special issue on ontologies and data management: Part I. KI - Künstliche Intelligenz **34**(3), 287–289 (2020). https://doi.org/10.1007/s13218-020-00682-7

Sherimon, V., et al.: COVID-19 ontology engineering-knowledge modeling of severe acute respiratory syndrome coronavirus 2 (SARS-COV-2). Int. J. Adv. Comput. Sci. Appl.Comput. Sci. Appl. **11**(11), (2020). https://doi.org/10.14569/IJACSA.2020.0111115

Sonntag, D.: Ai in medicine, covid-19 and Springer Nature's open access agreement. KI - Künstliche Intelligenz **34**(2), 123–125 (2020). https://doi.org/10.1007/s13218-020-00661-y

Wang, Z., He, Y.: Precision Omics Data Integration and analysis with interoperable ontologies and their application for covid-19 research. Brief. Funct. GenomicsFunct. Genomics **20**(4), 235–248 (2021). https://doi.org/10.1093/bfgp/elab029

AMS: Applied Mathematics in Sciences

Steps Towards Fuzzy Homotopy Based on Linguistic Variables

Nguyen Van Han[1,2](✉) and Phan Cong Vinh[1]

[1] Faculty of Information Technology, Nguyen Tat Thanh University, 300A Nguyen Tat Thanh Street, Ward 13, District 4, Ho Chi Minh City, Vietnam
{nvhan,pcvinh}@ntt.edu.vn

[2] Faculty of Electrical Engineering and Computer Science, VSB-Technical University of Ostrava, 17, listopadu 15, 708 33 Ostrava, Czech Republic

Abstract. This paper studies on linguistic topological sapces which are generate from Hedge algebra. We also indicate homotopy classes of homotopic functions on this spaces as well as its equivalence relations.

Keywords: Linguistic variable · Linguistic topological sapce · Homotopic function

1 Introduction

Natural language processing (NLP) holds significant significance in the realm of artificial intelligence (AI) as it aids in the analysis, logical deduction, and decision-making processes. Within this context, "Computing with words" (CWW), a mathematical approach, addresses computational challenges framed in natural language. CWW draws from fuzzy set theory and fuzzy logic, initially proposed by L. A. Zadeh, offering an approximation technique within the range of values between 0 and 1. Notably, within the linguistic domain, linguistic hedges assume a crucial role in forming sets of linguistic variables.

An established utilization of fuzzy sets involves fuzzy graphs, fuzzy neural networks, and machine learning [2,8,11,12], which merge fuzzy sets with graph theory. Fuzzy graphs find numerous applications in modeling and deducing fuzzy knowledge, including scenarios like human trafficking, internet routing, and illegal immigration [10]. These applications operate within the range of values from 0 to 1, excluding linguistic values.

Nonetheless, numerous scenarios are not easily represented within the numerical context, such as linguistic summarization issues [9]. To address this challenge, the paper employs an abstract algebraic framework known as hedge algebra ($\mathbb{HA}$) to facilitate the analysis of linguistic content. The subsequent sections of the paper are structured as follows: Sect. 2 revisits key notions pertaining to word-based modeling using ($\mathbb{HA}$) and investigates the characteristics of topological

P. Cong Vinh and H. Mahfooz Ul Haque (Eds.): ICTCC 2023, LNICST 586, pp. 125–132, 2024.
https://doi.org/10.1007/978-3-031-59462-5_9

linguistic spaces. In the primary Sect. 3, different categories of homotopic functions and equivalence equations are explored. Finally, Sect. 4 outlines the paper's conclusions and outlines directions for future research endeavors.

2 Preliminary

In this segment, fundamental principles of $\mathbb{H}\mathbb{A}$ are introduced alongside crucial information utilized within this paper.

2.1 Hedge Algebra

First definition of a $\mathbb{H}\mathbb{A}$ is 3-Tuple $\mathbb{H}\mathbb{A} = (X, H, \leq)$ in [6]. In [5], to readily replicate fuzzy information, the 3-Tuple is augmented with the inclusion of two elements, denoted as G and C. So $\mathbb{H}\mathbb{A} = (X, G, C, H, \leq)$ where $H \neq \emptyset$, $G = \{c^+, c^-\}$, $C = \{0, W, 1\}$. Domain of X is $\mathbb{L} = Dom(X) = \{\delta c | c \in G, \delta \in H^*(\text{hedge string over H})\}$, $\{\mathbb{L}, \leq\}$ is a POSET (partial order set) and $x = h_n h_{n-1} \ldots h_1 c$ Is referred to as the canonical string corresponding to the linguistic variable x.

Example 1. Fuzzy subset X *is Age*, $G = \{c^+ = young; \ c^- = old\}$, $H = \{less; more; very\}$ *so term-set of linguistic variable Age X is* $\mathbb{L}(X)$ *or* $\mathbb{L}$ *for short:* $\mathbb{L} = \{less\ less\ young\ ;\ less\ more\ young\ ;\ young\ ;\ more\ more\ young\ ;\ very\ more\ young\ ;\ very\ very\ young\ \ldots\}$

Fuzziness properties of elements in $\mathbb{H}\mathbb{A}$, specified by $\mathscr{F}$ (fuzziness measure) [5] as follows:

Definition 1. *A mapping $\mathscr{F} : \mathbb{L} \to [0,1]$ is said to be the fuzziness measure of $\mathbb{L}$ if:*

1. $\sum_{c \in \{c^+, c^-\}} \mathscr{F}(c) = 1$, $\mathscr{F}(0) = \mathscr{F}(w) = \mathscr{F}(1) = 0$.
2. $\sum_{h_i \in H} \mathscr{F}(h_i x) = \mathscr{F}(x)$, $x = h_n h_{n-1} \ldots h_1 c$, *the canonical form.*
3. $\mathscr{F}(h_n h_{n-1} \ldots h_1 c) = \prod_{i=1}^{n} \mathscr{F}(h_i) \times \mu(x)$.

Truth and significance hold pivotal roles in fuzzy logic, artificial intelligence, and machine learning. Within RCT (restriction-centered theory) in [9], truth values are structured hierarchically, encompassing ground-level or first-order truth values as well as second-order ones. While first-order truth values adopt numerical expressions, second-order truth values assume the form of linguistic interpretations. A linguistic truth value, designated as "ℓ," constitutes a fuzzy set. We study linguistic truth values on POSET $\mathbb{L}$ whose elements are comparable [3].

Definition 2. *A $\mathfrak{L}$ STRUCT[ρ] on relational signature ρ is a tuple:*

$$\mathfrak{L} = \langle \mathbb{L}, f_{a_i}^{\mathfrak{L}}, c_j^{\mathfrak{L}} \rangle \tag{1}$$

Consists of a universe $\mathbb{L} \neq \emptyset$ together with an interpretation of:

- *each constant symbol c_j from ρ as an element $c_j^{\mathfrak{L}} \in \mathbb{L}$*
- *each a_i-ary function symbol f_{a_i} from ρ as a function:*

$$f_i^{\mathfrak{L}} : \mathbb{L}^{a_i} \to \mathbb{L} \qquad (2)$$

In $\mathbb{HA}$, $\ell \in \mathbb{L}$ and there are order properties:

Theorem 1. *In [6] let $\ell_1 = h_n \ldots h_1 u$ and $\ell_2 = k_m \ldots k_1 u$ be two arbitrary canonical representations of ℓ_1 and ℓ_2, then there exists an index $j \leq \bigwedge\{m, n\}+1$ such that $h_i = k_j$, for $\forall i < j$, and:*

1. *$\ell_1 < \ell_2$ iff $h_j x_j < k_j x_j$ where $x_j = h_{j-1} \ldots h_1 u$;*
2. *$\ell_1 = \ell_2$ iff $m = n = j$ and $h_j x_j = k_j x_j$;*
3. *ℓ_1 and ℓ_2 are incomparable iff $h_j x_j$ and $k_j x_j$ are incomparable;*

Example 2. Take into linguistic variables: $\{\mathcal{V}\text{high}, \mathcal{P}\text{high}, \mathcal{L}\text{high}\}$ belonging to the set $\mathbb{L}$, where $\{\mathcal{V}\text{high}, \mathcal{P}\text{high}, \mathcal{L}\text{high}\}$ correspond to linguistic truth values representing "very true," "possible true," and "less true," derived from the underlying truth of a variable pressure. Suppose there are propositions p = "Lucie is young is $\mathcal{V}$high" and q = "Lucie is smart is $\mathcal{P}$high." The interpretations over $\mathbb{L}$ are as follows:

- pressure$(p) = \mathcal{V}$high $\in \mathbb{L}$, pressure is a unary function.
- $p \wedge q = \mathcal{V}$high $\wedge \mathcal{P}$high $= \mathcal{P}$high $\in$. $\wedge$ is a binary function.
- $p \vee q = \mathcal{V}$high $\vee \mathcal{P}$high $= \mathcal{V}$high $\in$. $\vee$ is a binary function.

2.2 Linguistic Topological Spaces

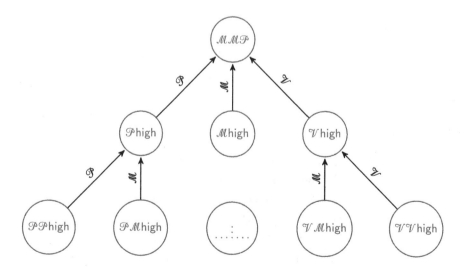

Fig. 1. Tree of hedges

Linguistic topological spaces (LTS), as presented in [4], can be regarded as a particular instance of a fuzzy topological space [1].

Definition 3. *[1] A fuzzy topological is a family T of fuzzy sets in X which satisfies the following condition:*

1. $\phi, X \in T$,
2. If $A, B \in T$, then $A \cap B \in T$,
3. If $A_i \in T$ for each $i \in I$ then $\bigcup_I A_i \in T$.

T is called a fuzzy topoloty for X and the pair $\langle X, T \rangle$ is a fuzzy topological space (FTS).

Definition 4. *[4] A linguistic fuzzy topological is a family T of linguistic term sets in L which the following condition holds:*

1. $\phi, L \in T$,
2. If $A, B \in T$, then $A \cap B \in T$,
3. If $A_i \in T$ for each $i \in I$ then $\bigcup_I A_i \in T$.

T is called a linguistic fuzzy topoloty for L.

Let L be a language which is generate from a ℍA with m hedges and T be a set of subset of leaf nodes on a complete m-ary tree as Fig. 1 then we have property

Property 1. [4]

1. T is a linguistic topology on L
2. Couple (L, T) is a linguistic topological space.

Example 3. Give a ℍA:

$$\mathbb{H}\mathbb{A} = \langle \mathscr{X} = \text{pressure}; c^+ = \text{high}; \mathscr{H} = \{\mathscr{P}, \mathscr{M}, \mathscr{V}\} \rangle \tag{3}$$

be an ℍA with order as $\mathscr{P} < \mathscr{M} < \mathscr{V}$ ($\mathscr{P}$ for possible, $\mathscr{M}$ for more and $\mathscr{V}$ for very are hedges). Let $\{h_i, h_j, h_i \in \mathscr{H} \cup W\}$ in which W is the neutral element, that is $Wc^+ = c^+$ ... then language L which generated from linguistic variable $\mathscr{X}$ is as follow Fig. 2:

$$
\begin{aligned}
L = &\{h_i h_j h_k \text{high} | h_i \neq h_j \wedge h_i \neq h_k \wedge h_j \neq h_k\} \\
= &\{\mathscr{P}\text{high}, \mathscr{M}\text{high}, \mathscr{V}\text{high}, \\
&\mathscr{P}\mathscr{M}\text{high}, \mathscr{M}\mathscr{P}\text{high}, \mathscr{P}\mathscr{V}\text{high}, \\
&\mathscr{V}\mathscr{P}\text{high}, \mathscr{M}\mathscr{V}\text{high}, \mathscr{V}\mathscr{M}\text{high}, \\
&\mathscr{P}\mathscr{M}\mathscr{V}\text{high}, \mathscr{V}\mathscr{P}\mathscr{M}\text{high}, \mathscr{P}\mathscr{V}\mathscr{M}\text{high}, \\
&\mathscr{V}\mathscr{M}\mathscr{P}\text{high}, \mathscr{M}\mathscr{V}\mathscr{P}\text{high}, \mathscr{M}\mathscr{P}\mathscr{V}\text{high}\}
\end{aligned}
$$

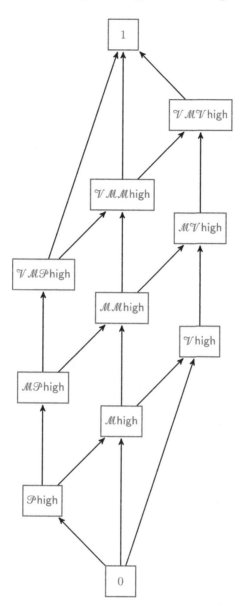

Fig. 2. Hasse diagram

3   Linguistic Homotopic Ralations

Fuzzy homotopy theory on numerical domain [0, 1] was presented in [7]. This paper study homotopic relations on linguistic domain $\mathbb{L}$ of linguistic topological space [4].

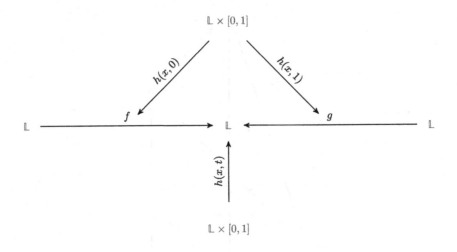

Fig. 3. Homotopic ralation diagram

Definition 5. *Given two functions* $f : \mathbb{L} \longrightarrow \mathbb{L}$ *and* $g : \mathbb{L} \longrightarrow \mathbb{L}$. *$f$ and g are said to be homotopic if there is a function h exists:*

$$h : \mathbb{L} \times [0,\ 1] \longrightarrow \mathbb{L} \tag{4}$$

such that:

$$h(x,t) \in \mathbb{L}$$
$$h(x,0) = f(x) \quad and \quad h(x,1) = g(x) \tag{5}$$

With functions f, g, h are illustrated as in the Fig. 3.

Example 4. With the parameter $t \in [0,\ 1]$ and relationship between f and g as follows:

$$h(x,t) = f(x) + t \times [g(x) - f(x)]$$

Suppose f is the identity function

$$f(x) = x$$

and $g(x)$ denote a constant function:

$$g(x) = (\mathbb{W})$$

Let $M = (x_M)$ represent a point on line segment of fuzziness measure in Definition 1. Point $h(M,t) = N$ with $N = x_N$ is the point on the line so that $\mathcal{F}(x_N) = t \times \mathcal{F}(x_M)$. Then, we have:

$$h(M,0) = M$$
$$h(M,1) = \mathbb{W}$$

Property 2. The relation on $\mathbb{L}$, $f \sim g$ in which f is homotopic to g is an equivalence equation.

Proof. Prove the relation satisfying the properties $\mathbb{L}$, $f \sim g$: Reflexivity, symmetry and transitivity.

- Symmetry: Every function is homotopic to itself
  Define a function $h : \mathbb{L} \times [0, 1] \longrightarrow \mathbb{L}$ as

$$h(x, t) = t \times f(x) + (1 - t) \times f(x)$$

  This function satisfies the conditions for homotopy since $h(x, 0) = f(x)$ and $h(x, 1) = f(x)$
- Symmetry: If f is homotopic to g, then g is homotopic to f. Let h_1 be the homotopy between f and g.
  Define a function $h_1 : \mathbb{L} \times [0, 1] \longrightarrow \mathbb{L}$ as

$$h_1(x, t) = h(x, 1 - t)$$

$h_1(.)$ satisfies the conditions for homotopy since:

$$h_1(x, 0) = h(x, 1) = g(x) \text{ and } h_1(x, 1) = h(x, 0) = f(x)$$

- Transitivity: If f is homotopic to g and g is homotopic to h, then f is homotopic to h.
  Let h be the homotopy between f and g, and let h_1 be the homotopy between g and h. Define a function $h_2 : \mathbb{L} \times [0, 1] \longrightarrow \mathbb{L}$ as

$$h_2(x, t) = h(x, t) + (1 - t) \times (h_1(x, t) - h(x, t))$$

h_2 satisfies the conditions for homotopy since

$$h_2(x, 0) = h_1(x, 0) = f(x) \text{ and } h_2(x, 1) = h_1(x, 1) = h(x)$$

Since the relation $f \sim g$ of homotopy satisfies reflexivity, symmetry, and transitivity, it is indeed an equivalence relation.

4   Conclusion and Forthcoming Study

The paper study properties on linguistic topological space based on hedge algebra and fuzziness measure.

- Study homotopic functions on linguistic domain $\mathbb{L}$
- Show that the relationship between homotopic functions on $\mathbb{L}$ is an equivalence relation.

In the future, two studies will be:

- Research on homotopy classes.
- Apply linguistic homotopy in quantum logic and homotopy data analysis.

References

1. Chang, C.L.: Fuzzy topological spaces. Math. Anal. **24**(1), 182–190 (1968)
2. Glykas, M.: Fuzzy Cognitive Maps, Advances in Theory, Tools and Applications. Springer Heidelberg (2010). https://doi.org/10.1007/978-3-642-03220-2
3. Van Han, N., Cong Vinh, P.: Reasoning with words: a hedge algebra linguistic cognitive map approach. Concurrency Comput. Pract. Experience **33**(2), e5711 (2020)
4. Van Han, N., Cong Vinh, P.: Towards linguistic fuzzy topological spaces based on hedge algebra. EAI Endorsed Trans. Context-aware Syst. Appl. **8**(1), e5711 (2022)
5. Ho, N.C., Son, T.T., Khang, T.D., Viet, L.X.: Fuzziness measure, quantified semantic mapping and interpolative method of approximate reasoning in medical expert systems. J. Comput. Sci. Cybern. **18**(3), 237–252 (2002)
6. Ho, N.C., Wechler, W.: Hedge algebras: an algebraic approach to structure of sets of linguistic truth values. Fuzzy Sets Syst. **35**(3), 281–293 (1990)
7. Kandemir, M.B.: The foundations of homotopic fuzzy sets. Konuralp J. Math. **10**(1), 34–39 (2022)
8. Kosko, B.: Fuzzy cognitive maps. Int. J. Man-Machine Stud. **24**, 65–75 (1986)
9. Zadeh, L.A.: Computing with words - principal concepts and ideas. In: Studies in Fuzziness and Soft Computing. Springer, Heidelberg (2012). https://doi.org/10.1007/978-3-642-27473-2
10. John, N., Mordeson, J.N., Mathew, S.: Advanced Topics in Fuzzy Graph Theory, Springer, Cham (2019). https://doi.org/10.1007/978-3-030-04215-8
11. Papageorgiou, E.I.: Fuzzy Cognitive Maps for Applied Science and Engineering From Fundamentals to Extensions and Learning Algorithms. Springer-Verlag, Heidelberg (2014). https://doi.org/10.1007/978-3-642-39739-4
12. Rosenfeld, A.: Fuzzy graphs. Fuzzy Sets Appl. 77–95 (1975)

Reasoning with Words: Steps Towards Applying in Mobile System

Nguyen Van Han[1,2]([⊠])◉ and Phan Cong Vinh[1]◉

[1] Faculty of Information Technology, Nguyen Tat Thanh University, 300A Nguyen Tat Thanh Street, Ward 13, District 4, Ho Chi Minh, Vietnam
{nvhan,pcvinh}@ntt.edu.vn
[2] Faculty of Electrical Engineering and Computer Science, VSB-Technical University of Ostrava, 17. listopadu 15, 708 33 Ostrava, Czech Republic

Abstract. In this paper, we introduce two algorithms for reasoning with words on fuzzy dynamic system. The systems that use linguistic variables which are variables whose values may be expressed in terms of a specific natural or artificial language, for example $\mathbb{L} = \{very\ less\ true;\ less\ true;\ true;\ more\ true;\ very\ true;\ very\ very\ true \dots\}$. In language of hedge algebra ($\mathbb{HA}$), $\mathbb{L}$ set which is generated from $\mathbb{HA}$ is the POSET (partial order set). The algorithms are Static reasoning and Dynamic reasoning. The former traverses the branch of the fuzzy graph whereas the later transform according to the equation of state and create a space of states of the system. Algorithms performed on linguistic variables and applied labeling techniques. And finally, the application of the algorithm on the mobile network model is also investigated.

Keywords: Linguistic variable · Fuzzy system · Mobile system

1 Introduction

Fuzzy engineering has been studied and applied in artificial intelligence. Fuzzy set and fuzzy logic or "computing with words" (CWW) were introduced by Lotfi A. Zadeh in 1965 as an extension of the classical notion of set [12,18] and was just a tool to knowledge represent and reasoning in intelligent system [13]. As Zadeh indicates [13], human acknowledgment is nothing different from words. In daily activity, we see the real world through words. Many smart devices that established based on CWW such as fuzzy cognitive map, mobile payment system, fuzzy data mining, ... and so on have been studied [1–3,14–16] The rest of the paper is organized as follows: Section 2 recalls some of the main foundation concepts of fuzzy cognitive map and linguistic cognitive map. Section 3 proposes two algorithms for reasoning with words and applies the algorithms for Mobile Payment System Project. Section 4 summaries outlines the corollary as well as future work.

P. Cong Vinh and H. Mahfooz Ul Haque (Eds.): ICTCC 2023, LNICST 586, pp. 133–147, 2024.
https://doi.org/10.1007/978-3-031-59462-5_10

2   Preliminary

This section reviews the basic knowledge related to the article that is Fuzzy cognitive map (FCM) and Linguistic cognitive map (LCM).

2.1   Reasoning on Fuzzy Cognitive Map

An integration model between fuzzy logic and neural networks is fuzzy cognitive map (FCM) [11] in which, the inference process is mainly on the domain $[0, 1]$.

Example 1. The fuzzy knowledge base is described in Table 1 which is formalized into the FCM graph as shown in Fig. 1.

Graph FCMs operate as a neuro-fuzzy system (NFS) with static and dynamic reasoning.

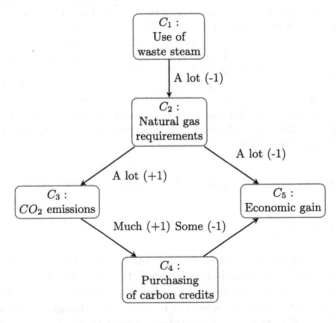

Fig. 1. FCM graph

1. *Static reasoning*: This method calculates the branches of the graph FCM.

Table 1. Knowledge Base

IF	Use of waste steam	THEN	Natural gas requirements
IF	Natural gas requirements	THEN	CO_2 emissions
IF	Natural gas requirements	THEN	Economic gain
IF	CO_2 emissions	THEN	Purchasing of carbon credits
IF	Economic gain	THEN	Purchasing of carbon credits

Example 2. Suppose there is a set of language values $\mathbb{L} = \{a\ lot,\ some,\ none,\ much\}$ with order $\{none < some < much < a\ lot\}$. The Fig. 1 shows that there are 2 paths between vertices C_1 and C_5, they are $P_1 = (1, 2, 5)$ and $P_2 = (1, 2, 3, 4, 5)$.

$$P_1(C_1, C_5) = \mathcal{M}in\{e_{12}, e_{25}\} \qquad = \mathcal{M}in\{a\ lot, a\ lot\}$$
$$= a\ lot$$
$$P_2(C_1, C_5) = \mathcal{M}in\{e_{12}, e_{23}, e_{3,4}, e_{4,5}\} \qquad = \mathcal{M}in\{a\ lot, a\ lot, much, some\}$$
$$= some$$

Total path ways :
$$T(C_1, C_5) = \mathcal{M}ax\{P_1(C_1, C_5), P_2(C_1, C_5)\} \qquad = \mathcal{M}ax\{a\ lot, some\}$$
$$= a\ lot$$

2. *Dynamic reasoning:* This method considers the transformation of the state vector according to the Eq. 1 [17]

$$[C_1 C_2 \ldots C_n]_{new} = [C_1 C_2 \ldots C_n]_{old} \otimes \begin{pmatrix} e_{11} & \cdots & e_{1,n} \\ \vdots & \ddots & \vdots \\ e_{n,1} & \cdots & e_{n,n} \end{pmatrix}. \tag{1}$$

Example 3. The adjacency matrix of the graph Fig. 1 is:

$$M = (e_{ij})_{5 \times 5} = \begin{pmatrix} 0 & -1 & 0 & 0 & 0 \\ 0 & 0 & +1 & 0 & -1 \\ 0 & 0 & 0 & +1 & 0 \\ 0 & 0 & 0 & 0 & -1 \\ 0 & 0 & 0 & 0 & 0 \end{pmatrix}.$$

Let $\mathfrak{C}^0 = [C_1 C_2 C_3 C_4 C_5] = [1\ 0\ 0\ 0\ 0]$ [17] be the initial term. Equation 2 is the recursive equation.

$$\mathfrak{C}^t = \mathfrak{C}^{t-1} \vee \mathfrak{C}^{t-1} \wedge M \tag{2}$$

With t=1, 2, 3, 4, we have:

$$\mathfrak{c}^0 = [1\ 0\ 0\ 0\ 0]$$

$$\mathfrak{c}^1 = [1\ 0\ 0\ 0\ 0] \vee [1\ 0\ 0\ 0\ 0] \wedge \begin{pmatrix} 0 & -1 & 0 & 0 & 0 \\ 0 & 0 & +1 & 0 & -1 \\ 0 & 0 & 0 & +1 & 0 \\ 0 & 0 & 0 & 0 & -1 \\ 0 & 0 & 0 & 0 & 0 \end{pmatrix} = [1\ -1\ 0\ 0\ 0]$$

$$\mathfrak{c}^2 = [1\ -1\ 0\ 0\ 0] \vee [1\ -1\ 0\ 0\ 0] \wedge \begin{pmatrix} 0 & -1 & 0 & 0 & 0 \\ 0 & 0 & +1 & 0 & -1 \\ 0 & 0 & 0 & +1 & 0 \\ 0 & 0 & 0 & 0 & -1 \\ 0 & 0 & 0 & 0 & 0 \end{pmatrix} = [1\ -1\ -1\ 0\ 1]$$

$$\mathfrak{c}^3 = [1\ -1\ -1\ 0\ 1] \vee [1\ -1\ -1\ 0\ 1] \wedge \begin{pmatrix} 0 & -1 & 0 & 0 & 0 \\ 0 & 0 & +1 & 0 & -1 \\ 0 & 0 & 0 & +1 & 0 \\ 0 & 0 & 0 & 0 & -1 \\ 0 & 0 & 0 & 0 & 0 \end{pmatrix} = [1\ -1\ -1\ -1\ 1]$$

$$\mathfrak{c}^4 = [1\ -1\ -1\ -1\ 1] \vee [1\ -1\ -1\ -1\ 1] \wedge \begin{pmatrix} 0 & -1 & 0 & 0 & 0 \\ 0 & 0 & +1 & 0 & -1 \\ 0 & 0 & 0 & +1 & 0 \\ 0 & 0 & 0 & 0 & -1 \\ 0 & 0 & 0 & 0 & 0 \end{pmatrix} = [1\ -1\ -1\ -1\ 1]$$

After four interactions using Eq. 2, the system converges to a fixed point since $\mathfrak{c}^4$'s state is a repeat of $\mathfrak{c}^3$'s state; that is, $\mathfrak{c}^4 = \mathfrak{c}^3 = [1\ -1\ -1\ -1\ 1]$. This indicates a hidden pattern.

Associating both static and dynamic reasoning results in our final NFS structure [17].

Example 4. Combining $T(C_1, C_5)=$ **a lot** from Example 2 and $C_5 \in \mathfrak{c}^4 = C_5 \in \mathfrak{c}^3 = 1$ from Example 3 to infer, then:

IF the use of waste steam increases **THEN** economic gain increases **alot**.

The FCM's structure in Fig. 1 is simple because only three values from the set $\{-1, 0, 1\}$ were used. This article expands to a set of linguistic values for a more natural representation.

2.2 Linguistic Fuzzy Cognitive Maps

Paper stands on LCM which is extended from fuzzy cognitive map FCM [11]. The LCM model, based on linguistic variables, is constructed from linguistic hedge of HA in [4–7].

Definition 1. *A linguistic cognitive map (LCM) is a 4- Tuple:*

$$LCM = \{C, E, C, f\} \tag{3}$$

In which:

1. $C = \{C_1, C_2, \ldots, C_n\}$ *is the set of concepts to form the nodes of a graph.*
2. $E : (C_i, C_j) \longrightarrow e_{ij} \in \mathbb{L}$; $e_{ij} = $ *directed edges' weight from C_i to C_j. The weighted matrix $E(N \times N) = \{e_{ij}\}_{N \times N} \in \mathbb{L}^{N \times N}$*
3. *The map:* $\mathbb{C} : C_i \longrightarrow C_i(t) \in \mathbb{L}, t \in N$
4. $\mathbb{C}(0) = [C_1(0), C_2(0), \ldots, C_n(0)] \in \mathbb{L}^N$ *is the initial vector, recurring transformation function f is defined as:*

$$C_j(t+1) = f(\sum_{i=1}^{N} e_{ij} C(t) \in \mathbb{L} \tag{4}$$

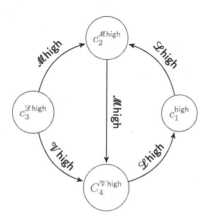

Fig. 2. A simple $\mathbb{LCM}$

Example 5. Figure 2 shows a simple $\mathbb{LCM}$. Let

$$\mathbb{HA} = \langle \mathcal{X} = SPEED; c^+ = \mathsf{high}; \mathcal{H} = \{\mathcal{L}, \mathcal{M}, \mathcal{V}\} \rangle \tag{5}$$

be an $\mathbb{HA}$ with order as $\mathcal{L} < \mathcal{M} < \mathcal{V}$ ($\mathcal{L}$ for less, $\mathcal{M}$ for more and $\mathcal{V}$ for very are hedges). $C = \{c_1, c_2, c_3, c_4\}$ is the set of 4 concepts with corresponding values $\mathcal{C} = \{\mathsf{high}, \mathcal{M}\mathsf{high}, \mathcal{L}\mathsf{high}, \mathcal{V}\mathsf{high}\}$

3   Algorithms

This section presents two reasoning algorithms on the $\mathbb{LCM}$ graph, which are branch-based and state-based reasoning.

3.1 Static Reasoning

Branch reasoning algorithm, Algorithm 1, find the weight of the path between any two vertices of the graph $\mathbb{LCM}$.

Example 6. The steps to implement Algorithm 1 are detailed step by step as shown in the Fig. 3 - Fig. 6

Algorithm 1. Branched Inference Algorithm

Input: Graph $\mathbb{LCM} = (V, E)$

    $\triangleright$ $\mathbb{LCM}$ has vetices: s=$C_1, \ldots, C_n = d$ and edges' weight $e(v_i, v_j) \in \mathbb{L}$

Ra: $\mathscr{L}(d)$

        $\triangleright$ $\mathscr{L}(d) \in \mathbb{L}$ is the length of the path from s to d

1: **foreach** $C_i \in V$ **do** $\triangleright$ initialize labels for vertices

2: $\mathscr{L}(C_i) \leftarrow 0$ $\triangleright$ Labels of vertices are assigned by zero

   $(0 = \mathcal{M}in\{\mathbb{L}\})$

3: **end foreach**

4: $\mathscr{L}(s) = 1$ $\triangleright$ The label of the source vertex is assigned 1 $(1 = \mathcal{M}ax\{\mathbb{L}\})$

5: $Q = \emptyset$ $\triangleright$ Initially, queue Q is empty

6: **while** $d \notin Q$ **do**

7: $u \leftarrow$ vertex in $V - Q$ and has the largest label $\mathscr{L}(u)$

8: $Q = Q \cup \{u\}$ $\triangleright$ Put in Q vertice with the largest label

9: **foreach** $v \notin Q$ **do**

10:   **if** $\mathscr{L}(u) \wedge e(u, v) \geq \mathscr{L}(v)$ **then**

11:    $\mathscr{L}(v) \leftarrow \mathscr{L}(u) \wedge e(u, v)$ $\triangleright$ update the label for vertex v

12:   **end if**

13: **end foreach**

14: **end while**

15: **return** $\mathscr{L}(d)$ $\triangleright$ $\mathscr{L}(d)$ is the length of the path from s to d

---

Property 1. Let $|V|$ be the size of the vertex set *fuzzy concept*, the complexity of Algorithm 1 is $\mathcal{O}(|V|)^2$.

Proof. The complexity of the Algorithm 1 depends on the number of $\leftarrow$ assignment operations in the iteration statements as follows:

Lines	Maximum number of assignment operations
Line 1 to 3	$\sum_{i=1}^{|V|} 1 = |V|$
Line 6 to 14	$\sum_{i=1}^{|V|} \sum_{i=1}^{|V|} 1 = (|V|)^2$

The total number of assignments of the loops is $(|V|)^2 + (|V|)$ so the complexity of the Algorithm 1 is $\mathcal{O}(|V|)^2$

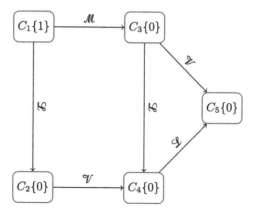

Fig. 3. Initialize label $s = C_1 = 1$ other vertices are labeled 0, set Q is empty

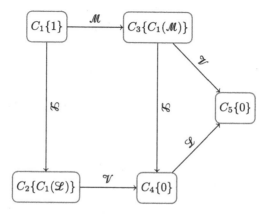

Fig. 4. Put $C_1 = 1$ into Q, $Q = \{C_1\}$, update labels for C_2 and C_3

3.2 Dynamic Reasoning

Different from branch reasoning algorithm, state reasoning algorithm, Algorithm 2, find the convergence vector of the system according to the state equation.

Example 7. Consider a graph $\mathbb{LCM}$ with 5 vertices and an adjacency matrix M:

$$
M = \begin{bmatrix}
0 & 0 & 0 & 0 & 0 \\
\mathcal{VV}\text{high} & 0 & \mathcal{VV}\text{low} & 0 & 0 \\
\mathcal{VV}\text{high} & \mathcal{VV}\text{high} & 0 & 0 & 0 \\
0 & \mathcal{L}\text{low} & \mathcal{L}\text{low} & 0 & \mathcal{V}\text{low} \\
0 & \text{low} & \text{low} & 0 & 0
\end{bmatrix}
$$

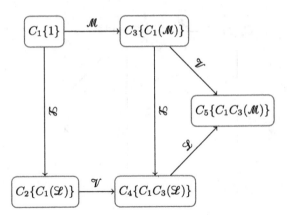

Fig. 5. Insert $C_3 = \mathcal{M}$ into $\mathcal{Q}$, $\mathcal{Q} = \{C_1, C_3\}$, update labels for C_4 and C_5

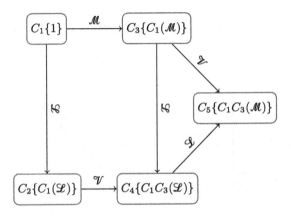

Fig. 6. Put $C_5 = \mathcal{M}$ into $\mathcal{Q}$, $\mathcal{Q} = \{C_1, C_3, C_5\}$, end the Algorithm 1

With an initial value of $\mathbb{C}(0) = \{\mathcal{M}\text{high}, \mathcal{L}\mathcal{M}\text{high}, \mathcal{L}\text{high}, \mathcal{M}\mathcal{V}\text{high}, \mathcal{L}\mathcal{M}\text{high}\}$. Applying the Algorithm 2, the steps will show as follows:

$$\mathbb{C}(1) = [C_1(1)..C_j(1)..C_5(1)] \text{ with } C_j(1) = \bigvee_{i=1}^{5} C_i(0) \wedge e_{ij}$$

$$= \bigvee([\mathcal{M}\text{high}, \mathcal{L}\mathcal{M}\text{high}, \mathcal{L}\text{high}, \mathcal{M}\mathcal{V}\text{high}, \mathcal{L}\mathcal{M}\text{high}] \wedge$$

$$\begin{bmatrix} 0 & 0 & 0 & 0 & 0 \\ \mathcal{V}\mathcal{V}\text{high} & 0 & \mathcal{V}\mathcal{V}\text{low} & 0 & 0 \\ \mathcal{V}\mathcal{V}\text{high} & \mathcal{V}\mathcal{V}\text{high} & 0 & 0 & 0 \\ 0 & \mathcal{L}\text{low} & \mathcal{L}\text{low} & 0 & \mathcal{V}\text{low} \\ 0 & \text{low} & \text{low} & 0 & 0 \end{bmatrix}$$

$$)$$

$$= [\mathcal{L}\mathcal{M}\text{high}, \mathcal{L}\text{high}, \mathcal{L}\text{low}, 0, \mathcal{V}\text{low}]$$

Algorithm 2. State dynamic reasoning

Input: Initialization vector $\mathbb{C}(0)$, matrix E
Output: Fixed point vector $\mathbb{C}(fix)$
1: **for** $i \leftarrow 1$ to n **do**   ▷ Initialize values for *fuzzy concept*
2:     $C_i \leftarrow C_i(0)$
3: **end for**
4: **for** $i \leftarrow 1$ to n **do**   ▷ Initialize values for edges
5:     **for** $j \leftarrow 1$ to n **do**
6:         $(C_i, C_j) \leftarrow e_{i,j}$
7:     **end for**
8: **end for**
9: $\mathcal{T}ime \leftarrow 0$
10: **while** $\mathbb{C}(\mathcal{T}ime + 1) \neq \mathbb{C}(\mathcal{T}ime)$ **do**
11:     **for** $j \leftarrow 1$ to n **do**
12:         $\mathcal{M}ax \leftarrow 0$ ▷ Calculate $\mathcal{M}ax = \bigvee_{i=1}^{n} C_i(\mathcal{T}ime) \wedge e_{ij}$
13:         **for** $i \leftarrow 1$ to n **do**
14:             $\mathcal{M}ax \leftarrow \mathcal{M}ax \vee C_i(\mathcal{T}ime) \wedge e_{ij}$
15:         **end for**
                                    ▷ Calculate $C_j(\mathcal{T}ime + 1) = \bigvee_{i=1}^{n} C_i(\mathcal{T}ime) \wedge e_{ij}$
16:         $C_j(\mathcal{T}ime + 1) \leftarrow \mathcal{M}ax$
17:     **end for**
18:     $\mathcal{T}ime \leftarrow \mathcal{T}ime + 1$
19: **end while**
20: $\mathbb{C}(fix) \leftarrow \mathbb{C}(\mathcal{T}ime)$
21: **return** $\mathbb{C}(fix)$

$$\mathbb{C}(2) = [C_1(2)..C_j(2)..C_5(2)] \quad \text{with } C_j(2) = \bigvee_{i=1}^{5} C_i(1) \wedge e_{ij}$$

$$= \bigvee \left([\mathcal{LM}\text{high}, \mathcal{L}\text{high}, \mathcal{L}\text{low}, 0, \mathcal{V}\text{low}] \right. \wedge$$

$$\begin{bmatrix} 0 & 0 & 0 & 0 & 0 \\ \mathcal{VV}\text{high} & 0 & \mathcal{VV}\text{low} & 0 & 0 \\ \mathcal{VV}\text{high} & \mathcal{VV}\text{high} & 0 & 0 & 0 \\ 0 & \mathcal{L}\text{low} & \mathcal{L}\text{low} & 0 & \mathcal{V}\text{low} \\ 0 & \text{low} & \text{low} & 0 & 0 \end{bmatrix}$$

$$\left. \right)$$

$$= [\mathcal{L}\text{high}, \mathcal{L}\text{low}, \mathcal{V}\text{low}, 0, 0]$$

$$\mathbb{C}(3) = [C_1(3)..C_j(3)..C_5(3)] \quad \text{with } C_j(3) = \bigvee_{i=1}^{5} C_i(2) \wedge e_{ij}$$

$$= \bigvee \left([\mathcal{L}\text{high}, \mathcal{L}\text{low}, \mathcal{V}\text{low}, 0, 0] \right. \wedge$$

$$\begin{bmatrix} 0 & 0 & 0 & 0 & 0 \\ \mathcal{VV}\text{high} & 0 & \mathcal{VV}\text{low} & 0 & 0 \\ \mathcal{VV}\text{high} & \mathcal{VV}\text{high} & 0 & 0 & 0 \\ 0 & \mathcal{L}\text{low} & \mathcal{L}\text{low} & 0 & \mathcal{V}\text{low} \\ 0 & \text{low} & \text{low} & 0 & 0 \end{bmatrix}$$

$$\left. \right)$$

$$= [\mathcal{L}\text{low}, \mathcal{V}\text{low}, \mathcal{VV}\text{low}, 0, 0]$$

$$\mathbb{C}(4) = [C_1(4)..C_j(4)..C_5(4)] \quad \text{with } C_j(4) = \bigvee_{i=1}^{5} C_i(3) \wedge e_{ij}$$
$$= \quad \bigvee(\ [\mathscr{L}\text{low}, \mathscr{V}\text{low}, \mathscr{V}\mathscr{V}\text{low}, 0, 0] \qquad\qquad \wedge$$

$$\begin{bmatrix}
0 & 0 & 0 & 0 & 0 \\
\mathscr{V}\mathscr{V}\text{high} & 0 & \mathscr{V}\mathscr{V}\text{low} & 0 & 0 \\
\mathscr{V}\mathscr{V}\text{high} & \mathscr{V}\mathscr{V}\text{high} & 0 & 0 & 0 \\
0 & \mathscr{L}\text{low} & \mathscr{L}\text{low} & 0 & \mathscr{V}\text{low} \\
0 & \text{low} & \text{low} & 0 & 0
\end{bmatrix}$$

$$)$$
$$= \quad [\mathscr{L}\text{low}, \mathscr{V}\mathscr{V}\text{low}, \mathscr{V}\mathscr{V}\text{low}, 0, 0]$$

$$\mathbb{C}(5) = [C_1(5)..C_j(5)..C_5(5)] \quad \text{with } C_j(5) = \bigvee_{i=1}^{5} C_i(4) \wedge e_{ij}$$
$$= \quad \bigvee(\ [\mathscr{L}\text{low}, \mathscr{V}\mathscr{V}\text{low}, \mathscr{V}\mathscr{V}\text{low}, 0, 0] \qquad\qquad \wedge$$

$$\begin{bmatrix}
0 & 0 & 0 & 0 & 0 \\
\mathscr{V}\mathscr{V}\text{high} & 0 & \mathscr{V}\mathscr{V}\text{low} & 0 & 0 \\
\mathscr{V}\mathscr{V}\text{high} & \mathscr{V}\mathscr{V}\text{high} & 0 & 0 & 0 \\
0 & \mathscr{L}\text{low} & \mathscr{L}\text{low} & 0 & \mathscr{V}\text{low} \\
0 & \text{low} & \text{low} & 0 & 0
\end{bmatrix}$$

$$)$$
$$= \quad [\mathscr{V}\mathscr{V}\text{low}, \mathscr{V}\mathscr{V}\text{low}, \mathscr{V}\mathscr{V}\text{low}, 0, 0]$$

$$\mathbb{C}(6) = [C_1(6)..C_j(6)..C_5(6)] \quad \text{with } C_j(6) = \bigvee_{i=1}^{5} C_i(5) \wedge e_{ij}$$
$$= \quad \bigvee(\ [\mathscr{V}\mathscr{V}\text{low}, \mathscr{V}\mathscr{V}\text{low}, \mathscr{V}\mathscr{V}\text{low}, 0, 0] \qquad\qquad \wedge$$

$$\begin{bmatrix}
0 & 0 & 0 & 0 & 0 \\
\mathscr{V}\mathscr{V}\text{high} & 0 & \mathscr{V}\mathscr{V}\text{low} & 0 & 0 \\
\mathscr{V}\mathscr{V}\text{high} & \mathscr{V}\mathscr{V}\text{high} & 0 & 0 & 0 \\
0 & \mathscr{L}\text{low} & \mathscr{L}\text{low} & 0 & \mathscr{V}\text{low} \\
0 & \text{low} & \text{low} & 0 & 0
\end{bmatrix}$$

$$)$$
$$= \quad [\mathscr{V}\mathscr{V}\text{low}, \mathscr{V}\mathscr{V}\text{low}, \mathscr{V}\mathscr{V}\text{low}, 0, 0]$$

Since $\mathbb{C}(6) = \mathbb{C}(5) = [\mathscr{V}\mathscr{V}\text{low}, \mathscr{V}\mathscr{V}\text{low}, \mathscr{V}\mathscr{V}\text{low}, 0, 0]$ the system reaches a fixed point after 6 iteration.

Property 2. For a graph $\mathbb{LCM} = (V, E)$ with vertex size $|V|$, the complexity of the algorithm 2 is $\mathcal{O}(|V|)^3$

Proof. The complexity of the algorithm depends on the number of $\leftarrow$ assignments in the iteration instructions and is detailed as follows:

Line	Maximum number of assignment operations
Line 1 to 3	$\sum_{i=1}^{n} 1 = n$
Line 4 to 8	$\sum_{i=1}^{n} \sum_{j=1}^{n} 1 = n^2$
Line 9 to 19	$\sum_{\mathcal{T}ime} \sum_{i=1}^{n} \sum_{j=1}^{n} 1 \leq n^3$

Since the variable $\mathcal{T}ime \leq n$ the total number of assignment operations $\leftarrow$ in the loops is at most: $n+n^2+n^3$, with $n = |V|$ so the complexity of the algorithm 2 is $\mathcal{O}(n^3) = \mathcal{O}(|V|)^3$

Property 3. At any time t, the system will reach a fixed point $\mathbb{C}(fix)$ when the vector $\mathbb{C}(t+1)$ depends recursively on the vector $\mathbb{C}(t)$ in the fields the following case:

$$\mathbb{C}(t+1) \geq \mathbb{C}(t) \tag{6}$$
$$\mathbb{C}(t+1) \leq \mathbb{C}(t) \tag{7}$$

Proof. Use mathematical induction to prove
Case 1: $\mathbb{C}(t+1) \geq \mathbb{C}(t)$

Base step: $With\ t = 0,$ we have $\mathbb{C}(1) \geq \mathbb{C}(0), so$

$$\mathbb{C}(2) = \bigvee_{i=0}^{N} C_i(1) \wedge e_{ij}$$

$$\geq \bigvee_{i=0}^{N} C_i(0) \wedge e_{ij}$$

$$= \mathbb{C}(1)$$

Induction step: Assume (6) is true for $t = k$

$$\text{Or} \ : C_j(k) \geq C_j(k-1)$$

$$\text{Then } C_j(k+1) = \bigvee_{i=0}^{N} C_i(k) \wedge e_{ij}$$

$$\geq \bigvee_{i=0}^{N} C_i(k-1) \wedge e_{ij}$$

$$= C_j(k), \text{therefore}$$

$$C_J(k+1) \geq C_j(k)$$

$C_j(k)$ is finite, monotonically increasing, and bounded on so $C_j(k)$ converges.
Case 2: $\mathbb{C}(t+1) \leq \mathbb{C}(t)$ The proof is similar to case 1.

Mobile Payment System

Mobile Payment System (MPS) is modeled to $\mathbb{FCM}$ [14,16]. Accordingly, the calculation must convert from numbers to words and vice versa. This process increases computational complexity. To reduce the number of mathematical operations in the calculation, the article proposes model of MPS in the form of $\mathbb{LCM}$ by applying domain transformations in the Table 2.

The Figure Fig. 7 indicates a $\mathbb{LCM} = (V, E)$ graph representing the MPS using linguistic variables. In which, $V = \{C_1, \ldots, C_{24}\}$ is the set of fuzzy concepts. The weight of edge (C_i, C_j) is e_{ij} which represents the causal relationship between two adjacent vertices C_i and C_j. By Definition 1, the weight matrix of the $\mathbb{LCM}$ graph in Fig. 7 has the form:

$$E = \begin{cases} e_{ij} \text{ if } (C_i, C_j) \in E \\ 0 \text{ if } (C_i, C_j) \notin E \end{cases} \tag{8}$$

Example 8. Apply Table 2, weight of edge (C_3, C_1) in $\mathbb{FCM}$ is $e_{31} = 0.68$ [16] will be changed to linguistic value in $\mathbb{LCM}$ is $e_{31} = \mathcal{LM}\text{high}$.

Table 2. Domains conversion

Range $[-1, 1]$	Positive range $[0, 1]$	Domain of $\mathbb{L}$	Meaning
$[-1, -0.7)$	$[0, 0.15)$	$\mathcal{VV}$low	very very low
$[-0.7, -0.4)$	$[0.15, 0.3)$	$\mathcal{LM}$low	less more low
$[-0.4, -0.1)$	$[0.3, 0.45)$	$\mathcal{LL}$low	less less low
$[-0.1, 0.1)$	$[0.45, 0.55)$	$\mathcal{W}$	Neutral
$[0.1, 0.4)$	$[0.55, 0.7)$	$\mathcal{VL}$high	very less high
$[0.4, 0.7)$	$[0.7, 0.85)$	$\mathcal{LM}$high	less more high
$[0.7, 1]$	$[0.85, 1]$	$\mathcal{VV}$high	more more high

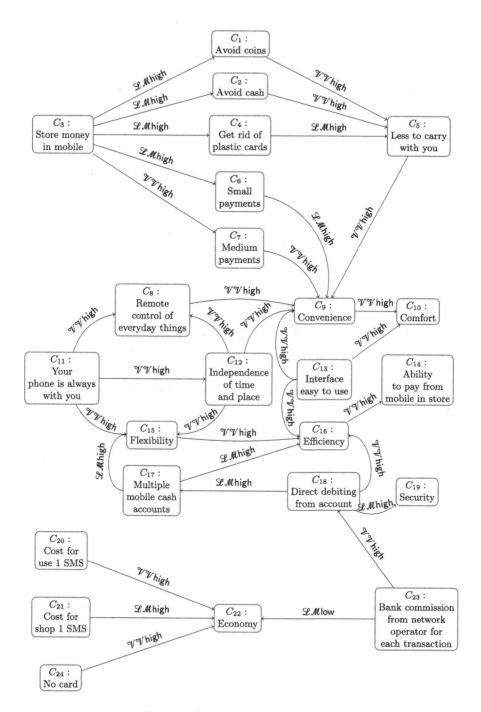

Fig. 7. LCM model for MPS Project

4   Conclusion and Forthcoming Study

The paper recommends two algorithms for reasoning with words on linguistic cognitive map.

- Static algorithm allows to find the path value between any two vertices of the graph 𝕃ℂ𝕄 on the linguistic value domain
- Dynamic algorithm allows to find the convergence vector in the state space over the linguistic domain
- Research and apply algorithms on Mobile Payment System

In the future, two studies will be:

- Research on modeling and reasoning methods on smart mobile systems based on lingistic variables.
- Prove the correctness and completeness of the algorithms.

References

1. Caarvalho, J.: On the semantics and the use of fuzzy cognitive maps and dynamic cognitive maps in social sciences. Fuzzy Sets Syst. **214**, 6–19 (2013)
2. Frias, M., Yaima, F., Nápoles, G., Vahoof, K., Bello, R.: Fuzzy cognitive maps reasoning with words: an ordinal approach. In: ISFUROS (2017)
3. Glykas, M.: Fuzzy Cognitive Maps, Advances in Theory, Tools and Applications. Springer, Heidelberg (2010). https://doi.org/10.1007/978-3-642-03220-2
4. Van Han, N., Hao, N.C., Vinh, P.C.: Toward aggregating fuzzy graphs a model theory approach. In: Vinh, P.C., Rakib, A. (eds.) ICCASA/ICTCC -2019. LNICST, vol. 298, pp. 215–222. Springer, Cham (2019). https://doi.org/10.1007/978-3-030-34365-1_17
5. Van Han, N., Cong Vinh, P.: Modeling with words based on hedge algebra. In: 7th EAI International Conference, ICCASA 2018 and 4th EAI International Conference, ICTCC 2018, pp. 266:211–217 (2018)
6. Van Han, N., Cong Vinh, P.: Toward modeling and reasoning with words based on hedge algebra. EAI Endorsed Trans. Context-aware Syst. Appl. **5**(15), e5 (2018)
7. Van Han, N., Cong Vinh, P.: Reasoning with words: a hedge algebra linguistic cognitive map approach. Concurrency Comput. Pract. Exp. **33**(2), e5711 (2020)
8. Nguyen Cat Ho and Nguyen Van Long: Fuzziness measure on complete hedge algebras and quantifying semantics of terms in linear hedge algebras. Fuzzy Sets Syst. **158**(4), 452–471 (2007)
9. Cat Ho, N., Thai Son, T., Dinh Khang, T., Xuan Viet, L.: Fuzziness measure, quantified semantic mapping and interpolative method of approximate reasoning in medical expert systems. J. Comp. Sci. Cybern. **18**(3), 237–252 (2002)
10. Cat Ho, N., Wechler, W.: Hedge algebras: an algebraic approach to structure of sets of linguistic truth values. Fuzzy Sets Syst. **35**(3), 281–293 (1990)
11. Kosko, B.: Fuzzy cognitive maps. Int. J. Man Mach. Stud. **24**, 65–75 (1986)
12. Zadeh, L.A.: The concept of a linguistic variable and its applications to approximate reasoning. Inf. Sci. **8**(3), 199–249 (1975)
13. Zadeh, L.A.: Computing with words - Principal Concepts and Ideas. Studies in Fuzziness and Soft Computing. Springer, Heidelberg (2012). https://doi.org/10.1007/978-3-642-27473-2

14. Frias, M., Filiberto, Y., Nápoles, G., Falcon, R., Bello, R., Vanhoof, K.: Comparative analysis of symbolic reasoning models for fuzzy cognitive maps. In: Bello, R., Falcon, R., Verdegay, J.L. (eds.) Uncertainty Management with Fuzzy and Rough Sets. SFSC, vol. 377, pp. 127–139. Springer, Cham (2019). https://doi.org/10.1007/978-3-030-10463-4_7

15. Papageorgiou, E.I. (ed.): Fuzzy Cognitive Maps for Applied Sciences and Engineering. ISRL, vol. 54. Springer, Heidelberg (2014). https://doi.org/10.1007/978-3-642-39739-4

16. Rodriguez-Repiso, L., Setchi, R., Salmeron, J.L.: Modelling it projects success with fuzzy cognitive maps. Expert Syst. Appl. **32**(2), 543–559 (2007)

17. Ross, T.J.: Fuzzy Logic With Engineering Applications. 3rd edn. Wiley (2010)

18. Zadeh, L.A., Kacprzyk, J.: Computing with Word in Information Intelligent System 1. Springer, Heidelberg (1999). https://doi.org/10.1007/978-3-7908-1873-4

Applying Design of Experiments to Evaluate the Influence of Parameters on the Economic Feasibility of the Eco-Industrial Parks

Kien Cao-Van[✉]

Faculty of Information Technology, Nguyen Tat Thanh University,
Ho Chi Minh City, Vietnam
cvkien@ntt.edu.vn

Abstract. This research employs the design of experimental (DoE) to examine how various parameters impact the economic feasibility and overall satisfaction of enterprises operating within eco-industrial parks (EIPs). A full factorial design is constructed, using economic feasibility and overall satisfaction as response variables, and experimental data is generated by simulating diverse scenarios. Each iteration of the experiment utilizes a single-leader multi-follower (SLMF) game optimization model, focusing on designing water exchange networks within EIPs. The investigation encompasses several parameters in a case study involving ten follower enterprises aiming to minimize their annual operational costs. Concurrently, the EIP authority assumes the leader role with the objective of reducing the collective freshwater consumption of the EIP. Furthermore, this study employs binary logistic and multi-linear regressions to establish causal relationships. These relationships link input parameters with economic feasibility and overall satisfaction of operating businesses within EIPs. Ultimately, the reliability of the DoE methodology is showcased, offering valuable insights into enterprise parameters, EIP design, economic feasibility, and overall satisfaction.

Keywords: Eco-industrial park · Design of experiments · Single-leader multi-follower game · Logistic regression · Multi-linear regression

1 Introduction

Design of Experiments (DoE) serves as a systematic and efficient approach, empowering researchers and engineers to comprehend the impact of experimental parameters (x_i, independent variables) on response variables (y, dependent variables). This is achieved by constructing mathematical models ($y = f(x_i)$). Originally formulated in the early 1920s, the research planning strategy, DoE, was pioneered by Sir Ronald Fisher in the field of agricultural research [6]. About 50 years for the DoE technique has been widely applied in different fields of medicine, biology, marketing research, and industrial production. We refer

© ICST Institute for Computer Sciences, Social Informatics and Telecommunications Engineering 2024
Published by Springer Nature Switzerland AG 2024. All Rights Reserved
P. Cong Vinh and H. Mahfooz Ul Haque (Eds.): ICTCC 2023, LNICST 586, pp. 148–172, 2024.
https://doi.org/10.1007/978-3-031-59462-5_11

the reader to references [9,16,17,19] for a survey on different applications of DoE. DoE allows using a minimum experiments, in which several experimental parameters are systematically varied to determine their effects on the response variables. Utilizing the acquired data, we construct a regression model for the analyzed procedure. This regression model serves the purpose of comprehending how the experimental parameters impact the response variables and identifying the optimal conditions for the process.

We refer the reader to [12] for general guidelines and procedures for implementing DoE. In fact, the practical steps required to plan and conduct a DoE include: stating the objectives, defining response variables, determining factors and levels, determining experimental design type, performing the experiment, data analysis, and practical conclusions and recommendations. Furthermore, the selection of factors and levels in the DoE usually depends on the type of investigation, the type of process, and the available resources. Thus, different selections of levels or factors will result in different DoEs that could theoretically be appropriate for the type of investigation. In a very recent publication [8], the authors recommend procedures for preparing input data for various types of experimental designs to select the most successful and the most efficient designs.

Due to the growing concern about the limitation of the available resources (steam, water, electricity, ...) and the need for more sustainable industrial development, the concept of Industrial Ecology (IE) has emerged [4]. IE is described as a group of interconnected industries in a certain region where waste production and resource consumption are reduced by allowing waste products from one sector to be used as raw materials for another. One of its main practical applications is the design of eco-industrial parks (EIPs) and a definition commonly admitted was given by Lowe [10] as: "A community of manufacturing and service businesses seeking enhanced environmental and economic performance through collaboration in managing environmental and resource issues including energy, water, and materials. By working together, the community of businesses seeks a collective benefit that is greater than the sum of the individual benefits each company would realize if it optimized its individual performance only". As we can see, enterprises operating in eco-industrial parks not only gain economic benefits but also achieve environmental benefits. To achieve these benefits, it is necessary to design an optimal resource exchange network between enterprises.

Based on a literature review, Boix et al. [4] classified resource exchanges in EIPs into three types: water, energy, and material. Moreover, water exchange constitutes the predominant form of interaction within EIPs, where the optimization of water distribution and the reduction of freshwater consumption often revolve around the strategic inclusion of a wastewater treatment facility alongside its associated network for the discharge of treated water. Most of the resource exchange network models proposed in the EIP have been modeled as an SLMF game [1,14,15]. In the SLMF game, the upper-level optimization subproblem represents the leader's decision-making viewpoint in order to minimize the consumption of natural resources while the lower-level optimization subproblems represent the followers' viewpoint in order to minimize their operating cost. Figure 1 shows the general scheme of such a model.

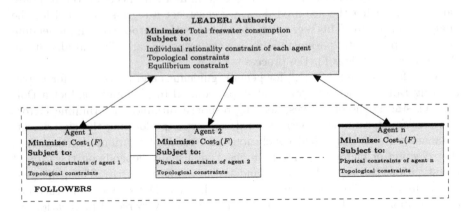

Fig. 1. General scheme of SLMF Game

In SLMF game model, the system variables are divided into those controlled by the leader and by the followers. The objective functions of both upper- and lower-level subproblems involve the controlled variables of both leader and followers. The constraint of the upper-level subproblems contains the lower-level subproblem. At the upper-level subproblem, the authority of the park chooses the connections of the exchange network, whereas at the lower-level subproblem, each enterprise manages the distribution of its output flux and natural resource consumption. In accordance with determinations by the EIP authority, all enterprises engage in a parametric non-cooperative generalized Nash game, where the strategies of the EIP authority are treated as external parameters. As exemplified in prior works [1,14,15], the robustness of this approach is evident, as it allows for the comprehensive assessment of multiple criteria within the model. Of paramount significance, the equilibrium solution ensures economic gains for each constituent enterprise engaged in the EIP.

The primary objective of this study is to combine the concepts of experimental design and the SLMF game model proposed in [15]. This fusion aims to assess how distinct parameters affect both the economic feasibility and the overall satisfaction of operational enterprises in eco-industrial parks.

The forthcoming sections of this paper are structured as follows: Sect. 2 explores the water exchange network model within eco-industrial parks, utilizing a single-leader multi-follower game framework. The conversion of the eco-industrial park modeling challenge into a mixed integer linear programming formulation is covered in Sect. 3. Moving on to Sect. 4, an empirical investigation is carried out using statistical experimental design to analyze the influence of various parameters on the economic feasibility and overall satisfaction of operating enterprises in eco-industrial parks. Finally, concluding thoughts and prospects for the future are presented in Sect. 5.

2 EIP Problem Statement and Model

In this section, we follow the ideas from papers [1,14,15].

2.1 EIP Problem Statement

From a number of specific enterprises in the EIP, it is possible to create a suitable network of connections between them. Each enterprise is required to comply with predefined parameters for the quantity and quality of incoming water, as well as the quantity and quality of the output wastewater. For each enterprise, the water input may include fresh water and/or water supplied from other enterprise units. In fact, wastewater from one enterprise can be transferred to other enterprise and/or released into the environment immediately. The main goal of the EIP model is to define an efficient water connection system between units, ensuring both reduction of global freshwater consumption and cutting operating costs for individual companies on the industrial premises, while still complying with all process and environmental constraints.

2.2 Enterprise's Problem

Assume n is the fixed number of firms in the EIP. We use the index set $I := \{1, \ldots, n\}$ to represent enterprises and 0 to represent a sink node representing a polluted water treatment pit. Importantly, we determine that $I_0 = \{0\} \cup I$. Each enterprise $i \in I$ receives water throughput from partners in the EIP. However, due to technical limitations on the P_i process, the pollutant concentration delivered by the other enterprises is limited to a maximum value here denoted by $C_{i,\text{in}}$ [ppm]. In contrast, each firm $i \in I$ produces a fixed amount of pollutant M_i [g/h] which, from its in-house production process, needs to be diluted before discharge. To do this, enterprise i must consume a sufficient amount of fresh water z_i [T/h] to ensure that the concentration of pollution in the exit flux after dilution is always lower than $C_{i,\text{out}}$. This means that, when considering enterprise i in I, they will optimize their processes to ensure that the output contaminant concentration always reaches the $C_{i,\text{out}}$ value. Obviously we have that $C_{i,\text{in}} \leq C_{i,\text{out}}$. This structure is illustrated in Fig. 2.

Within eco-industrial parks (EIPs), enterprises engage in the exchange of materials. Conversely, an exchange network within the EIP context takes the form of a simple directed graph denoted as (I_0, E), where the presence of a link $(i, j) \in E$ signifies that enterprise i has the capability to direct its output water to enterprise j. In a similar vein, the utilization of the connection $(i, 0)$ by enterprise i signifies the disposal of water from the park, releasing it into the environment.

The *stand-alone* and *complete* configurations are defined as follows:

$$E_{\text{st}} := \{(i, 0) : i \in I\} \quad \text{and} \quad E_{\text{max}} := \{(i, j) : i \in I, j \in I_0\},$$

a valid exchange network E must satisfy that $E_{\text{st}} \subset E \subset E_{\text{max}}$. This definition yields that:

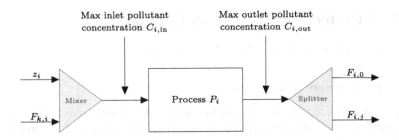

Fig. 2. Water mixture description for a given enterprise. Here $C_{i,\text{in}} \leq C_{i,\text{out}}$.

1. Every enterprise $i \in I$ maintains a connection to the sink node, i.e., $(i, 0) \in E$.
2. The sink node doesn't possess any outgoing connections, signifying that $(0, i) \notin E$ for all $i \in I$.

The collection of permissible networks within the EIP framework is represented as $\mathcal{E}$. Subsequently, for any E belonging to $\mathcal{E}$, the collection of unutilized connections, distinct from those in E, is denoted as E^c, where $E^c = E_{\max} \setminus E$.

Let $F_{i,j}$ [T/h] symbolize the water flow across the link (i, j) for every $(i, j) \in E_{\max}$. Furthermore, we establish $F = (F_{i,j} : (i, j) \in E_{\max})$ as the comprehensive flux vector across the network.

Moreover, considering each enterprise denoted as $i \in I$, we represent F as (F_i, F_{-i}), with $F_i = (F_{i,j} : j \in I_0)$ and $F_{-i} = (F_{k,j} : k \in I \setminus i)$. This representation underscores the array of flows associated with enterprise i. Consequently, given a fixed network E, a permissible flow vector F must adhere to the subsequent set of constraints:

1. **Use of connections in E:** Given that E denotes the feasible connections, it becomes imperative to enforce the following constraint:

$$\forall (i, j) \in E^c, \; F_{i,j} = 0. \tag{1}$$

2. **Water Mass Conservation:** Considering enterprise $i \in I$, the following equation holds true for water mass balance:

$$z_i + \sum_{(k,i) \in E} F_{k,i} = \sum_{(i,j) \in E} F_{i,j}. \tag{2}$$

3. **Contaminant Mass Conservation:** In the context of enterprise $i \in I$, the ensuing equation reflects the equilibrium of contaminant mass:

$$M_i + \sum_{(k,i) \in E} C_{k,\text{out}} F_{k,i} = C_{i,\text{out}} \sum_{(i,j) \in E} F_{i,j}. \tag{3}$$

4. **Inlet/outlet concentration constraints:** for an enterprise $i \in I$ we have

$$\sum_{(k,i) \in E} C_{k,\text{out}} F_{k,i} \leq C_{i,\text{in}} \left(z_i + \sum_{(k,i) \in E} F_{k,i} \right). \tag{4}$$

5. **Positivity of fluxes:** It is a requisite that all fluxes within the park maintain a positive value:

$$\forall (i,j) \in E, \; F_{i,j} \geq 0 \qquad \text{and} \qquad \forall i \in I, \; z_i \geq 0. \tag{5}$$

Note that by amalgamating Eqs. (2) and (3), we derive:

$$M_i + \sum_{(k,i)\in E} C_{k,\text{out}} F_{k,i} = C_{i,\text{out}} \left(z_i + \sum_{(k,i)\in E} F_{k,i} \right), \qquad \forall i \in I, \tag{6}$$

Thus, the quantity of fresh water procured by enterprise $i \in I$ is determined by the flows originating from other enterprises, indicating:

$$z_i(F_{-i}) = \frac{1}{C_{i,\text{out}}} \left(M_i + \sum_{(k,i)\in E} (C_{k,\text{out}} - C_{i,\text{out}}) F_{k,i} \right). \tag{7}$$

Each enterprise i strives to minimize its operational cost, as defined by the following expression:

$$\text{Cost}_i(F_i, F_{-i}, E) = A \left[c_f \cdot z_i(F_{-i}) + \delta \sum_{(k,i)\in E} F_{k,i} + \delta \sum_{\substack{(i,j)\in E \\ j \neq 0}} F_{i,j} + \beta F_{i,0} \right]. \tag{8}$$

In this context, A [h] represents a time constant that characterizes the park's lifecycle analysis, while c_f [\$/T] pertains to the procurement cost of freshwater. Additionally, δ [\$/T] accounts for the expenditure associated with pumping contaminated water between enterprises, and β [\$/T] denotes the expense linked to discharging polluted water. It is noteworthy that the model adopts an assumption wherein the cost β significantly outweighs δ.

With all of these considerations, the problem of each enterprise i, for a given network $E \in \mathcal{E}$, is given by:

$$P_i(F_{-i}, E) = \begin{cases} \min_{F_i} \text{Cost}_i(F_i, F_{-i}, E) \\ \text{s.t.} \begin{cases} z_i + \sum_{(k,i)\in E} F_{k,i} = \sum_{(i,j)\in E} F_{i,j}, \\ \sum_{(k,i)\in E} C_{k,\text{out}} F_{k,i} \leq C_{i,\text{in}} \left(z_i + \sum_{(k,i)\in E} F_{k,i} \right), \\ z_i(F_{-i}) \geq 0, \\ F_i \geq 0, \\ F_i \big|_{E^c} = 0. \end{cases} \end{cases} \tag{9}$$

In the context of a network $E \in \mathcal{E}$, we define a vector F as an equilibrium for the enterprises at the lower-level problem if and only if

$$\forall i \in I, \; F_i \text{ solves the problem } P_i(F_{-i}, E).$$

The collection of such equilibria for network E is symbolized as $Eq(E)$.

Remark 1. *Note that in cases where enterprise i does not receive contaminated water, its freshwater consumption z_i is determined as follows:*

$$z_i = \frac{M_i}{C_{i,\text{out}}}.$$

This subsequently leads to the formulation of the standalone operational cost, represented as STC_i [$\$$/h], according to the equation:

$$\text{STC}_i = A \cdot (c_f + \beta) \frac{M_i}{C_{i,\text{out}}}. \tag{10}$$

2.3 Authority's Problem

At the upper-level problem, the EIP authority wants to reduce the entire use of natural resources, thus he attempts to reduce the function:

$$Z(F) = \sum_{i \in I} z_i(F_{-i}). \tag{11}$$

In order to incentivize an enterprise $i \in I$ to participate in the EIP, the EIP authority needs to offer a proportional cost reduction of $\alpha \in]0, 1[$ compared to the expenses of standalone operation. This entails ensuring that:

$$\text{Cost}_i(F_i, F_{-i}, E) \leq \alpha \cdot \text{STC}_i. \tag{12}$$

The concept of this minimal relative enhancement was initially introduced in [15]. Subsequently, the problem of the EIP authority is

$$\min_{F \in \mathbb{R}^{|E_{\max}|}, E \in \mathcal{E}} Z(F)$$

$$s.t. \begin{cases} F \in Eq(E), \\ \text{Cost}_i(F_i, F_{-i}, E) \leq \alpha \cdot \text{STC}_i, \quad \forall i \in I. \end{cases} \tag{13}$$

Interpreting optimization problem (13) reveals the following scenario: The EIP authority will offer enterprises a feasible exchange network denoted as E and a corresponding operation $F \in \mathbb{R}^{|E_{\max}|}$ that adheres to all physical constraints. Importantly, this operation ensures that no enterprise has the motivation to independently deviate from the proposal due to constraint $F \in Eq(E)$, while simultaneously securing the participation of all enterprises. This participation is effectively guaranteed by the precondition established in constraint (12).

3 Solution Methodologies

The authority's problem (13) is formulated in the form of mathematical programming with equilibrium constraints (MPEC) (see, e.g., [2,11,18]). This section is dedicated to illustrating the transformation of the challenging-to-solve MPEC formulation into a single Mixed-Integer programming problem.

3.1 Characterization of Equilibria

Given a topology E, we will write

$$E_{i,\text{in}} := \{(k,i) : (k,i) \in E\} \quad \text{and} \quad E_{i,\text{out}} := \{(i,j) : (i,j) \in E\}.$$

We define the set of active and inactive of i, denoted by I_{act} and I_{inact} respectively as follows:

$$I_{act} := \{i \in I \mid \exists j \in I \text{ with } (i,j) \in E_{i,\text{ out}} \}$$
$$I_{inact} := \{i \in I \mid E_{i,\text{ out}} = \{(i,0)\}\}.$$

If each enterprise $i \in I_{act}$, we define the set of active arcs of i, denoted by $E_{i,\text{act}}$, that is,

$$E_{i,act} := \{(i,j) \in E_{i,\text{ out}} : j \neq 0\}.$$

If each enterprise $i \in I_{\text{inact}}$, we define the set of inactive arcs of i, denoted by $E_{i,\text{ inact}}$, that is,

$$E_{i,\text{ inact}} := \{(i,0)\}.$$

Theorem 2. *For any valid exchange network $E \in \mathcal{E}$ and denoting $S(E)$ by the set*

$$S(E) = \left\{ F \; : \; \forall i \in I, \begin{cases} z_i(F_{-i}) + \displaystyle\sum_{(k,i)\in E} F_{k,i} = \displaystyle\sum_{(i,j)\in E_{i,\text{act}}} F_{i,j}, & \text{if } i \in I_{act} \\[2mm] F_{i,0} = 0, \\[2mm] z_i(F_{-i}) + \displaystyle\sum_{(k,i)\in E} F_{k,i} = F_{i,0}, & \text{if } i \in I_{inact} \\[4mm] \displaystyle\sum_{(k,i)\in E} C_{k,\text{out}} F_{k,i} \leq C_{i,\text{in}} \left(z_i + \displaystyle\sum_{(k,i)\in E} F_{k,i} \right) \\[2mm] z_i(F_{-i}) \geq 0 \\[1mm] F_i \geq 0 \end{cases} \right\}$$

(14)

then, one has $S(E) = \text{Eq}(E)$. Additionally, any optimal solution (F, E) of the mathematical programming problem

$$\min_{F \in \mathbb{R}^{|E_{\max}|}, E \in \mathcal{E}} Z(F)$$

$$\text{s.t.} \begin{cases} F \in S(E), \\ \text{Cost}_i(F_i, F_{-i}, E) \leq \alpha \cdot \text{STC}_i, & \forall i \in I. \end{cases}$$

(15)

constitutes an optimal solution for the SLMF problem (13).

Proof. The proof follows a similar path as outlined in [15, Theorem 4.1]. Our focus centers on demonstrating the equivalence $S(E) = \text{Eq}(E)$, as the latter aspect naturally emerges by substituting the constraint "$F \in \text{Eq}(E)$" with "$F \in S(E)$".

Hence, our objective is to demonstrate the inclusion $S(E) \subseteq \text{Eq}(E)$. Let's consider an arbitrary $F \in S(E)$. Because $E_{i,\text{act}} \subset E$ for all $i \in I_{\text{act}}$ and $E_{i,\text{inact}} \subset E$ for all $i \in I_{\text{inact}}$, it follows that F_i serves as a feasible solution for $P_i(F_{-i}, E)$ across all $i \in I$.

Now, fix $i \in I$ and let F_i' be another feasible point of $P_i(F_{-i}, E)$. Then, $F_i' \geq 0$ and the water mass balance constraint (2) is satisfied. Therefore,

– if $i \in I_{\text{act}}$, one has

$$\text{Cost}_i(F_i', F_{-i}, E) - \text{Cost}_i(F_i, F_{-i}, E) = A \left[\delta \sum_{(i,j) \in E} F_{i,j}' + \beta F_{i,0}' - \delta \sum_{(i,j) \in E_{i,\text{act}}} F_{i,j} \right]$$

$$\geq A\delta \left[\sum_{(i,j) \in E} F_{i,j}' + F_{i,0}' - \sum_{(i,j) \in E_{i,\text{act}}} F_{i,j} \right].$$

Moreover, the mass balance constraint (2) is satisfied for F_i' and F_i for any $i \in I_{\text{act}}$, thus

$$\sum_{(i,j) \in E, j \neq 0} F_{i,j}' + F_{i,0}' = z_i(F_{-i}) + \sum_{(k,i) \in E} F_{k,i} = \sum_{(i,j) \in E} F_{i,j} = \sum_{(i,j) \in E_{i,\text{act}}} F_{i,j}.$$

Hence, $\text{Cost}_i(F_i', F_{-i}, E) \geq \text{Cost}_i(F_i, F_{-i}, E)$ for any $i \in I_{\text{act}}$.

– if $i \in I_{\text{inact}}$, one has

$$\text{Cost}_i(F_i', F_{-i}, E) - \text{Cost}_i(F_i, F_{-i}, E) = A \left[\beta F_{i,0}' - \beta F_{i,0} \right]$$

$$= A\beta \left[F_{i,0}' - F_{i,0} \right].$$

Moreover, the mass balance constraint (2) is satisfied for F_i' and F_i for any $i \in I_{\text{inact}}$, thus

$$F_{i,0}' = z_i(F_{-i}) + \sum_{(k,i) \in E} F_{k,i} = F_{i,0}.$$

Hence, $\text{Cost}_i(F_i', F_{-i}, E) = \text{Cost}_i(F_i, F_{-i}, E)$ for any $i \in I_{\text{inact}}$.

Thus, F_i solves $P_i(F_{-i}, E)$, and since this holds for every $i \in I$, we conclude that $F \in \text{Eq}(E)$.

Now, let us prove that $\text{Eq}(E) \subseteq S(E)$. Let $F \in \text{Eq}(E)$, and assume that $F \notin S(E)$. Since for each $i \in I$ the vector F_i is a feasible point of $P_i(F_{-i}, E)$, so $F \notin S(E)$ if there exists $i_0 \in I_{\text{act}}$ such that $F_{i_0,0} > 0$. Let $(i_0, j) \in E_{i,\text{act}}$ and let us consider the vector F_{i_0}' given by

$$F_{i_0,k}' = \begin{cases} F_{i_0,k} & \text{if } k \in I \setminus \{0, j\}, \\ 0 & \text{if } k = 0, \\ F_{i_0,j} + F_{i_0,0} & \text{if } k = j. \end{cases}$$

We have that $F_{i_0}' \geq 0$ and also

$$z_i(F_{-i_0}) + \sum_{(k,i_0) \in E} F_{k,i_0} = \sum_{(i_0,j) \in E} F_{i_0,j} = \sum_{(i_0,j) \in E} F_{i_0,j}'.$$

Thus, since F_{-i_0} remains the same, F'_{i_0} is a feasible point of $P_i(F_{-i_0}, E)$. Furthermore, we have that

$$\text{Cost}_{i_0}(F'_{i_0}, F_{-i_0}, E) - \text{Cost}_{i_0}(F_{i_0}, F_{-i_0}, E) = \delta \sum_{(i_0,j) \in E, j \neq 0} F'_{i_0,j} + \beta F'_{i_0,0} - \left(\delta \sum_{(i_0,j) \in E} F_{i_0,j} + \beta F_{i_0,0} \right)$$

$$= (\delta - \beta) F_{i_0,0}$$

$$< 0.$$

This yields that F_{i_0} doesn't solve $P_i(F_{-i_0}, E)$, which is a contradiction. Thus, $F \in S(E)$. Finishing the proof.

3.2 Mixed-Integer Formulation

Theorem 2 establishes the remarkable revelation that the authority's problem can be reformulated into a "classical" programming problem through the MPEC formula. Yet, due to the presence of exchange network topologies as variables in this programming context, a numerical implementation might pose a challenge. Consequently, within this section, we will illustrate the process of effectively dealing with a more conventional mixed-integer programming problem.

Let's start by introducing the crucial idea? what we refer to as arc classes? that we will employ to arrive at the final formulation: We define the arc classes exiting from each enterprise $i \in I$ as the sets:

$$C_{i,p} = \{(i,j) \in E_{\max} : j \in I\} \quad \text{and} \quad C_{i,0} = \{(i,0)\}.$$

The family of all arc classes that exit from i is denoted by the symbol C_i, which is defined as $C_i = \{C_{i,p}, C_{i,0}\}$.

Observe that, for each enterprise $i \in I_{\text{act}}$, the class $C_{i,p}$ is always satisfied

$$E_{i,\text{act}} \subseteq C_{i,p}. \tag{16}$$

This class is given by $C = C_{i,p}$ where (i,p) is any element of $E_{i,\text{act}}$.

Now, for each enterprise $i \in I$, we add two integer variables, $y_{i,p}, y_{i,0} \in \{0,1\}$ with the following interpretation:

- When $y_{i,p}$ is equal to 1, it signifies the inclusion of the connections within $C_{i,p}$ in the network structure.
- Similarly, when $y_{i,0}$ is set to 1, it denotes that the connection $(i,0)$ serves as the exclusive exit pathway for node i, while also denoting the involvement of node i in the EIP.

We establish the following constraints with this new boolean variable:

1. For each enterprise i within the set I, we assign the condition:

$$y_{i,p} + y_{i,0} = 1, \tag{17}$$

indicating that only one class is in an active state.

2. For each enterprise i in the set I, we establish the following condition to hold:

$$\sum_{(i,j)\in C_{i,p}} F_{i,j} \leq K \cdot y_{i,p}, \tag{18}$$

where $K > 0$ is a sufficiently large constant ensuring that all fluxes within the park remain below K. This constraint guarantees that when the connections $C_{i,p}$ are excluded from the network, the flow values $F_{i,j}$ become zero for any $j \in I$.

3. For each enterprise i in the set I, we establish the following condition to hold:

$$F_{i,0} \leq K \cdot y_{i,0}, \tag{19}$$

for some constant $K > 0$ large enough. This constraint ensures that, whenever $C_{i,0}$ are not included in the network, then $F_{i,0} = 0$.

Starting from the binary vector $y \in \{0,1\}^{2n}$, we proceed to construct the graph associated with y as depicted by the equation:

$$E(y) = \left(\bigcup (i,p) \ : \ y_{i,p} = 1\right) \cup (i,0) \ : \ i \in I. \tag{20}$$

We consider then the following Mixed-Integer optimization problem:

$$\min_{F \in \mathbb{R}^{|E_{\max}|}, y \in \{0,1\}^{2n}} Z(F)$$

$$s.t. \begin{cases} z_i + \displaystyle\sum_{(k,i)\in E_{\max}} F_{k,i} = \sum_{(i,j)\in E_{\max}} F_{i,j}, & \forall i \in I \\[2ex] \displaystyle\sum_{(k,i)\in E_{\max}} C_{k,\text{out}} F_{k,i} \leq C_{i,\text{in}} \left(z_i + \sum_{(k,i)\in E_{\max}} F_{k,i}\right), & \forall i \in I \\[2ex] y_{i,p} + y_{i,0} = 1, & \forall i \in I \\ \displaystyle\sum_{(i,j)\in C_{i,p}} F_{i,j} \leq K \cdot y_{i,p}, & \forall i \in I \\[2ex] F_{i,0} \leq K \cdot y_{i,0}, & \forall i \in I \\ z_i(F_{-i}) \geq 0, & \forall i \in I \\ F \geq 0, & \\ \text{Cost}_i(F_i, F_{-i}, E(y)) \leq \alpha \cdot \text{STC}_i, & \forall i \in I \end{cases} \tag{21}$$

Theorem 3. *For every feasible point (F, y) that satisfies (21), the corresponding pair $(F, E(y))$ is a feasible point for (15). Conversely, given any feasible point (F, E) that adheres to (15), the associated pair (F, y^E) is a feasible point for (21), where $y^E = (y^E_{i,p}, y^E_{i,0})_{i\in I} \in \{0,1\}^{2n}$ is defined as follows:*

$$y^E_{i,p} = \begin{cases} 1 & \text{if the connections in } C_{i,p} \text{ are part of the network } E, \\ 0 & \text{otherwise}, \end{cases}$$

and

$$y_{i,0}^E = \begin{cases} 1 & \textit{if the connection } (i,0) \textit{ is the sole exit connection for } i, \\ 0 & \textit{otherwise.} \end{cases}$$

In light of this, the implications are as follows:

1. *If (F, E) represents an optimal solution for (15), then (F, y^E) stands as an optimal solution for (21).*
2. *If (F, y) constitutes an optimal solution for (21), then $(F, E(y))$ serves as an optimal solution for (15).*

Proof. The proof follows a similar path as outlined in [15, Theorem 4.2]. Consider a feasible point (F, y) in the context of (21).

- Let's take an enterprise $i \in I_{\text{act}}$ and denote the unique class within Ci for which $y_{i,p} = 1$ as $C_{i,p}$. By construction, we can ascertain that

$$E(y)_{i,\text{act}} = C_{i,p} \quad \text{and} \quad \sum_{(i,j) \in E_{\max} \setminus C_{i,p}} F_{i,j} \leq K \cdot \sum_{C \in C_i \setminus \{C_{i,p}\}} y_C = 0.$$

Consequently, we derive that

$$F_i \big|_{E(y)_{i,\text{act}}^c} = 0 \iff F_{i,0} = 0, \quad \forall i \in I_{\text{act}}. \tag{22}$$

Since this constraint holds for all active enterprises $i \in I_{\text{act}}$, we can reformulate the balance constraint within problem (21) as

$$z(F_{-i}) + \sum_{(k,i) \in E(y)} F_{k,i} = \sum_{(i,j) \in E(y)_{i,\text{act}}} F_{i,j}, \quad \forall i \in I_{\text{act}}. \tag{23}$$

- Now, for an enterprise $i \in I_{\text{inact}}$, we can express the balance constraint in problem (21) as

$$z_i(F_{-i}) + \sum_{(k,i) \in E(y)} F_{k,i} = F_{i,0}, \quad \forall i \in I_{\text{inact}}. \tag{24}$$

By combining (22), (23), and (24), we then infer that $(F, E(y))$ qualifies as a feasible point for problem (15).

Now, let (F, E) be a feasible point of problem (15). Let us define $y^E = (y_{i,p}^E, y_{i,0}^E)_{i \in I} \in \{0,1\}^{2n}$ as in the statement of the theorem. Then, for every $i \in I$, $y_{i,p} + y_{i,0} = 1$.

- Now, let $i \in I_{\text{act}}$, we have that

$$\sum_{(i,j) \in C_{i,p}} F_{i,j} \leq \begin{cases} K = K \cdot y_{i,p}^E & \text{if the connections in } C_{i,p} \text{ are included in } E, \\ 0 = K \cdot y_{i,p}^E & \text{otherwise,} \end{cases}$$

For an enterprise $i \in I_{\text{act}}$, the fact that $E_{i,\text{act}} \subseteq E(y^E)$ lead us to the fact that

$$\text{Cost}_i(F_i, F_{-i}, E(y^E)) = \text{Cost}_i(F_i, F_{-i}, E),$$

and so, the constraint (12) is satisfied for any $i \in I_{\text{act}}$.
– For each enterprise $i \in I_{\text{inact}}$,

$$F_{i,0} \leq \begin{cases} K = K \cdot y_{i,0}^E & \text{if the connections in } C_{i,0} \text{ are included in } E, \\ 0 = K \cdot y_{i,0}^E & \text{otherwise,} \end{cases}$$

For an enterprise $i \in I_{\text{inact}}$, we have

$$\text{Cost}_i(F_i, F_{-i}, E(y^E)) = \text{Cost}_i(F_i, F_{-i}, E),$$

and so, the constraint (12) is satisfied for any $i \in I_{\text{inact}}$.

Consequently, we establish that (F, y^E) is a valid solution for (21), as all other constraints are automatically fulfilled when (F, E) proves to be feasible for (15).

The final two implications of the theorem are a direct result of the preceding developments.

3.3   Null Class as Exit Option

Perceiving that the network consistently possesses a viable configuration in the form of the standalone setup E_{st}, it's worth noting that the introduction of constraint (12) can potentially render problem (15) unfeasible.

The infeasibility of (15) implies that the authority faces a challenge in achieving a solution that abides by the constraint (12) across all enterprises. This prompts the need to consider the possibility of excluding certain enterprises from the network.

To address this, we introduce a boolean variable $y_{i,\text{null}} \in \{0, 1\}$ for each enterprise $i \in I$, defined as follows:

$$y_{i,\text{null}} = \begin{cases} 1 & \text{if } i \text{ violates the contract (12),} \\ 0 & \text{otherwise.} \end{cases}$$

We modify problem (21) with this extra variable, adding the following constraints:

1. For every enterprise i within the set I, we establish

$$y_{i,\text{null}} + y_{i,p} + y_{i,0} = 1, \tag{25}$$

which signifies that either a single arc class is operational, or the enterprise remains unlinked to the network.

2. For every enterprise i within the set I, we put

$$F_{i,0} \le K \cdot (y_{i,0} + y_{i,\text{null}}), \tag{26}$$

$$\sum_{(i,j)\in E_{\max}, j\neq 0} F_{i,j} \le K \cdot (1 - y_{i,\text{null}}), \tag{27}$$

for some constant $K > 0$ large enough. This ensures that if the enterprise violates contract (12), he will employ the discharge arc $(i,0)$.

3. For every enterprise i within the set I, we put

$$\sum_{(k,i)\in E_{\max}} F_{k,i} \le K \cdot (1 - y_{i,\text{null}}), \tag{28}$$

for some large enough constant $K > 0$. This constraint ensures that in the event of an enterprise contravening the contract stipulated in (12), no other entity is allowed to transmit any flux to it.

4. For each enterprise $i \in I$, we establish

$$\text{Cost}_i(F_i, F_{-i}, E(y)) \le \alpha_i \cdot \text{STC}_i \cdot (1 - y_{i,\text{null}}) + \text{STC}_i \cdot y_{i,\text{null}}. \tag{29}$$

In this context, the constraint of individual rationality holds true exclusively when $y_{i,\text{null}} = 0$. Conversely, when the enterprise is not integrated into the network, its cost aligns with STC_i.

Denoting

$$\text{STC}_i(y_{i,\text{null}}) := \alpha_i \cdot \text{STC}_i \cdot (1 - y_{i,\text{null}}) + \text{STC}_i \cdot y_{i,\text{null}},$$

the new optimization problem becomes

$$\min_{F,y} \quad Z(F)$$

$$\text{s.t.} \begin{cases} z_i + \displaystyle\sum_{(k,i)\in E_{\max}} F_{k,i} = \sum_{(i,j)\in E_{\max}} F_{i,j}, & \forall i \in I \\[2mm] \displaystyle\sum_{(k,i)\in E_{\max}} C_{k,\text{out}} F_{k,i} \le C_{i,\text{in}}\left(z_i + \sum_{(k,i)\in E_{\max}} F_{k,i} \right), & \forall i \in I \\[2mm] y_{i,\text{null}} + y_{i,p} + y_{i,0} = 1, & \forall i \in I \\[2mm] \displaystyle\sum_{(i,j)\in C_{i,p}} F_{i,j} \le K \cdot y_{i,p}, & \forall i \in I \\[2mm] F_{i,0} \le K \cdot (y_{i,0} + y_{i,\text{null}}), & \forall i \in I \\[2mm] \displaystyle\sum_{(i,j)\in E_{\max}, j\neq 0} F_{i,j} \le K \cdot (1 - y_{i,\text{null}}), & \forall i \in I \\[2mm] \displaystyle\sum_{(k,i)\in E_{\max}} F_{k,i} \le K \cdot (1 - y_{i,\text{null}}), & \forall i \in I \\[2mm] z_i(F_{-i}) \ge 0, & \forall i \in I \\[2mm] F \ge 0, & \\[2mm] \text{Cost}_i(F_i, F_{-i}, E(y)) \le \alpha \cdot \text{STC}_i(y_{i,\text{null}}), & \forall i \in I \end{cases} \tag{30}$$

Given that the optimization problem (30) can yield multiple solutions, we incorporate an additional term into the objective function to guide the selection towards the solution with a greater number of participating enterprises. We replace $Z(F)$ with the following expression:

$$Z(F) + \text{Coef} \cdot \sum_{i \in I} y_{i,\text{null}}, \tag{31}$$

where $\text{Coef} \geq 0$ serves as a coefficient to penalize optimal solutions that exclude a larger number of enterprises from the park.

In the upcoming sections, we will tackle the MILP problem (30) through the utilization of the programming language `Julia v1.0.5`, employing the `Cplex` solver.

4   Design of Experiments

As mentioned in Sect. 1, the objective of this study is to establish a cause-and-effect relationship between a number of input factors and the economic feasibility, as well as between a number of input parameters and the overall satisfaction of operating enterprises in EIPs. To identify these input factors, we use the design of experimental (DoE) techniques. Thus, we conduct a series of experimental runs with the change of the inputs and test the results in order to collect the outputs to evaluate the corresponding change. Each run of an experiment involves a combination of the levels of the investigated factors. The DoE inputs are studied based on the original parameter values given in Table 1. In fact, the parameters in Table 1 include part of the hypothetical literature example originally developed by Olesen and Polley [13]. The DoE consists of 7 levels regarding factors $C_{i,\text{in}}$, $C_{i,\text{out}}$, and M_i of enterprises 5, 6, 7, 8, 9, and 10, being values in Table 1 as the base level. Other levels correspond to 0.5, 0.8, 0.9, 1.1, 1.2, 1.5 times the base value for $C_{i,\text{in}}$, $C_{i,\text{out}}$, and M_i. Additionally, we define $\rho = \frac{c_f}{\delta}$ as another factor considered in the DoE evaluated in five levels, i.e., 0.2, 0.5, 2.1, 3.1, and 12.4. Then, for evaluation purposes, it is assumed that $c_f = 6.2000$ [\$/T] and $\beta = 34.875$ [\$/T]. Furthermore, assume that the EIP operates for one hour, i.e., $A = 1\,\text{h}$.

Since the DoE consists of 7 levels regarding factors $C_{i,\text{in}}$, $C_{i,\text{out}}$, M_i and 5 levels regarding factor ρ, thus the DoE will require 1715 experimental runs. For each experimental run, the MILP problem (30) was solved in proper sequence. Then the economic satisfaction of each enterprise was checked for each combination of levels. For such a purpose, the level of satisfaction of each enterprise is defined as:

$$L_i = \begin{cases} 1 & \text{if } \text{Cost}_i{}^* \leq \text{Cost}_i{}^{\text{LOW}}, \\ \dfrac{\text{Cost}_i{}^* - \text{Cost}_i{}^{\text{UP}}}{\text{Cost}_i{}^{\text{LOW}} - \text{Cost}_i{}^{\text{UP}}} & \text{if } \text{Cost}_i{}^{\text{LOW}} < \text{Cost}_i{}^* < \text{Cost}_i{}^{\text{UP}}, \\ 0 & \text{if } \text{Cost}_i{}^* \geq \text{Cost}_i{}^{\text{UP}}, \end{cases} \tag{32}$$

Table 1. Parameters of the Network.

Enterprise i	$C_{i,\text{in}}$(ppm)	$C_{i,\text{out}}$(ppm)	M_i(g/h)
1	0	100	2000
2	50	80	2000
3	50	100	5000
4	80	800	30000
5	400	800	4000
6	10	100	2000
7	60	80	2000
8	80	400	5000
9	100	800	30000
10	400	1000	4000

where $\text{Cost}_i{}^*$ is the optimal operating cost of enterprise i when operating inside the EIP, $\text{Cost}_i{}^{\text{UP}}$ is the operating cost of enterprise i when operating stand-alone, while $\text{Cost}_i{}^{\text{LOW}}$ is the desired cost of enterprise i. Note that, for each combination of levels of the factors, the MILP problem (30) was solved to obtain a generalized Nash equilibrium point (F_i, F_{-i}, y) then the value of $\text{Cost}_i{}^*$ is defined by $\text{Cost}_i(F_i, F_{-i}, E(y))$, on the other hand the value of $\text{Cost}_i{}^{\text{LOW}}$ is determined by 80% of the operating stand-alone cost $\text{Cost}_i{}^{\text{UP}}$.

Now, the overall satisfaction of operating enterprises in EIPs is measured by

$$L_{tot} = \sum_{i \in I} L_i. \tag{33}$$

For the EIP economic feasibility study, all 1715 simulations were included on the DoE built with the 4 variable mentioned above ($C_{i,\text{in}}$, $C_{i,\text{out}}$, M_i, ρ), as well as their interactions and the squared terms. When enterprises operate in an EIP, there are two possibilities either the EIP is economically feasible or the EIP is not economically feasible. So, we introduce a categorical variable Y defined as

$$Y = \begin{cases} 1 & \text{if } L_{tot} > 0 \\ 0 & \text{otherwise} \end{cases} \tag{34}$$

where $Y = 1$ means that the EIP is economically feasible while $Y = 0$ means that the EIP is not economically feasible.

4.1 Binary Logistic Regression Model

In this part, we present a logistic regression model to evaluate whether the predictors (i.e., $C_{i,\text{in}}$, $C_{i,\text{out}}$, M_i, and ρ), their interactions, and squared terms affect the economic feasibility of the operating enterprises in EIPs or not. The model built was of the following form:

$$\ln\left[\frac{P(Y=1)}{P(Y=0)}\right] = \beta_0 + \beta_1 C_{i,\text{in}} + \beta_2 C_{i,\text{out}} + \beta_3 M_i + \beta_4 \rho$$
$$+ \beta_5 C_{i,\text{in}}^2 + \beta_6 C_{i,\text{out}}^2 + \beta_7 M_i^2 + \beta_8 \rho^2$$
$$+ \beta_9 C_{i,\text{in}} \times C_{i,\text{out}} + \beta_{10} C_{i,\text{in}} \times M_i + \beta_{11} C_{i,\text{in}} \times \rho$$
$$+ \beta_{12} C_{i,\text{out}} \times M_i + \beta_{13} C_{i,\text{out}} \times \rho + \beta_{14} M_i \times \rho, \tag{35}$$

where P is the probability, Y is the categorical variable defined as in equation (34), $C_{i,\text{in}}$, $C_{i,\text{out}}$, M_i and ρ are the predictors, β_0 is the Y intercept, and $\beta_1, \beta_2, \ldots, \beta_{14}$ are the regression coefficients of the independent variables to the dependent variable Y. In literature, the coefficients $\beta_0, \beta_1, \ldots, \beta_{14}$ are typically estimated by maximum likelihood method. For the survey of binary logistic regression, we prefer the reader to [7].

For each combination of levels of factors, the MILP problem (30) is solved and the categorical variable Y is determined. Thus, we have a set of 1715 response variables Y_i corresponding to 1715 different sets of 4 input factors ($C_{i,\text{in}}$, $C_{i,\text{out}}$, M_i and ρ). Based on this collected data set, the logistic regression analysis was carried out by the Logistic procedure in SPSS software version 22 [5]. The result showed that

$$\ln\left[\frac{P(Y=1)}{P(Y=0)}\right] = 18.447 + 3.502 C_{i,\text{in}} - 50.245 C_{i,\text{out}} - 10.949 M_i + 3.053\rho$$
$$- 2.985 C_{i,\text{in}}^2 + 14.684 C_{i,\text{out}}^2 - 4.097 M_i^2 - 0.210\rho^2$$
$$+ 4.794 C_{i,\text{in}} \times C_{i,\text{out}} - 0.826 C_{i,\text{in}} \times M_i - 0.104 C_{i,\text{in}} \times \rho$$
$$+ 14.207 C_{i,\text{out}} \times M_i + 0.120 C_{i,\text{out}} \times \rho + 2.057 M_i \times \rho. \tag{36}$$

The model (36) is not selected because the terms of $C_{i,\text{in}}$, $C_{i,\text{in}} \times M_i$, $C_{i,\text{in}} \times \rho$, $C_{i,\text{out}} \times \rho$ are not statistically significant because there are large sig numbers, respectively 0.311, 0.573, 0.872, and 0.870. Now, we remove the terms of $C_{i,\text{in}}$, $C_{i,\text{in}} \times M_i$, $C_{i,\text{in}} \times \rho$, $C_{i,\text{out}} \times \rho$ from the model (35), then continue to run SPSS with the remaining terms, we get the following result

$$\ln\left[\frac{P(Y=1)}{P(Y=0)}\right] = 20.873 - 50.475 C_{i,\text{out}} - 11.947 M_i + 3.011\rho$$
$$- 2.104 C_{i,\text{in}}^2 + 14.695 C_{i,\text{out}}^2 - 4.054 M_i^2 - 0.205\rho^2$$
$$+ 5.332 C_{i,\text{in}} \times C_{i,\text{out}} + 14.193 C_{i,\text{out}} \times M_i + 2.081 M_i \times \rho \tag{37}$$

The model (37) was chosen because all terms are statistically significant at the standard error of regression of 5%. Thus, the model (37) is the optimal logistic regression model in this study.

After estimating the coefficients of the binary linear regression model as shown in model (37), there are several steps involved in assessing the appropriateness, adequacy and usefulness of the model (37). Therefore, to evaluate the logistic regression model, one must attend to (a) overall model evaluation,

(b) goodness-of-fit statistics, (c) validations of predicted probabilities, and (d) statistical tests of individual predictors.

Overall model evaluation. A logistic regression model is considered to exhibit an enhanced fit to the data when it shows advancement over the intercept-only model, which lacks our explanatory variables and is commonly referred to as the null model.

Table 2. Omnibus Tests of Model Coefficients.

		Chi-square	df	Sig.
Step 1	Step	1743.079	10	0.000
	Block	1743.079	10	0.000
	Model	1743.079	10	0.000

The Omnibus Tests of Model Coefficients as shown in Table 2 will be used to check whether model (37) (with explanatory variable included) is an improvement over the intercept-only model. Here the chi-square is highly significant (chi-square = 1743.079, df=10, $p < 0.000$) so the logistic regression model (37) is significantly better the intercept-only model.

Goodness-of-fit statistics. The prevalent evaluation of the comprehensive model fit in logistic regression involves the likelihood ratio test, essentially indicating the chi-square disparity between the model with just the intercept and the one encompassing the predictors. In the context of the Model Summary depicted in Table 3, the -2 Log Likelihood statistic registers a value of 485.903. This metric gauges the model's efficacy in forecasting decisions, signifying that a lower value signifies a more proficient model prediction.

Table 3. Model Summary.

Step	−2 Log likelihood	Cox & Snell R Square	Nagelkerke R Square
1	485.903	0.638	0.877

Most statistical software packages offer supplementary statistics akin to the coefficient of determination (R^2) in linear regression, though not an exact analogy [3]. Among these, the Cox & Snell R^2 and the Nagelkerke R^2 stand out. The Cox and Snell R^2 outcome, indicating that 63.8% of the variance in the dependent variable is accounted for by the predictor variable, is considered satisfactory. It's worth noting that a limitation of the Cox-Snell R^2 is its maximum value being less than 1.

In contrast, the Nagelkerke R^2 represents a modified rendition of the Cox & Snell R^2 and encompasses a full range from 0 to 1, which makes it generally more preferred. The R^2 statistic doesn't measure the model's goodness of fit, rather it assesses the utility of explanatory variables in predicting the response variable, serving as a measure of effect size. With a value of 0.877, it indicates that the model effectively predicts the economic viability of operating enterprises within EIPs.

Table 4. Goodness-of-Fit Statistics

Step	Chi-square	df	Sig
1	3.388	8	0.908

In Table 4, the Hosmer-Lemeshow test, an inferential measure of goodness-of-fit, is also provided. The Hosmer-Lemeshow test statistic of 3.388 yielded insignificance ($p = 0.908 > 0.05$), implying that the logistic regression model (37) exhibited a satisfactory fit to the dataset.

Table 5. Classification Table.

			Predicted		
			Economic feasibility		Percentage Correct
	Observed		0.0	1.0	
Step 1	Economic feasibility	0.0	1029	79	92.9
		1.0	57	550	90.6
	Overall Percentage				92.1

Validations of predicted probabilities. In Table 5, the classification table showcases the alignment between anticipated probabilities and real outcomes. The overall accuracy of predictions, at 92.1%, signifies an enhancement beyond the 50% baseline probability level. This classification table facilitates the assessment of sensitivity, specificity, false positive, and false negative rates. Sensitivity gauges the fraction of accurately identified events, while specificity quantifies the ratio of accurately identified nonevents. False positive denotes the proportion of observations wrongly classified as events among those classified as such. On the other hand, false negative quantifies the portion of observations inaccurately labeled as nonevents within the nonevent cate

Statistical tests of individual predictors. However the most important of all output is the Variables in the Equation as shown in Table 6. Within the confines of Table 6, crucial information is presented, encompassing regression coefficients (denoted as βs), the Wald statistic for assessing statistical significance, and the pivotal Odds Ratio (Exp (β)) pertaining to each of the input variables.

According to Table 6, the factors $(C_{i,\text{out}}, M_i, \rho)$, their interactions $(C_{i,\text{in}} \times C_{i,\text{out}}, C_{i,\text{out}} \times M_i, M_i \times \rho)$ and squared terms $(C^2_{i,\text{in}}, C^2_{i,\text{out}}, M^2_i, \rho^2)$ were significant and they influence the economic feasibility of operating enterprises in EIPs.

Table 6. Statistical Tests of Individual Predictors

		B	S.E.	Wald	df	Sig.	Exp(B)	95% C.I for EXP(B)	
								Lower	Upper
Step 1	C_{out}	−50.475	4.757	112.561	1	0.000	0.000	0.000	0.000
	M	−11.947	3.178	14.131	1	0.000	0.000	0.000	0.003
	ρ	3.011	0.769	15.352	1	0.000	20.315	4.504	91.624
	C^2_{in}	−2.104	0.613	11.767	1	0.001	0.122	0.037	0.406
	C^2_{out}	14.695	1.599	84.494	1	0.000	2408641.387	104960.835	55273506.03
	M^2	−4.054	1.156	12.297	1	0.000	0.017	0.002	0.167
	ρ^2	−0.205	0.048	18.520	1	0.000	0.815	0.742	0.894
	$C_{\text{in}} \times C_{\text{out}}$	5.332	1.234	18.683	1	0.000	206.886	18.436	2321.600
	$C_{\text{out}} \times M$	14.193	1.748	65.961	1	0.000	1458833.066	4745.852	44826871.12
	$M \times \rho$	2.081	0.693	9.011	1	0.003	8.015	2.059	31.193
	Constant	20.873	3.041	47.123	1	0.000	1161411149		

Moreover, from Table 6, a cause-and-effect relationship between a number of input factors and the economic feasibility of operating enterprises in EIPs is given by

$$\ln \left[\frac{P(Y=1)}{P(Y=0)} \right] = 20.873 - 50.475 C_{i,\text{out}} - 11.947 M_i + 3.011\rho$$

$$- 2.104 C^2_{i,\text{in}} + 14.695 C^2_{i,\text{out}} - 4.054 M^2_i - 0.205\rho^2$$

$$+ 5.332 C_{i,\text{in}} \times C_{i,\text{out}} + 14.193 C_{i,\text{out}} \times M_i + 2.081 M_i \times \rho \quad (38)$$

As observed from (38), the effect of each input factor ($C_{i,\text{in}}$, $C_{i,\text{out}}$, M_i and ρ respectively) on the economic feasibility of operating enterprises in EIPs depends on the value(s) of one or more other input factors.

A very powerful application of binary logistic regression is predictability. From the regression equation (38), we have the probability function to evaluate the economic feasibility of operating enterprises in EIPs as follows:

$$P(Y=1) = \frac{e^{20.873-50.475C_{i,\text{out}}-11.947M_i+3.011\rho-2.104C^2_{i,\text{in}}+14.695C^2_{i,\text{out}}-4.054M^2_i-0.205\rho^2+5.332C_{i,\text{in}}\times C_{i,\text{out}}+14.193C_{i,\text{out}}\times M_i+2.081M_i\times\rho}}{1+e^{20.873-50.475C_{i,\text{out}}-11.947M_i+3.011\rho-2.104C^2_{i,\text{in}}+14.695C^2_{i,\text{out}}-4.054M^2_i-0.205\rho^2+5.332C_{i,\text{in}}\times C_{i,\text{out}}+14.193C_{i,\text{out}}\times M_i+2.081M_i\times\rho}}.$$

To demonstrate how the economic feasibility of enterprises in EIPs is sensitive when changing the levels of input parameters $(C_{i,\text{in}}, C_{i,\text{out}}, M_i, \rho)$, we consider the following two scenarios:

– First, the levels of $C_{i,\text{in}}$, $C_{i,\text{out}}$, M_i, ρ are 0.5, 0.5, 0.5, 12.4, respectively. Then the probability of the economic feasibility of enterprises in EIPs for this scenario is given by

$$P(Y = 1) = 0.99$$

– Second, the levels of $C_{i,\text{in}}$, $C_{i,\text{out}}$, M_i, ρ are 0.5, 0.5, 0.5, 0.2, respectively. Then the probability of the economic feasibility of enterprises in EIPs for this scenario is given by

$$P(Y = 1) = 0.07$$

As we can observe, the economic feasibility of enterprises in EIPs is very sensitive when changing the levels of input parameters. More precisely, when the levels of $C_{i,\text{in}}$, $C_{i,\text{out}}$, M_i, ρ are 0.5, 0.5, 0.5, 12.4 then the probability of the economic feasibility of enterprises in EIPs is 0.99. However, when the levels of $C_{i,\text{in}}$, $C_{i,\text{out}}$, M_i, ρ are 0.5, 0.5, 0.5, 0.2 then the probability of the economic feasibility of enterprises in EIPs is 0.07.

4.2 Multiple Linear Regression Model

In this part, we present a multiple linear regression model to predict the value of overall satisfaction L_{tot} based on the variables $C_{i,\text{in}}$, $C_{i,\text{out}}$, M_i, and ρ. The data consists of only 607 simulations (economically feasible configurations) built with the same 4 variables, their interactions, and the square terms.

To ensure the credibility and validity of our analysis when performing a multiple linear regression, it is imperative to assess our data against various assumptions. These prerequisites encompass:

1. The dependent variable must be measured on a continuous scale.
2. There should be a presence of two or more independent variables, which could either be continuous or categorical in nature.
3. The residuals' values need to exhibit independence.
4. The connection between the dependent and independent variables ought to be linear.
5. The residuals' variance should remain constant.
6. The data should be devoid of multicollinearity issues.
7. The model should not be unduly influenced by outlier cases.
8. The residuals, or errors, should approximate a normal distribution.

Considering none of the eight previously mentioned assumptions were violated, multiple regression outputs for the given data were generated through the following steps performed in SPSS statistical software.

Determining how well the model fits. The first table of interest is the *model summary* (Table 7). Within this table, essential metrics such as R, R^2, and adjusted R^2 are presented, aiding in the assessment of the regression model's goodness of fit to the data.

Table 7. Model Summary

Model	R	R Square	Adjusted R Square	Std. Error of the Estimate	Durbin Watson
1	0.905	0.819	0.817	0.5582011102	1.518

In the "R" column, you will find the R value, denoting the *multiple correlation coefficient* between the actual and projected values of the dependent variable. R can be considered one gauge of how accurately the dependent variable, in this instance, *overall satisfaction*, is predicted. A value of $R = 0.905$ suggests a commendable level of prediction.

The "R Square" column represents the value of R^2, the *coefficient of determination*. R Square is the proportion of variance in the dependent variable (overall satisfaction) that can be explained by the independent variables ($C_{i,\text{in}}, C_{i,\text{out}}, M_i, \rho$). This value indicates that 81.9% of the variance in overall satisfaction can be predicted from the variables $C_{i,\text{in}}, C_{i,\text{out}}, M_i$, and ρ. It also means that 18.1% of the variation is caused by factors other than the predictors included in this model.

A greater R^2 value indicates a more optimal fit. Nonetheless, a higher R^2 doesn't necessarily signify a robust fit or a superior regression model, as including additional variables consistently elevates the R^2 value, leading to less effective predictions. To address this, the adjusted R^2 is introduced, which isn't swayed by mere variable additions and provides a more reliable gauge.

Furthermore, a notable disparity between the R-squared and Adjusted R Square values implies a subpar model fit. In the current instance, the value stands at 0.817, not significantly distant from 0.819, signifying a reasonably good fit.

Statistical significance of the model. The F-ratio within ANOVA evaluates the suitability of the entire regression model concerning the dataset. As illustrated in Table 8, the independent variables exhibit a statistically significant predictive influence on the dependent variable, with $F(4, 602) = 679.108$, $p < 0.0005$ (indicating a strong alignment between the regression model and the data).

Table 8. ANOVA

Model		Sum of Squares	df	Mean Square	F	Sig.
1	Regression	846.408	4	211.602	679.108	0.000
	Residual	187.576	602	0.312		
	Total	1033.985	606			

Estimated model coefficients. The "B" column displays the coefficients corresponding to the regression equation, used to predict the dependent variable based on the independent variables (Table 9).

Table 9. Coefficients

Model		Unstandardized Coefficients		Standardized Coefficients	t	Sig.	95% C.I for B		Collinearity Statistics	
		B	Std. Error	Beta			Lower Bound	Upper Bound	Tolerance	VIF
1	Constant	1.433	0.134		10.708	0.000	1.170	1.695		
	C_{in}	0.524	0.080	0.115	6.593	0.000	0.368	0.681	0.995	1.005
	C_{out}	−0.449	0.071	−0.112	−6.356	0.000	−0.588	−0.310	0.972	1.028
	M	−0.659	0.081	−0.143	−8.155	0.000	−0.818	−0.501	0.980	1.020
	ρ	0.246	0.005	0.892	51.142	0.000	0.237	0.256	0.992	1.008

The "Sig." column contains the p-values for each of the independent variables $(C_{i,\text{in}}, C_{i,\text{out}}, M_i, \rho)$. A p-value < 0.05, provides evidence that the coefficient is different to 0. Thus $C_{i,\text{in}}, C_{i,\text{out}}, M_i$, and ρ are all significant predictors of *overall satisfaction*.

Therefore, the general form of the equation to predict *overall satisfaction* from $C_{i,\text{in}}, C_{i,\text{out}}, M_i, \rho$ is:

$$L_{tot} = 1.433 + 0.524C_{i,\text{in}} - 0.449C_{i,\text{out}} - 0.659M_i + 0.246\rho \qquad (39)$$

These regression coefficients tell us about the relationship between the independent variables $(C_{i,\text{in}}, C_{i,\text{out}}, M_i, \rho)$ and the dependent variable (overall satisfaction L_{tot}). These regression coefficients provide the expected change in the dependent variable for a one-unit increase in the independent variable. The coefficient for $C_{i,\text{in}}$ is 0.524. So, for every unit increase in $C_{i,\text{in}}$, there is 0.524 unit increase in overall satisfaction, holding all other variables constant. But each unit increase in $C_{i,\text{out}}$ (resp. M_i) causes reduction (the negative sign of the coefficient) in overall satisfaction by 0.449 (resp. 0.659) unit. the coefficient for ρ is 0.246. Hence, for every unit increase in ρ we expect a 0.246 unit increase in overall satisfaction, holding all other variables constant. Thus, we can use equation (39) to find the estimated *overall satisfaction*, based on the level of $C_{i,\text{in}}$, $C_{i,\text{out}}, M_i$, and ρ.

5   Conclusions and Future Work

This study evaluated the influence of different input parameters on the economic feasibility and overall satisfaction of operating enterprises in EIPs. The proposed method integrated the design of experiments (DoE) method and the SLMF game model to identify and quantify the impact of different parameters on the economic feasibility and overall satisfaction of operating enterprises in EIPs. As the results show the most critical parameters in a potential EIP environment are those related to process constraints and those related to the inherent production of each enterprise. Moreover, the economic feasibility of enterprises operating in eco-industrial parks is quite sensitive to changing input parameters, which can produce a variety of scenarios that can be a potential reason to reject EIP cooperation between different enterprises. However, by combining the DoE method and the SLMF model, we can adjust the input parameters so that enterprises operating in the eco-industrial park become economically feasible. Thus, it's an advantage in the design of EIPs.

For future research, the results of this study can be extended to the assessment of the influence of input parameters on the economic feasibility and overall satisfaction of other resource exchanges in the eco-industrial park, such as the exchange of steam, electricity, energy, ...

Acknowledgments. This research is funded by Nguyen Tat Thanh University, Ho Chi Minh city, Vietnam.

References

1. Aussel, D., Van Cao, K., Salas, D.: Optimal design of exchange water networks with control inputs in eco-industrial parks. Energy Econ. **120**, 106480 (2023). https://doi.org/10.1016/j.eneco.2022.106480, https://www.sciencedirect.com/science/article/pii/S0140988322006090
2. Baumrucker, B.T., Renfro, J., Biegler, L.: MPEC problem formulations and solution strategies with chemical engineering applications. Comput. Chem. Eng. **32**(12), 2903–2913 (2008)
3. Bewick, V., Cheek, L., Ball, J.: Statistics review 7: Correlation and regression. Critical Care (London, England) **7**, 451–459 (2004). https://doi.org/10.1186/cc2401
4. Boix, M., Montastruc, L., Azzaro-Pantel, C., Domenech, S.: Optimization methods applied to the design of eco-industrial parks: a literature review. J. Clean. Prod. **87**, 303–317 (2015)
5. Field, A.: Discovering Statistics Using IBM SPSS Statistics. SAGE Publications (2018). https://books.google.com.vn/books?id=JIrutAEACAAJ
6. Fisher, R.: The Design of Experiments, 9th edn. MacMillan, New York (1971)
7. Hosmer, D., Lemeshow, S., Sturdivant, R.: Applied Logistic Regression. Wiley Series in Probability and Statistics, Wiley (2013). https://books.google.com.vn/books?id=64JYAwAAQBAJ
8. Jankovic, A., Chaudhary, G., Goia, F.: Designing the design of experiments (doe) - an investigation on the influence of different factorial designs on the characterization of complex systems. Energy Build. **250**, 111298 (2021). https://doi.org/10.1016/j.enbuild.2021.111298, https://www.sciencedirect.com/science/article/pii/S037877882100582X
9. Laoun, B., Kasat, H.A., Ahmad, R., Kannan, A.M.: Gas diffusion layer development using design of experiments for the optimization of a proton exchange membrane fuel cell performance. Energy **151**, 689–695 (2018). https://doi.org/10.1016/j.energy.2018.03.096, https://www.sciencedirect.com/science/article/pii/S036054421830505X
10. Lowe, E.A.: Creating by-product resource exchanges: Strategies for eco-industrial parks. J. Clean. Prod. **5**(1), 57–65 (1997)
11. Luo, Z.Q., Pang, J.S., Ralph, D.: Mathematical Programs with Equilibrium Constraints. Cambridge University Press, Cambridge (1996)
12. Montgomery, D.: Design and Analysis of Experiments. Design and Analysis of Experiments. John Wiley & Sons, Hoboken (2008). https://books.google.de/books?id=kMMJAm5bD34C
13. Olesen, S., Polley, G.: Dealing with plant geography and piping constraints in water network design. Process Saf. Environ. Prot. **74**(4), 273–276 (1996). https://doi.org/10.1205/095758296528626

14. Ramos, M., Boix, M., Aussel, D., Montastruc, L., Domenech, S.: Water integration in eco-industrial parks using a multi-leader-follower approach. Comput. Chem. Eng. **87**, 190–207 (2016)
15. Salas, D., Van Cao, K., Aussel, D., Montastruc, L.: Optimal design of exchange networks with blind inputs and its application to eco-industrial parks. Comput. Chem. Eng. **143**, 107053 (2020)
16. Sieira, P., Mendes, P., Castro, A., Pradelle, F.: Impact of spinning conditions on the diameter and tensile properties of mesophase petroleum pitch carbon fibers using design of experiments. Mater. Lett. **285**, 129110 (2021). https://doi.org/10.1016/j.matlet.2020.129110, https://www.sciencedirect.com/science/article/pii/S0167577X20318176
17. Suchana, S., Passeport, E.: Optimization of a solid-phase microextraction technique for chloro- and nitro- substituted aromatic compounds using design of experiments. J. Chromatogr. A **1621**, 461083 (2020). https://doi.org/10.1016/j.chroma.2020.461083, https://www.sciencedirect.com/science/article/pii/S0021967320303046
18. Tseveendorj, I.: Mathematical programs with equilibrium constraints: a brief survey of methods and optimality conditions. In: Chinchuluun, A., Pardalos, P., Enkhbat, R., Pistikopoulos, E. (eds.) Optimization, Simulation, and Control. Springer Optimization and its Applications, vol. 76, pp. 49–61. Springer, New York (2013). https://doi.org/10.1007/978-1-4614-5131-0_4
19. Zaibi, M., Cherif, H., Champenois, G., Sareni, B., Roboam, X., Belhadj, J.: Sizing methodology based on design of experiments for freshwater and electricity production from multi-source renewable energy systems. Desalination **446**, 94–103 (2018). https://doi.org/10.1016/j.desal.2018.08.008, https://www.sciencedirect.com/science/article/pii/S0011916418305812

Comparing LSTM Models for Stock Market Prediction: A Case Study with Apple's Historical Prices

Ha Minh Tan, Le Gia Minh, Tran Cao Minh, Tran Thi Be Quyen, and Kien Cao-Van[✉]

Faculty of Information Technology, Nguyen Tat Thanh University, Ho Chi Minh City, Vietnam
cvkien@ntt.edu.vn

Abstract. Stock market prediction holds significant importance in the world of finance, captivating the attention of both investors and financial researchers. The integration of artificial intelligence and advancements in computational power has led to substantial improvements in predicting stock prices, surpassing the effectiveness of traditional programmed prediction methods. In this paper, we explore three distinct and innovative methods for stock price prediction: Long Short-Term Memory (LSTM), LSTM combined with Simple Moving Average (LSTM-SMA), and LSTM combined with Exponential Moving Average (LSTM-EMA). Our analysis is conducted using a comprehensive historical dataset of Apple's stock prices, and the performance of each model is rigorously evaluated using critical metrics, including Mean Absolute Percentage Error (MAPE), Mean Absolute Error (MAE), Root Mean Square Error (RMSE), and R2 score. Additionally, the training time for each model is taken into account. The results show that all three models LSTM, LSTM-SMA, and LSTM-EMA give good prediction results for Apple's stock price, in which the LSTM model gives the best prediction results for the 21-day cluster. However, in terms of computational time, the LSTM-SMA model and LSTM-EMA model are more efficient than the LSTM model. These findings highlight the potential of integrating advanced techniques to achieve more accurate and efficient stock price predictions.

Keywords: Long Short-Term Memory · Simple Moving Average · Exponential Moving Average · Neural Network · Prediction · Stock Price

1 Introduction

Stock prediction is a significant challenge in the field of finance. Investors and risk managers alike desire the ability to accurately forecast the trends and fluctuations of stock prices in order to make intelligent and effective investment decisions. In the digital age, the development of technology has generated a vast amount of stock market data and advanced analytical tools, thereby creating

P. Cong Vinh and H. Mahfooz Ul Haque (Eds.): ICTCC 2023, LNICST 586, pp. 173–185, 2024.
https://doi.org/10.1007/978-3-031-59462-5_12

opportunities to apply database-driven prediction methods to provide forecasts for the stock market.

In recent years, many researchers have explored this topic from various perspectives. They have employed different approaches such as statistical methods [3,7,9,15], supervised learning methods, with Long Short-Term Memory (LSTM) being a typical example [4,8,14,16], and unsupervised learning [13]. Statistical methods require several factors to achieve good results, such as data reliability and adherence to standards and assumptions. On the other hand, neural networks, especially LSTM, have the capability to learn complex patterns and process time series data. LSTM is able to store long-term information and capture relationships in past data, enabling it to learn and predict trends, fluctuations, and complex patterns in stock market time series data.

When trained on historical stock market data, neural networks have the ability to outperform traditional methods such as simple statistical models in terms of prediction. Through continuous learning and updating during the training process, neural networks can enhance prediction capabilities and provide more accurate results. However, the effectiveness of both statistical methods and neural networks in stock market prediction can be influenced by various factors, including sample size, data quality, and training methods.

We conducted experiments on a historical dataset of Apple Inc. stock obtained from the website https://finance.yahoo.com/, spanning from January 2, 2019, to June 29, 2023, comprising 1,131 data points. This dataset provides detailed information on the price fluctuations of Apple Inc. stock over the past four years, enabling investors and financial analysts to analyze trends and forecast prices for future periods.

In this paper, we focus on researching and comparing the performance of three stock prediction methods: LSTM, LSTM combined with SMA technique, and LSTM combined with EMA technique. Our objective is to evaluate and compare the predictive capabilities of these methods, while determining which method is the most effective in predicting stock prices.

The remainder of the article is structured as follows: Sect. 2 describes the methodology of the applied techniques. Section 3 presents the experimental evaluation of the methods' results, and Sect. 4 concludes the paper.

2   Methodology

2.1   Description of Data

The historical stock price data for Apple was downloaded from the website https://finance.yahoo.com/ from January 02, 2019, to June 29, 2023, comprising 1,131 rows of data. The dataset contains information such as Date, Open, High, Low, Close, Adj Close, and Volume, which are used for analyzing and tracking stock prices and other assets in the financial market. Some of the stocks shown in Table 1. Moreover, the data has been checked and does not contain any empty, null, or NaN values.

Table 1. Dataset

Date	Open	High	Low	Close	Adj Close	Volume
02/01/2019	38.72	39.71	38.56	39.48	37.99	148,158,800
03/01/2019	35.99	36.43	35.50	35.55	34.21	365,248,800
...	...	...	...	...	...	...
28/06/2023	187.93	189.90	187.60	189.25	189.25	51,216,800
29/06/2023	189.08	190.07	188.94	189.59	189.59	46,347,300

In the world of trading, the final trading price signifies the latest value at which a stock is exchanged during regular trading hours. This closing price serves as a pivotal reference point for investors to monitor the stock's performance over an extended period. The objective of this study is to forecast the closing price of Apple's stock market. Figure 1 illustrates the closing price of Apple's stock market spanning from January 02, 2019, to June 29, 2023.

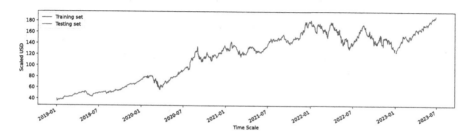

Fig. 1. Closing price of the Apple stock market.

A set of six additional variables has been developed to enhance the accuracy of predicting stock closing prices, as implemented in the research [17]. These newly introduced variables were utilized in the training process of the model. Here are the details of these fresh variables:

- Stock High minus Low price (H-L)
- Stock Close minus Open price (O-C)
- Stock price's seven days' moving average (7 DAYS MA)
- Stock price's fourteen days' moving average (14 DAYS MA)
- Stock price's twenty one days' moving average (21 DAYS MA)
- Stock price's standard deviation for the past seven days (7 DAYS STD DEV)

2.2   Min-max Scaling

Min-max scaling is a widely recognized technique used for normalization. It involves mapping variables to a specific range, typically [0, 1], where the minimum and maximum values of a variable are set to 0 and 1, respectively. The primary objective is to ensure that variables are measured on a consistent scale, enabling each variable to contribute proportionally during model fitting. This normalization method helps align the scales of different variables, facilitating fair comparisons and accurate analysis. The mathematical formula is,

$$x_{scale} = \frac{x - x_{min}}{x_{max} - x_{min}} \tag{1}$$

where x_{scale} and x are scaled and the original input respectively. Similarly, x_{max} and x_{min} are the maximum and minimum value of each feature, respectively.

2.3 Moving Average

Moving Average (MA) is an essential technique for analyzing time series data as it effectively smooths the input data by averaging values over a specified time period, thereby revealing their underlying price trend. Subsequently, a new time series is generated based on these average values. There are several approaches to calculating MA, with the two most prevalent methods being the Simple Moving Average (SMA) and the Exponential Moving Average (EMA), both of which have been extensively applied [2,5] in this field.

SMA is a method to predict the value of the next data point based on the mean of the previous "n" data points. It involves calculating the average of the past "n" data points, denoted as P_1 to P_n, and using this average as the predicted value for the next data point. Namely,

$$SMA = \frac{P_1 + P_2 + \cdots + P_n}{n}. \tag{2}$$

The choice of "n" significantly impacts the precision of the prediction. A higher "n" means considering a more extended period in the past to compute the present value. For instance, with $n = 2$, the average of the past two days' stock prices is taken, while with $n = 50$, fifty days' worth of stock prices are considered. Naturally, using more data points provides more information about the stock's trends, leading to better predictions. However, using an excessively large "n" can also destabilize the model, as it smoothes out finer fluctuations, and looking too far back in time, such as the past 300 days, may not be optimal for prediction accuracy.

On the other hand, EMA is a method for calculating a moving average by giving greater weight to recent values rather than assigning equal weights to the entire data.

$$EMA = k * P_t + (1 - k) * EMA_{(t-1)}, \tag{3}$$

where P_t represents the price at time t, and k denotes the weight assigned to that particular data point. $EMA_{(t-1)}$ corresponds to the value computed from the previous $t-1$ data points. The number of time points in the EMA is denoted by N, and the weighting factor is calculated as $k = 2/(N + 1)$.

The EMA has an edge over the SMA as it exhibits greater responsiveness to price fluctuations. This characteristic renders it particularly valuable for short-term trading strategies.

2.4 Long Short Term Memory

The Recurrent Neural Network (RNN) was initially designed to handle sequential or time-related data effectively. However, when propagated through multiple time steps, the gradient may experience either an exponential decrease or a significant increase. The issue of diminishing gradients can result in ineffective weight updates and the loss of distant information, commonly referred to as vanishing gradients [10].

In 1997, Hochreiter and Schmidhuber introduced the LSTM model [11], a significant advancement in the realm of RNNs, specifically designed to address challenges related to vanishing gradients and long-term dependencies. While an RNN model comprises a sequence of recurrent neural network modules, the standard RNN models often employ a simple structure, typically using a *tanh* layer as the repeating module. In contrast, LSTM models also follow a sequential structure akin to RNNs but with slightly different configurations for the repeating modules. As shown in Fig. 2, LSTM incorporates four key components (cell, forget gate, input gate, output gate) that interact in a specialized manner to enhance its capabilities.

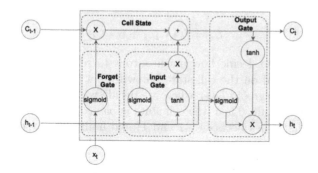

Fig. 2. Architecture of a cell Long Short-Term Memory

The sequence of steps in the LSTM model is as follows:

- The first step in LSTM determines which information is allowed to pass through the cell state. It is controlled by a sigmoid function in a layer called the forget gate. It takes inputs h_{t-1} and x_t and outputs a value between 0 and 1 for each value in the cell state C_{t-1}. A value of 1 indicates "keep all information", and 0 indicates "discard all of it".

$$f_t = \sigma \left(W_f \cdot [h_{t-1}, x_t] + b_f \right), \tag{4}$$

where σ denotes the sigmoid function, W_f denotes the weight of forget gate, b_f denotes the bias of forget gate, x_t is input at time t, and h_{t-1} is the output of the hidden layer at time $t-1$.

- Next, we decide what information to store in the cell state. This step consists of two parts. The first part is a hidden layer of the sigmoid function called the input gate layer, which decides what values to update. Then, a *tanh* function generates a vector of a new state value C_t that can be added to the cell state. The results of these two layers are combined to form an update for the cell state.

$$i_t = \sigma\left(W_i \cdot [h_{t-1}, x_t] + b_i\right) \tag{5}$$

$$\tilde{C}_t = \tanh\left(W_C \cdot [h_{t-1}, x_t] + b_C\right) \tag{6}$$

where σ denotes the sigmoid function, W_f denotes the weight of forget gate, b_i denotes the bias of input gate, x_t is input at time t, h_{t-1} is the output of the hidden layer at time $t-1$, W_c is the weight of cell, and b_c is the bias of cell.

- At this point, we update the old cell state C_{t-1} to a new state C_t, which has been decided in the previous steps, and in this step, we simply carry out that decision.
- We multiply the old cell state by f_t, which corresponds to forgetting the parts that we decided to forget early on. The candidate element $i_t * \tilde{C}_t$ is a newly computed value corresponding to how much should be added to each cell state value.

$$C_t = f_t * C_{t-1} + i_t * \tilde{C}_t. \tag{7}$$

- Finally, we need to decide how much output to return. The output at this stage will be based on the cell state but will be a filtered version. First, we run it through a sigmoid layer where we decide which parts of the cell state will be in the output. Then, the cell state is passed through a tanh function (to squash the values between -1 and 1) and multiplied by the output of a sigmoid gate, thus outputting only the parts we decided.

$$o_t = \sigma\left(W_o\left[h_{t-1}, x_t\right] + b_o\right) \tag{8}$$

$$h_t = o_t * \tanh\left(C_t\right), \tag{9}$$

where σ denotes the sigmoid function, W_o denotes the weight of output gate, and b_o denotes the bias of output gate.

Based on its operating mechanism, LSTM is considered superior to RNN. LSTM can access information from a larger set of data, making it highly suitable for long-term time series forecasting. The LSTM model has found applications in various fields due to its ability to capture long-term dependencies in sequential data. Some notable applications of LSTM include: Time Series Forecasting [1], Speech Recognition [6], Natural Language Processing [12], etc.

3   Experimental Results

During the model construction phase, we will establish three distinct models, each corresponding to one of the following methods: LSTM, LSTM combined with SMA, and LSTM combined with EMA. More precisely, the LSTM model will be trained using data organized into clusters of 7-day, 14-day, and 21-day intervals. For the LSTM with the SMA method, we will first apply a simple moving average to smooth the data within 7-day, 14-day, and 21-day clusters before feeding it into the LSTM model. On the other hand, the LSTM with EMA approach will involve smoothing the data within 7-day, 14-day, and 21-day clusters using exponential moving averages before inputting it into the LSTM model. These models will exhibit diverse performances and outcomes when applied. Through careful observation and evaluation, we aim to identify the optimal model for predicting the closing price of Apple's stock.

Parameter Configuration: The LSTM network will have a consistent setup across all three methods. The input layer will contain 128 units, with "return_sequences" set to True and the "input_shape" taking values from the training set. A Dropout rate of 0.2 will be applied. Intermediate layers 2, 3, and 4 will share the same configuration, each with 128 units and a Dropout rate of 0.2. The output layer of the LSTM will be a fully connected layer (Dense), resulting in a model size of 461,441 parameters.

Data Splitting: The training set will encompass closing price data from January 02, 2019, to December 30, 2022, while the test set will cover data from January 03, 2023, to June 29, 2023. To implement the early stopping method, Early Stopping callbacks with "monitor" set to 'loss' and a "patience" of 30 will be used. Additionally, the validation set will consist of 10% of the data for all methods.

The hardware setup for the project comprises a Ryzen 3 2200G processor, a 256 GB SSD, 16 GB RAM, and an RX570 graphics card. For coding and experimentation, we utilize the Google Colab v2.15.0 platform along with the Python programming language. Additionally, we incorporate essential libraries such as TensorFlow v2.6.0, Numpy v1.22.2, and Scikit-learn v1.0.2 to facilitate the construction and experimentation processes.

3.1   Evaluation Criteria

To assess the model's performance, we will use the following metrics: MAPE (Mean Absolute Percentage Error), MAE (Mean Absolute Error), RMSE (Root Mean Square Error), and R2 score. These metrics are commonly used in forecasting and statistics to evaluate the accuracy of prediction models. They measure the level of deviation between predicted values and actual values. With n representing the number of samples in the dataset, Y_t denoting the actual value of the t-th sample, and $\widehat{Y_t}$ representing the predicted value of sample t.

- **MAPE**, which measures prediction accuracy, calculates the ratio of the sum of absolute errors of predictions to the sum of the actual values. A lower MAPE value indicates a more accurate model assessment.

$$MAPE = \frac{1}{n} \sum_{t=1}^{n} \left| \frac{Y_t - \widehat{Y}_t}{Y_t} \right| \tag{10}$$

- **MAE** quantifies the average deviation between predicted values and actual values, using absolute values for computation. A lower MAE value signifies a better model accuracy.

$$MAE = \frac{1}{n} \sum_{t=1}^{n} \left| Y_t - \widehat{Y}_t \right| \tag{11}$$

- **RMSE** assesses the accuracy of a prediction model in comparison to real data. A lower RMSE value indicates a higher level of model accuracy.

$$RMSE = \sqrt{\frac{1}{n} \sum_{t=1}^{n} \left(Y_t - \widehat{Y}_t \right)^2} \tag{12}$$

- **R2 score** score evaluates how well a model fits the data. It is computed by taking the sum of the squares of the differences between the predicted and actual values, dividing it by the sum of the squares of the differences between the mean of the actual values and the actual values, and subtracting this result from 1. A higher R2 score indicates a better fit of the model to the data, serving as a metric for model accuracy assessment.

$$R2 = 1 - \frac{\sum_{t=1}^{n} \left(Y_t - \widehat{Y}_t \right)^2}{\sum_{t=1}^{n} \left(Y_t - \bar{Y} \right)^2}. \tag{13}$$

3.2   Analysis of Results

In this study, we conducted stock price predictions of Apple using three different methods: LSTM, LSTM combined with the SMA technique, and LSTM combined with the EMA technique. Specifically, we used data clusters of 7 days, 14 days, and 21 days to input into the prediction models and evaluated the results using several performance evaluation metrics such as MAPE, MAE, RMSE, and R2.

Subsequently, we compared the experimental results to gain a better understanding of the performance of each method. Additionally, testing with different data clusters allowed us to identify the most suitable data cluster to achieve the highest accuracy. The general results of the three methods can be found in Table 2.

Table 2. Experimental Results for Stock Price Prediction of Apple using Different Methods and Data Clusters.

Method	Cluster	Value				Epochs	Training time
		MAPE	MAE	RMSE	R2		(seconds)
LSTM	**7-days**	0.0237	3.8823	4.4520	0.9167	236	529.1066
	14-days	0.0171	2.7637	3.3151	0.9550	256	977.6710
	21-days	0.0140	2.2685	2.7940	0.9672	277	1637.5458
LSTM-SMA	**7-days**	0.0170	2.8032	3.5610	0.9487	206	150.6537
	14-days	0.0156	2.5766	3.3633	0.9546	258	192.8566
	21-days	0.0169	2.7848	3.6121	0.9480	205	142.0111
LSTM-EMA	**7-days**	0.0188	3.1369	4.0096	0.9357	149	114.1174
	14-days	0.0170	2.8194	3.6231	0.9463	166	107.8286
	21-days	0.0162	2.6887	3.5321	0.9504	182	130.1446

Below is a comment on the prediction results of three methods LSTM, LSTM combined with SMA and LSTM combined with EMA based on evaluation indicators and training time:

Prediction Method Using the LSTM Model: The best results are achieved when using a data cluster of 21 days, with MAPE = 0.0140, MAE = 2.2685, RMSE = 2.7940, R2 = 0.9672. This indicates that the LSTM model has the ability to accurately predict with a large data cluster.

Training time increases with the data cluster, ranging from 529 s for a 7-day cluster to 1637 s for a 21-day cluster. The LSTM model requires longer training time when using larger data clusters (Figs. 3 and 4).

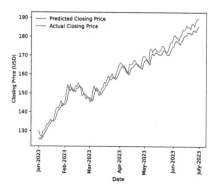

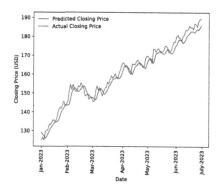

Fig. 3. Closing price Apple's stock is predicted by pure LSTM in 7-day clusters

Fig. 4. Closing price Apple's stock is predicted by pure LSTM in 14-day clusters

Prediction Method Using LSTM Combined with SMA Technique: The results show that this model performs better than the pure LSTM method with smaller data clusters (Figs. 5, 6, 7 and 8).

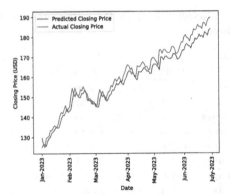

Fig. 5. Closing price Apple's stock is predicted by pure LSTM in 21-day clusters

The best results are achieved when using a data cluster of 14 days, with MAPE = 0.0156, MAE = 2.5766, RMSE = 3.3633, R2 = 0.9546.

The training time of the model with SMA technique is significantly faster compared to the pure LSTM model, ranging from 142 s (for a 21-day cluster) to 192 s (for a 14-day cluster).

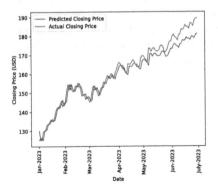

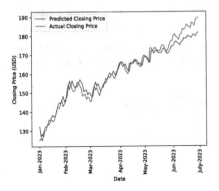

Fig. 6. Closing price Apple's stock is predicted by LSTM with SMA in 7-day clusters

Fig. 7. Closing price Apple's stock is predicted by LSTM with SMA in 14-day clusters

Prediction Method Using LSTM Combined with EMA Technique: The results also show improvements compared to the LSTM method with smaller data clusters (Figs. 9, 10 and 11).

The best results are obtained when using a data cluster of 21 days, with MAPE = 0.0162, MAE = 2.6887, RMSE = 3.5321, R2 = 0.9504.

Fig. 8. Closing price Apple's stock is predicted by LSTM with SMA in 21-day clusters

The LSTM model combined with EMA technique is also faster than the pure LSTM model, with training times ranging from about 107 s (for a 14-day cluster) to 130 s (for a 21-day cluster).

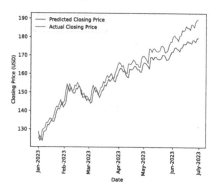

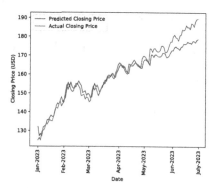

Fig. 9. Closing price Apple's stock is predicted by LSTM with EMA in 7-day clusters

Fig. 10. Closing price Apple's stock is predicted by LSTM with EMA in 14-day clusters

In summary, the findings indicate that all three models, namely LSTM, LSTM-SMA, and LSTM-EMA, yield favorable predictions for Apple's stock price. Among them, the LSTM model stands out with the most accurate predictions within the 21-day cluster. Nevertheless, when considering computational time, both the LSTM-SMA and LSTM-EMA models outperform the LSTM model. Nonetheless, the choice of suitable techniques and data clusters for achieving precise predictions still hinges on the unique objectives and requirements of the model.

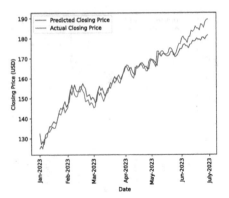

Fig. 11. Closing price Apple's stock is predicted by LSTM with EMA in 21-day clusters

4   Conclusions and Future Work

In this study, we have demonstrated the feasibility and performance of applying the data smoothing methods, SMA and EMA, to the Apple Stock dataset. Our results show promising values in terms of accuracy, time, training speed, and data processing when using SMA and EMA instead of directly inputting data into the LSTM model. For future research, we aim to enhance the capability of the LSTM with the EMA method to achieve even higher performance and potentially surpass the traditional LSTM's capabilities. Additionally, we will apply this approach to a broader range of datasets to provide more comprehensive and rigorous evaluations.

Acknowledgments. This research is funded by Nguyen Tat Thanh University, Ho Chi Minh city, Vietnam.

References

1. AL-Alimi, D., et al.: Tlia: time-series forecasting model using long short-term memory integrated with artificial neural networks for volatile energy markets. Appl. Energy **343**, 121230 (2023). https://doi.org/10.1016/j.apenergy.2023.121230
2. Altarawneh, G.A., Hassanat, A.B., Tarawneh, A.S., Abadleh, A., Alrashidi, M., Alghamdi, M.: Stock price forecasting for Jordan insurance companies amid the Covid-19 pandemic utilizing off-the-shelf technical analysis methods. Economies **10**(2), 43 (2022)
3. Ariyo, A.A., Adewumi, A.O., Ayo, C.K.: Stock price prediction using the Arima model. In: 2014 UKSim-AMSS 16th International Conference on Computer Modelling and Simulation, pp. 106–112. IEEE (2014)
4. Bhandari, H.N., Rimal, B., Pokhrel, N.R., Rimal, R., Dahal, K.R., Khatri, R.K.: Predicting stock market index using LSTM. Mach. Learn. App. **9**, 100320 (2022)
5. Biswas, M., Shome, A., Islam, M.A., Nova, A.J., Ahmed, S.: Predicting stock market price: a logical strategy using deep learning. In: 2021 IEEE 11th IEEE Symposium on Computer Applications & Industrial Electronics (ISCAIE), pp. 218–223 (2021). https://doi.org/10.1109/ISCAIE51753.2021.9431817

6. Chien, J.T., Misbullah, A.: Deep long short-term memory networks for speech recognition. In: 2016 10th International Symposium on Chinese Spoken Language Processing (ISCSLP), pp. 1–5 (2016). https://doi.org/10.1109/ISCSLP.2016.7918375

7. Fattah, J., Ezzine, L., Aman, Z., El Moussami, H., Lachhab, A.: Forecasting of demand using Arima model. Int. J. Eng. Bus. Manage. **10**, 1847979018808673 (2018)

8. Gülmez, B.: Stock price prediction with optimized deep LSTM network with artificial rabbits optimization algorithm. Expert Syst. Appl. **227**, 120346 (2023)

9. Haining, R.: The moving average model for spatial interaction. Trans. Inst. Br. Geograph. **3**, 202–225 (1978)

10. Hochreiter, S.: The vanishing gradient problem during learning recurrent neural nets and problem solutions. Int. J. Uncertain. Fuzziness Knowl. Based Syst. **06**(02), 107–116 (1998). https://doi.org/10.1142/S0218488598000094

11. Hochreiter, S., Schmidhuber, J.: Long short-term memory. Neural Comput. **9**(8), 1735–1780 (1997)

12. Kasthuri, E., Balaji, S.: Natural language processing and deep learning chatbot using long short term memory algorithm. Mater. Today Proc. **81**, 690–693 (2023)

13. Leangarun, T., Tangamchit, P., Thajchayapong, S.: Stock price manipulation detection using deep unsupervised learning: the case of Thailand. IEEE Access **9**, 106824–106838 (2021)

14. Md, A.Q., Kapoor, S., A.V., C.J., Sivaraman, A.K., Tee, K.F., H., S., N., J.: Novel optimization approach for stock price forecasting using multi-layered sequential LSTM. Appl. Soft Comput. **134**, 109830 (2023). https://doi.org/10.1016/j.asoc.2022.109830, https://www.sciencedirect.com/science/article/pii/S1568494622008791

15. Mondal, P., Shit, L., Goswami, S.: Study of effectiveness of time series modeling (Arima) in forecasting stock prices. Int. J. Comput. Sci. Eng. App. **4**(2), 13 (2014)

16. Tan, H.M., Wang, J.C.: Single channel speech separation using enhanced learning on embedding features. In: IEEE 10th Global Conference on Consumer Electronics (GCCE), pp. 430–431. IEEE (2021)

17. Vijh, M., Chandola, D., Tikkiwal, V., Kumar, A.: Stock closing price prediction using machine learning techniques. Proc. Comput. Sci. **167**, 599–606 (2020). https://doi.org/10.1016/j.procs.2020.03.326

Author Index

P. Cong Vinh and H. Mahfooz Ul Haque (Eds.): ICTCC 2023, LNICST 586, p. 187, 2024.
https://doi.org/10.1007/978-3-031-59462-5

Printed in the United States
by Baker & Taylor Publisher Services